CHARACTER AND THE NOVEL

CHARACTER AND THE NOVEL

By

W. J. HARVEY

Professor of English
The Queen's University of Belfast

CORNELL UNIVERSITY PRESS

Ithaca, New York

© W. J. Harvey 1965

First published in the United States of America 1965
CORNELL UNIVERSITY PRESS

Second printing 1966

Library of Congress Catalog Card Number: 65–23933

Printed in Great Britain

To Reed College

Contents

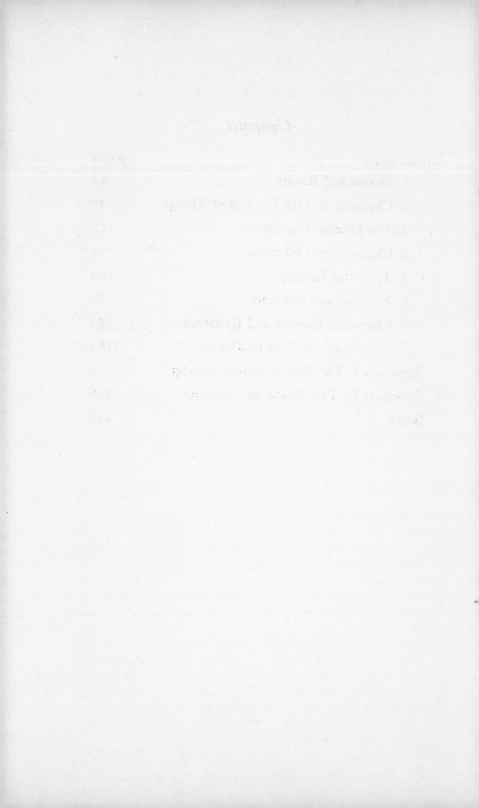

Acknowledgements

My primary debt is to those students of Reed College (Portland, Oregon) with whom I first discussed the subject of this book in 1959–60. I owe much to friends and colleagues who have subsequently read sections of it: notably Professors J. J. Lawlor and R. North, Mrs. B. Hardy and Mr. D. Hewitt. My debt to other writers on fiction can hardly be sufficiently indicated in the footnotes. Inevitably, there must be many critics, not directly mentioned, to whom I owe much; some of them—for example Lionel Trilling in *The Liberal Imagination* or John Bayley in *The Characters of Love*—I am acutely aware of; to the anonymous others I give inadequate thanks.

Parts of this book have been published, in another form, in *Essays in Criticism* and in *Dickens and the Twentieth Century* (ed. J. Gross and G. Pearson, Routledge and Kegan Paul, 1962).

Acknowledgements for extracts quoted in this book are due to the following:

Edward Arnold Ltd., for *Two Cheers for Democracy* by E. M. Forster; the Cambridge University Press for *An Experiment in Criticism* by C. S. Lewis and *Principia Ethica* by G. E. Moore; the Oxford University Press for *A Preface to Paradise Lost* by C. S. Lewis and *E. M. Forster: The Perils of Humanism* by F. C. Crews; Weidenfeld and Nicolson Ltd., for *The Hedgehog and the Fox* by I. Berlin and *Image and Idea* by P. Rahv; Faber and Faber Ltd., for *Tolstoy or Dostoevsky* by G. Steiner; Hamish Hamilton Ltd., *Nausea, The Age of Reason, The Reprieve, Iron in the Soul*, all by J. P. Sartre and for *J. P. Sartre* by P. Thody; Chatto and Windus Ltd., for *Marcel Proust and Deliverance from Time* by G. Brée, *The Great Tradition* by F. R. Leavis, *Fiction and the Reading Public* by Q. D. Leavis, *The Tragic Sense in Shakespeare* by J. J. Lawlor and *The Poetry of Experience* by R. Langbaum; Routledge and Kegan Paul Ltd., for *Technics and Civilization* by L. Mumford, *In Defence of Reason* by Y. Winters and *The Charted Mirror* by J. Holloway; William Heinemann Ltd., for D. H. Lawrence's *Letters* and *On the Contrary* by M. MacCarthy; Methuen and Co., Ltd., for *What is Literature* by J. P. Sartre; Rider and Co., Ltd., for *Literary and Philosophical Essays* by J. P. Sartre; Secker and Warburg Ltd., for *The Genesis of a Novel* by T. Mann;

Julliard (Paris) for *Haute-École* by J. L. Curtis; the University of Chicago Press for *A Rhetoric of Fiction* by W. Booth; the Harvard University Press for *The Dehumanization of Art* and *Notes on the Novel* by Ortega y Gasset; the University of California Press for *Time and Literature* by H. Meyerhoff; Prentice-Hall Inc., for *A Grammar of Motives* by K. Burke; Holt Rinehart and Winston for *The English Novel; Form and Function* by D. van Ghent; the *Kenyon Review* for "The Understanding of Fiction" by J. C. Ransom and the *Yale Review* for "The Sublime and the Beautiful Revisited" by I. Murdoch.

CHAPTER I

Fiction and Reality

A PROFOUND theologian may not make a good pastor nor need a brilliant advocate know much about the philosophy of law. So it is with the literary critic. Many good literary critics are eclectic in their methods and assumptions, caring little for theoretical consistency. Many even distrust critical theory. They prefer to use theories, taking what they want or what is momentarily useful; they fear, above all, that the theories may use them. If criticism be regarded as a committee of differing views, interests, methods, then the critic as chairman rules with a light hand, conveniently disregarding points of order, working to a very flexible agenda and knowing that he is likely, at best, to produce no more than a rough draft of an interim report.

One reason for this state of affairs is the critic's awareness that a great many systems or theoretical models potentially exist within the manifold data represented by particular acts of criticism. He knows that one may spend too much time and energy in constructing such models, in endlessly discriminating and multiplying categories; that such activity, though fascinating, soon becomes abstract and arid; that no terminology is stable enough to pin down the complex and shifting processes involved and that such theories may carry in themselves a concealed emotional potential which will discharge through any particular act of judgment. If, therefore, I begin by opposing two theories of art, this must be seen as no more than a provisional and convenient abstraction; in actual fact most critics carry on a good deal of traffic—some of it in the nature of smuggling—across the boundaries between these two theories.

We may call the two systems I am thus isolating the theories of autonomy and mimesis. The autonomy theory lies behind such slogans as "A poem should not mean but be" (Archibald MacLeish), or "It is not what a poem says that matters but what it *is*" (I. A. Richards). It lies behind most variants of the idea of Significant Form. It views the work of art as a created *thing*, a self-sufficient artefact containing its meaning and value within itself. Art is valuable "because it has to do with order, and creates little worlds of its own, possessing internal harmony, in the bosom of this disordered planet".[1] Criticism deriving from this theory will tend to be of a technical or formalist kind, concerned with the internal morphology of the work, demonstrating the relation of part to part and of part to whole. If the truth of the work is discussed, it will be largely in terms of internal coherency and consistency. Words like *probability* and *plausibility* will refer back to the initial assumptions or terms of reference upon which the work is built and which we are asked, quite simply, to accept. We may parody the autonomy theory of artistic truth by saying that in its terms all art aspires to the condition of geometry. This theory has been immensely popular and influential during the last seventy or eighty years; from it much good has sprung. I will not discuss it further here since I have attacked it in some detail in the second of the two appendices to this book.

My concern is with the theory of mimesis; that is to say, with critical acts which if traced back to their theoretical assumptions derive in some way from the root proposition that "Art imitates Nature". We must see what sense can be made of words like *truth*, *probability*, *realism* when they operate within the context of a mimetic system, in what ways they are valid and useful and to what dangers of misuse and confusion they are subject. More particularly, I shall discuss these problems as they apply primarily to the concept of *character* and to the sense of character we derive from our reading of prose fiction.

It is only fair at this point to declare my own interest and bias. As I have said, most critics very sensibly behave as if there were no discontinuity between the theories of autonomy and mimesis; they cross and recross the theoretical boundaries apparently without being aware that any frontier exists. They emphasize—again very sensibly—one or other critical method depending on the nature of the work under discussion; clearly, an autonomy theory will tend to prove more fruitful with an abstract painting whereas a mimetic theory is the better base of operations from which to explore

[1] E. M. Forster, *Two Cheers For Democracy*, p. 59.

Middlemarch. Given this freedom, most critics are understandably reluctant to be argued into a situation where they have to declare an ultimate allegiance to one or other of these theories. These are the polar regions of criticism, they will reply, where all statements must begin, "In the last analysis"; but there are many useful critical jobs to be done without ever setting foot in such a bleak and rigorous clime. Some would argue that such a region lies altogether outside the latitudes of criticism. Nevertheless, I suspect that if one manoeuvres a critic into such a situation he will ultimately have to make this either/or choice, to commit himself finally to one or other of these theories. It seems only honest, therefore, to say that in the last analysis I find myself firmly on the side of mimesis, that this defines the kind of critic I am and limits the kind of critical activity available to me. One hopes, of course, that in any *particular* critical task this commitment does not deny the happy eclecticism, the free traffic of the mind without which criticism would be a dour application of rigid principles.

Given this ultimate commitment, we must face squarely all the difficulties and limitations of the mimetic theory. The proposition, "Art Imitates Nature" may mean two things, depending on the way in which it is used. It may be descriptive or normative, stating either what is or what ought to be the relation of art to reality. The latter sense is not my prime concern and may be briefly discussed. One version of the normative proposition derives from the assumption that there is some essential nature or ideal order beyond or within the manifold and discrete data of our experience. Behind the apparently actual lurks the "really real". Much neo-classical criticism is based on this assumption, but it is hardly appropriate to the novel, which of all major art-forms adheres most stubbornly to the manifold and the discrete. Nevertheless, from this neo-classical simplicity (and largely, I suspect, in response to the new critical challenge posed by the growth of the novel) has developed a more flexible version of the normative proposition, one that wins wide acceptance today. The root of this credo is the assumption that art is to be judged by reference to something external to itself; from this a rough but working theory of value may be evolved through the following stages:

(*a*) That the value of art lies in its openness and fidelity to what one knows of life oneself, when one's sensibility and intelligence are at their finest pitch.

(*b*) That this fidelity is not, of course, literal; that art by its form directs our attention to what is central or most important in life itself. The parody of the mimetic position is the "slice-of-life" theory; a theory held, so far as I know, by no one today and which I shall not discuss.

(*c*) That by responding to the discipline of art our sympathy, insight and experience of life are imaginatively extended. Thus the mimetic theory sees critical judgment as essentially a two-way process; in judging a work of art we are at the same time testing and judging ourselves. Here it seems to me to score heavily over the autonomy theory.

(*d*) That this imaginative extension is a moral good.

(*e*) That ultimately, therefore, all criticism is rooted in our moral natures. Whereas the autonomy theory presupposes a unique kind of aesthetic response, the mimetic theory sees no final discontinuity between our responses to art and to life. They may differ in degree but not in kind; critical judgments demand the same qualities of intelligence, sensibility, rational control and emotional response that we deploy in our actual lives, though no doubt at a greater pitch and with more concentration and purity than in life itself.

Such a theory of value may have logical imperfections. These do not greatly worry me since the theory seems justified on pragmatic grounds—it works, not perfectly, but well enough as an account of the kinds of satisfaction I find in art. A more precise calculus of imaginative pleasure seems neither desirable nor necessary. I am more concerned lest this view be dismissed as a variant of Puritanism, austere, intolerant, afraid of simple pleasures. Let me stress, therefore, the primacy of enjoyment, both in the sense of immediate entertainment and of lasting satisfaction. The pleasures of the imagination, viewed from within this sytem, are what Dr. Johnson took them to be, those of Truth and of Novelty —or in my terms, fidelity to experience and the imaginative extension of experience. But these are linked to a third kind of pleasure, namely the response to the discipline of art. Professor C. S. Lewis has finely described it as like

taking part in a choric dance invented by a good choreo-
grapher. There are many ingredients in our pleasure. The
exercise of our faculties is itself a pleasure. Successful
obedience to what seems worth obeying and is not quite
easily obeyed is a pleasure. . . . Looking back on the
whole performance, we shall feel that we have been led
through a pattern or arrangement of activities which our
nature cried out for.[1]

The autonomy theory might claim this disciplined response as proof of its own validity; but it seems to me that
such qualities of pleasure must sustain *any* theory of art.
Without it, theories are nothing.

Let us now return to the proposition that "Art imitates
Nature", when taken descriptively. Here there are real
difficulties of substance and logic which *must* be faced—else
we shall be lost in the semantic labyrinths of both *Imitation*
and *Nature*. The trouble with the concept of Imitation is
that it covers so many different relationships between art and
life. Again, C. S. Lewis has posed the problem cogently:

> We must first decide what sort of fictions can justly be
> said to have truth to life. I suppose we ought to say that a
> book has this property when a sensible reader, on finish-
> ing it, can feel, "Yes. This—thus grim, or splendid, or
> empty, or ironic—is what our life is like. This is the sort
> of thing that happens. This is how people behave."
> But when we say "The sort of thing that happens", do
> we mean the sort of thing that usually or often happens,
> the sort of thing that is typical of the human lot? Or do we
> mean "The sort of thing that might conceivably happen
> or that, by a thousandth chance, may have happened
> once"? For there is a great difference in this respect be-
> tween the *Oedipus Tyrannus* or *Great Expectations* on the
> one hand and *Middlemarch* or *War and Peace* on the other.
> In the first two we see (by and large) such events and such
> behaviour as would be probable and characteristic of
> human life, given the situation. But the situation itself is
> not. It is extremely unlikely that a poor boy should be
> suddenly enriched by an anonymous benefactor who later
> turns out to be a convict. The chances against anyone's

[1] C. S. Lewis, *An Experiment in Criticism*, p. 134. Cambridge: C.U.P., 1961.

being exposed as an infant, then rescued, then adopted by a king, then by one coincidence killing his father, and then by another coincidence marrying his father's widow, are overwhelming. The bad luck of Oedipus calls for as much suspension of disbelief as the good luck of Monte Cristo. In George Eliot's and Tolstoy's masterpieces, on the other hand, all is probable and typical of human life. These are the sort of things that might happen to anyone. Things like them have probably happened to thousands. These are such people as we might meet any day. We can say without reservation, "This is what life is like."[1]

I would modify this account only to the extent of introducing a third mediating category between the normal and the exceptional. There is a kind of work, which includes many great novels, of which we neither say simply, "Life is like this", nor "Let us pretend that life is like this", but rather, "Life is not normally like this but it could be in certain circumstances. The quality of life here represented is of extreme intensity and concentration; we ordinary mortals could not for long endure it. Yet we realize that it involves no inherent improbabilities. It represents the possible, but the possible distilled to a quite unusual degree of purity."

These three categories are, of course, very rough and ready; part of the uniqueness of any work of art lies in its individual mimetic relationship to life. To convey this complexity I wish to coin for future use a trope derived from geometry and speak of the *angle* of mimesis. The "normal" work—a member of the *Middlemarch* family—we may metaphorically regard as lying very nearly parallel to life itself— it has a narrow mimetic angle. On the other hand, a fantasy like *Alice in Wonderland* stands almost at right-angles to life. The novel is the most inclusive and plastic of art-forms; if, for example, we move from *War and Peace* to *The Possessed* to *Moby Dick* to *The Trial*, we can see the novel subtending a wider and wider mimetic arc. But in each of these cases we must make sense of the idea that the "truth" of the novel resides not merely in its internal consistency but in its relationship to life. Clearly, then, the notion of Imitation must vary in meaning, depending on the angle of mimesis; the

---

[1] C. S. Lewis, *An Experiment in Criticism*, pp. 61–2.

greater the angle, the more difficult the problem for the mimetic critic. Conversely, autonomy theories have greater difficulty in coping with novels like *War and Peace*. Our problem, therefore, is to seek some general sense of "truth to life" which, without being totally abstract, may account for as great a mimetic arc as possible.

Alas, it is not only the central term in our root equation—Art Imitates Nature—that is a variable. *Nature*, that which is imitated, is even less constant. The variability of Nature differs from that of Imitation in that it is much more obviously caused by historical change.[1] Thus an Elizabethan would have found it hard to comprehend the shifting, evanescent reality described by Virginia Woolf; his own concept of Mutability refers to a quite different state of affairs.[2] Newton, Darwin, Freud (to take only three obvious points of reference) have all caused significant shifts in what is commonly thought to be the "real" state of things. Such historical flux drives the critic between the Scylla of historical relativism and the Charybdis of some form of absolute criteria. On the one hand, the critic may say that the truth and value of any work must be located in the contemporary society and world-view that produced it. Put thus bluntly, this seems inadequate. On the other hand, the critic may say that whatever meaning and value the work possesses reside in his own sense of the real. A work is thus great only in so far as it seems contemporary, relevant to the critic's own knowledge, interests and assumptions. Put thus bluntly, this seems arrogant even if the critic goes on to acknowledge that he, too, is historically limited, so that what seems to him absolutely true will be recaptured by history and become a relative thing, a phenomenon of time and changing taste. Moreover, if historicism may lead to an academic timidity which refuses to make *any* judgments, then the anti-historicist's judgments will often be based on incomplete and

[1] I am, of course, not saying that the concept of Imitation is unaffected by historical factors. For a brilliant historical study of this subject, see E. Auerbach's *Mimesis*. But in any age and in any single art form there can be a tremendous range of mimetic angle, e.g. *Wuthering Heights, Vanity Fair* and *Dombey and Son* are very nearly comtemporary novels, yet they differ considerably in their mimetic relationship to life.

[2] See Appendix I, pp. 194–5. For a discussion of this problem in a different area of literature, see R. Tuve, *Elizabethan and Metaphysical Imagery*.

B

misleading evidence. Great works are Janus faced; we must always recognize their pastness even if they seem great to us by virtue of their being eternally present.

How, then, can we hope to discover the stability of meaning necessary to any mimetic theory? Even if we limit ourselves to the novel, maintaining that it becomes a major artform *circa* 1700, our problem is not made very much easier—enough water has flowed under the bridge since then. I have dismissed slice-of-life theories as unworthy of serious discussion. Mere historicism is not enough. In its terms, even if we could define precisely what Nature and Imitation meant for Jane Austen and Virginia Woolf, still we should have no grounds for a comparative judgment. We could not praise either novelist on the basis of her greater "truth to life". Yet without historicism we are trapped within our own contemporary scene. How, then, may we resolve this dilemma?

It might seem that the most obvious way out would be to take an empirical and descriptive path. This would involve describing as fully as possible everything that we would commonly regard as a constituent of character. I shall, indeed, attempt precisely this in my next three chapters; it is a humble but necessary step in the endeavour to give substance to the concept of mimesis. But it is only *one* step; in itself it would not be sufficient and would be vulnerable to two serious objections. However careful we may be, the results of such an enquiry will inevitably have the appearance of a list, of a static table of ingredients. As such it can hardly convey two essential aspects of any novel—the interaction of these ingredients and our sense of this interaction as a dynamic process, of the novel as a thing moving massively forward in time. It will stand in much the same relation to an actual work of art as the Periodic Table does to a living organism. Moreover, this list of constituent elements will be long and complex; by what standards are we then to compare the novel which treats a wide range of such elements in a dilute manner with the novel which concentrates intensely on a few? How can we judge the relative mimetic adequacy of *Le Rouge et le Noir* and *Adolphe*, *Anna Karenina* and *Madame Bovary*, *Ulysses* and *Mrs Dalloway*?

Clearly something more is required. The great temptation

for the mimetic critic seeking stability in a bewildering world of flux is to fall back upon some variety of what has been called "the doctrine of the eternal human heart". This doctrine, stated crudely, holds that human nature, at its deepest levels, never essentially changes, that there is some common human denominator which "shackles accidents and bolts up change". But in so far as this is true are we left with more than a bare and uninteresting abstraction? "The thing itself," as King Lear says, "unaccommodated man is no more but such a poor, bare, forked animal". We must, it seems, dismiss the eternal human heart in the words of C. S. Lewis:

> The truth is that when you have stripped off what the human heart actually was in this or that culture, you are left with a miserable abstraction totally unlike the life really lived by any human being. To take an example from a simple matter, human eating, when you have abstracted all that is peculiar to the social and culinary practice of different times and places, resolves itself into the merely physical. Human love, abstracted from all the varying taboos, sentiments, and ethical discriminations which have accompanied it, resolves itself into something capable only of medical treatment, not of poetical.

Lewis's solution is that of the thorough-going historicist:

> It is better to study the changes in which the being of the Human Heart largely consists than to amuse ourselves with fictions about its immutability.[1]

Certainly the plea for the use of the historical imagination commands respect. It is continuous with that imaginative extension of the self which any great literary work compels and which is the basis of any moral theory of aesthetic value. We cannot deny or ignore it. Yet it seems to thrust us back into the world of flux and historical relativity. Must we then abandon the Eternal Human Heart? Can we salvage anything from this doctrine? Given that we are dealing with a specific form, the novel, which flourishes during a relatively short cultural period, cannot we find some significant and unchanging qualities of human nature which lie between the

[1] C. S. Lewis, *A Preface To Paradise Lost*, p. 63. London: O.U.P., 1942.

particular but transient details of social fashion and the eternal but abstract qualities of "unaccommodated man"?

The profitable areas to explore might seem to be the regions of man's moral and affective natures. The values we cherish, the experiences which prompt us to laugh, weep, pity, fear, admire or love—surely these things are the very pith and texture of life as rendered by the novel and are therefore immune to critical abstraction? While manners may change, while social structures may flourish or decay, surely these are but the vehicles of man's moral life, the varying outward forms of a constant inner experience? May we not find here a touchstone, a sufficiently stable frame of reference, at least for the relevant cultural epoch?

I would like to believe this but I hardly think it to be so. The human heart, if this is what we mean by it, *does* change and change both rapidly and radically. The fact that the novel is a relatively recent art form does not make it less vulnerable to quite startling shifts in sensibility and outlook; I have met many undergraduates who find the *Iliad* less alien than *Clarissa*. How, they ask, can the eighteenth century make such a fuss about chastity and yet be so casual about brutality? The moral world has so shifted that it needs a real effort of realignment on their part before any contact is made with the past. Again, any teacher who has had to tackle the problem of sentimentality in Dickens's novels will know what barriers a mere century can throw up. Is not the extreme pathos extracted from the death of little children obsessive and morbid? Is it credible that the death of Little Nell could have caused tough men of the world, like Lord Jeffrey, to weep? These are typical reactions. One may attempt historical explanations of such phenomena, pointing out that unlike the Victorians we are largely insulated from death as a domestic fact. Death for us takes place on the battlefield or in the hospital; the death of a small child is not a common family experience. We may point out, too, that intellectually Dickens was writing at a time when the firm belief in personal immortality was beginning to be assailed by agnostic doubts and that perhaps the hectic quality of his death-bed scenes is a quasi-religiose response to this conflict. But such explanations, in my experience, do little to bridge the gap between Victorian and modern attitudes to death.

This gap has real critical consequences; many readers, I think, find it hard to distinguish between the sentimentality of uncontrolled pathos and the sentimentality of pathos created or exploited by a cool and calculating mind. Certainly, many readers cannot discriminate between varying degrees of aesthetic success—between the deaths, say, of Jo, Little Nell and Paul Dombey.

Further examples would be redundant. But although the doctrine of the Eternal Human Heart in any form is a disappointment, it does help us to define more closely what we are looking for. Any notion of a mimetic theory must satisfy two conditions; it must be both particular and general. By particular I mean something which inheres in the detail of individual experience, which meshes inextricably with the dense patterns of life itself. These patterns differ with each of us and with each individual work of art, so that what we are looking for must accommodate these differences. If we start from the bare statement that "All men fear" (hope, pity, love, etc.), we go nowhere, since what interests us in fiction as in life is how *this* man fears and *that* man loves. Thus we must look for something which allows for the *thisness* and *thatness* of experience and yet which is general in the sense that experience—of whatever individual quality— would be meaningless without it. It must also be something which is so little conditioned by history, which changes so slowly in time, that it allows us a sufficiently stable frame of reference, at least for the period during which the novel has flourished. Finally, this frame of reference must be flexible as well as stable; it must not lop the facts to fit a Procrustean bed of theory.

It will scarcely surprise the reader if I now produce a modest and rather commonplace rabbit out of the hat. In doing so, I must coin my second and, I hope, my last piece of technical jargon and introduce the notion of the "constitutive category".[1] By this I mean something which, though not in itself often the object of experience, is inherent in everything we do actually experience. It is that which constitutes and orders experience for us; without it life would be

---

[1] Strictly speaking, this is not a coinage but a theft from Kant's *Critique of Pure Reason*. The meaning I have given the term overlaps, but is not identical with that of Kant; thus Freedom is for him not a category but an Idea of Reason.

entirely random and chaotic. It is, so to speak, the type-face by which we spell out and make sense of the words printed on our individual *tabulae rasae*; better still, it is the grammar which determines the raw data of our lives. The sense of what we *read* (i.e. the experiences we have) is private and unique; but at least we are reading the same language, governed by a syntax sufficiently common for us to communicate with each other.

The four categories with which I shall deal—the list, of course, is far from complete—are Time, Identity, Causality and Freedom. They seem to me to satisfy the conditions I have just laid down. They are inherent in all experience and thus enforce upon us that concern for particularity without which theories become useless or dangerous. They have important and immediate aesthetic concomitants; the novel is a temporal art, dealing with identities and largely concerned with the processes of motive, cause and effect. While these categories, as they operate in art and life, are not sharply discontinuous they are sufficiently distinct to provide us with a standard beyond the work of art, a frame of reference located in life itself. By this means we may judge any work more or less adequate as an imitation of reality and we may compare different works in these terms. These categories control and regulate experience, so that if a novelist convinces us that his handling of them is truthful, then there is a good chance that the particular experience he portrays as the end-product of these categories will also strike us as true to life. The texture of the created fictional world—the society portrayed, the values assumed, the emotions rendered—may be alien, but the shape of that world will be familiar. To use my linguistic metaphor, while the novelist's vocabulary may be new to us, his grammar will be recognizably our own. Finally, these categories—because they are so basic to our consciousness—change more slowly than manners or morals. They are not eternal, but within the history of the novel they are stable enough for all practical purposes. Where historical change is important I shall take note of it; in particular I shall consider whether the revolution through which we seem to be living is not in part precisely the radical derangement of these categories. In this sense, the exciting experiments of the modern novel may be seen as an imaginative response to the profound dislocation of the very terms in which experience is constituted for us.

To sum up; experience may be seen in terms of texture and structure. The texture of our lives—manners, morals, passions, thoughts—is structured by those regulating principles I have called constitutive categories. Mimetic theories which relate art to life only in terms of its texture are precarious, since this texture is infinitely varied and liable to rapid historical change. Therefore, we must attempt a mimetic theory in terms of the structure of experience. Structure is relatively stable; only in terms of it does the texture of life make any sense. Such is my thesis and the main object of this book.

The trajectory of the argument is, however, conditioned by two other considerations. I shall concentrate on character since most great novels exist to reveal and explore character. It may be objected that to treat character as an isolable element within the total pattern of the novel is misleading and ridiculous. Of course it is; in any particular case I shall be led on from character to consider other structural features of the work. It may also be argued that other features of the work—plot, for example—are in themselves mimetically significant. This, too, I accept; clearly the plots (or rejection of plot) in the novels of Arnold Bennett and Virginia Woolf reflect two very different notions of reality and imitation. It also seems true that the bare outlines of a plot may imitate reality—the more so, as the work approaches primitive levels of myth or ritual. The story of an Oedipus or a Faustus may be deeply significant, even when the protagonist seems almost anonymous, drained of almost all human content in the sense of complex characterization. It is true that some novels have this quality of myth or ritual—*Moby Dick*, for instance, or *The Trial*. But most novels seem to me antiprimitivistic in direction; hence the Aristotelian emphasis on plot as the prime mimetic agent seems to me misplaced in the case of this art form.[1] However, we are here valuably

[1] This can be seen if we compare Lawrence's *Sons and Lovers* or Mann's *Doctor Faustus* with the more primitive versions of the Oedipus and Faustus legends. The plots of the novels, abstractly considered, do not have the disturbing quality of myth; the deeper and wider significances of these works—their "symbolic" value—depend upon our primary sense of character. In other words, in fiction the archetype must be apprehended through the individual case. I would maintain this

reminded of the scope and plasticity of the novel; as a major
art form it contains within itself a multitude of literary kinds.
The boundaries of this form are not sharply defined; it
shades off into epic, chronicle, drama, fable, romance, ideological debate. Each of these sub-species has its own mimetic
angle which widens as the frontiers of the novel are approached. While I shall be primarily concerned with the
classical, central regions of the novel I shall do my best, in
my choice of examples, to acknowledge this variety.

II

One of the few Marxist generalizations about literature to
hold up reasonably well when put to the test of detailed
historical examination is the thesis that the development of
the novel is intimately connected with the growth of the
bourgeoisie in a modern capitalist system. From this social
process derive the assumptions and values we may conveniently if crudely lump together as liberalism. We may
fairly say that the novel is the distinct art form of liberalism,
by which I mean not a political view or even a mode of
social and economic organization but rather a state of mind.
This state of mind has as its controlling centre an acknow-
ledgment of the plenitude, diversity and individuality of
human beings in society, together with the belief that such
characteristics are good as ends in themselves. It delights in
the multiplicity of existence and allows for a plurality of beliefs and values; as Presswarden notes in Durrell's *Clea*, "At
each moment of time all multiplicity waits at your elbow."
Tolerance, scepticism, respect for the autonomy of others
are its watchwords; fanaticism and the monolithic creed its
abhorrence. Kant's second general principle of morality is
its first commandment.[1] By scepticism I do not mean intellectual scepticism of a Pyrrhonic kind; indeed, historically
considered, the liberal state of mind has been distinguished
by a belief in the dignity and potentiality of reason. The
attempt to assimilate the growing awareness of the *irration-*

despite Mann's remarks on the mythic qualities of his work in his *Genesis of a
Novel. Cf.* Appendix II, p. 210.
    [1] "So act as to treat humanity, whether in thine own person or in that of any
other, in every case as an end withal, never as means only." Kant, *Groundwork of
Morals.*

ality of existence and of human behaviour has in fact constituted a major crisis of liberalism, a crisis reflected artistic-
ally in the novels of a Dostoevski or a Lawrence, and intellectually—the case is classic and symbolic—in the work of
Freud. Irrationality is sensed as dangerous since it so often
leads to some intuitively grasped and intellectually unassail-
able variety of monism. In Isaiah Berlin's formulation,
novelists are usually foxes by nature and the fascination
offered us by many modern novelists is the internal conflict
displayed in their work between the pluralistic fox and the
monistic hedgehog.[1]

I am not, of course, maintaining that the novel cannot
flourish in an illiberal or monolithic society, particularly an
inefficient one. The nineteenth-century Russian novel
proves the opposite; indeed, part of the distinctive quality of
much literature may derive from the delightful or sombre
evasions and obliquities of an author asserting his freedom in
a closed society. What I am maintaining is that the novel
cannot be written out of a monolithic or illiberal mind. Because of the range of his subject matter, because he must see
all life as *divers et ondoyant*, because he must accept his
characters as asserting their human individuality and uniqueness in the face of all ideology (including his own limited
point of view), the novelist must tend to be liberal, pluralistic, foxy.

Consider the two greatest systems of beliefs which are
liable to evoke a monistic commitment in their adherents,
Christianity and Marxism. Where is the truly great Christian
or Marxist novel—that is to say, the novel written out of a
sensibility entirely ordered by one or other of these ideo-
logies? The nearest thing we can find to fit either of these
categories is the work of Dostoevski and even here one
must say that his religion was distinctively individual and
odd and that he could only attempt a Christian novel because he was of the devil's party and knew it. The novelist
must acknowledge, if he is to create a faithful imitation of

[1] "There exists a great chasm between those . . . who relate everything to a
single central vision . . . and . . . those who pursue many ends, often unrelated
and even contradictory . . . . The first kind of intellectual and artistic personality
belongs to the hedgehogs, the second to the foxes."

I. Berlin, *The Hedgehog and the Fox*, pp. 1–2. London: Weidenfeld and Nicolson,
1953.

mankind, that most human beings will always elude or overflow the categories of *any* ideology; such a belief is part of
what I have called the liberal state of mind. It may well be,
of course, that we are moving towards a form of society
where such a state of mind is no longer viable, that liberalism
is a luxury rarely allowed by history. In this case the novel
will, like other art forms in the past, cease to be an available
imaginative mode and will be supplanted by other art forms,
either entirely new or drastic mutations of the novel itself.
Considered in this way, the radical experiments of many
modern novelists may be seen as the first attempts at such
mutation, the first imaginative responses to a changing
world view which involves the gradual death of liberalism.

Certainly, if such a change *is* taking place, the novel will
probably prove the most vulnerable of the major literary
modes. Poetry is much less affected by this state of affairs;
great poems have often been written from a monistic position. If we shift our terms a little we can easily relate the
monistic to Keats's idea of the "egotistical sublime" and the
pluralistic to his "negative capability". The novelist, much
more than the poet, *must* be endowed with "negative capability"; as he surveys the crowded human scene he must
much more be able to withhold final judgment, to suspend
his attachment to a particular point of view, to reconcile
disparities, to encompass the multitudinous and conflicting
interests, values, assumptions of the world if he is to allow
this full weight within the world of his novel. A poet *can*, if
he wants to, make a final and total commitment to a single
ideology; the novelist cannot. The dramatist—I am much
less certain about this—hovers between the two although
tending, at least in post-Renaissance drama, much more to
the novelist.

We can see this difference more clearly if we examine
particular aspects of the problem. Consider the question of
Literature and Belief which arises most acutely when the
artist is committed to a monistic ideology, is a hedgehog
rather than a fox, is characterized by the "egotistical sublime" rather than by "negative capability". Supposing, for
example, that we find T. S. Eliot's theology repulsive, how
can we maintain that *Four Quartets* is a great poem? The
usual answer, I suppose, would be that while we reject

Eliot's theology, while we may not even be able "to suspend disbelief for the moment", we can still maintain that the real subject of the poem is the human experience of what it is like to be thus committed; we attend not to the doctrine but to the man grappling with the doctrine. But that the monistic mind finds it much more difficult to cope with its total commitment in another medium can be seen by placing *Four Quartets* beside *The Family Reunion* or *The Cocktail Party*. We cannot now, I think, take the same escape route; somehow the task of imagining the interplay of a number of characters has thrown up the doctrine as something unassimilable in human terms, as something simply and stubbornly there. The problem would be even more acute if the form were that of the novel; indeed a novel written out of the position of *Four Quartets* is difficult to imagine.

Let us now consider the case where although the writer may not subscribe to such a belief, some variety of monism forms part of his subject matter. The pluralist constantly weighs and balances one outlook or set of values against another; hence the clash and conflict in his work and hence, frequently, the kind of irony which pervades it. But the conflict and the irony deriving from a monistic position is quite different. For one thing, metaphysical or final issues are much more likely to arise. Where a total commitment to one ideology is envisaged, the characters will often be confronted with some absolute which demands their total allegiance; the absolute, say, of historical necessity or the commands of God. In such a case human values may well be suddenly superseded or abrogated by some more-than-human *fiat*. Prince Hal *must* reject Falstaff; the duties of kingship assert an imperative which allows of no alternative. Adam and Eve *must* be condemned for sinning by their Fall; whatever Adam's motives, for example—and they may be the noblest possible within the limits of a merely human imagination—they must seem trivial when measured against divine injunction. Hence the difficulty of the reader who happens to be a pluralist, since he will stress the value of the merely human, will remember Falstaff's life or Adam's love rather than the metaphysical necessity stemming from an outlook he cannot accept. Again, given the different medium of the novel, such final issues become even more difficult to handle successfully; there are few great metaphysical novels. For the novelist is, as I have said, by nature liberal, pluralist, foxy; his typical subject is the partial, the limited, the relative, the imperfect—in other words, the merely human rather than the overarching non-human absolutes. The monist is hot for certainties, the pluralist content with a more or less dusty answer.

As with the novelist, so with the critic; his answers, too, must be more dusty than certain. For me to assert that my initial assumptions are universally true would clearly be a subversion of the liberal and pluralist viewpoint deriving from those very assumptions. Equally clearly they do need *some* qualification and I have tried to show some of the problems which will then arise. But from my reading in the main traditions of the novel I would conclude that if a novelist does not share these assumptions, then he tends to write a *kind* of fiction—romance, fable, the novel of ideas—in which the angle of mimetic relationship between art and life is more oblique than in what I have called the realistic novel. The realistic novel I take to be the central, classic tradition of modern fiction; it is with this kind of work that the question of mimetic adequacy is most important and such a question seems to me to depend primarily on the validity of my initial assumptions.

III

I trust that the reader now has a reasonably clear idea of the assumptions on which this book is based, the values to which it adheres. It is written from within what Lionel Trilling has called "the liberal imagination". The book is compounded of theoretical argument and practical demonstration; although I have tried everywhere to enrich abstraction with an abundance of concrete examples, it may be worthwhile indicating the general theoretical drift. Chapters II–IV attempt to describe the main constituents of character; Chapters V–VI deal with the four constitutive categories I have isolated, Time and Identity, Freedom and Causality. But since, as I have said, we live in a revolutionary age when traditional assumptions are being challenged and subverted, I have in Chapter VII re-surveyed my argument from the quite different viewpoint of existentialism; to focus discussion here, I have concentrated on the theories and creative practice of Sartre. Finally the two appendices deal with the historical reasons for the devaluation of the concept of character and with a rebuttal of critical objections to this concept, culminating with a consideration of autonomy theories of art as represented by Ortega y Gasset's remarks on the novel. These appendices are largely polemical in tone and may appeal only to a rather specialised taste for critical in-fighting; hence their location where the general reader can conveniently ignore them, if he wishes to do so. In all that follows, I have tried to remember as my motto and talisman a dictum of Orlo Williams: "Theories are like omnibuses, useful when you want to go in the same direction as they, not otherwise."

CHAPTER II

Character and the Context of Things

I N the next three chapters I shall deal with elements of character rather than with techniques of characterization. Of course, the two can never really be separated. In real life our sense of character naturally varies with our powers of perception and understanding. We see in others only what we are able to see and this ability then forms for others part of our own character. We value qualities of sensitivity, tact, sympathy, the unafraid acceptance of intensity or contradiction—qualities, we say, which make us more fully human in that through them we respond more fully to others. There is no *necessary* connection between many of these qualities and the power to express them. We probably all know the man whose profound knowledge of human nature expresses itself only in silence or in platitude. We certainly know the man whose brilliant epigrams only disguise his ignorance or fear or hatred of anything beneath the surface.

As in life, so in art. We do not mean enough by technique if we mean only those particular skills or methods of articulation—control of dialogue, point of view, stream of consciousness and so on. Behind these particular skills may or may not lie the really valuable qualities of human vision, understanding and response. On the one hand, a novelist may conscientiously include in his work every aspect of character and yet remain finally unperceptive because he lacks the technique whereby these elements are composed into a living whole. Technical inadequacy here points to a more radical failure of the imagination. If we are to choose only from the first order of art, then *Romola* strikes me as a failure of this kind; of course, such failures become more common as we descend the ladder of talent. On the other hand, we know that an elegant technician may corruscate in a human void while someone like Dreiser—clumsy, technically outrageous—still has the power of deeply moving the reader because the life he has imagined is indeed alive. Imagination here stands for the incalculable and indescribable factor in the creative process. As I have said, I shall try to describe what might be called the raw material of character rather than techniques of characterization. But even here language may betray us if it suggests a process of manufacture; a more appropriate metaphor is that of conception, gestation, birth and growth—more appropriate because more mysterious. As critics we can never do more than guess or hint at what happens with the conjunction of vision and technique.

II

When, in real life, we try to describe a person's character we generally speak in terms of a discrete identity. We think of it as something unique and separable from all other identities. We do this, of course, because the most intimate sense of character we can possibly have—our knowledge of self—is of this kind. No matter what image we have of our own identity—as the secret, central ego lurking behind a gallery of social personae, as the ghost in the machine, as a pattern, as a flux, as a hard, stable core within the flux—we still think of it as unique, isolate, discrete. From this we extrapolate a similar sense of the characters of others; they may be private and unknowable but they are like us at least in this respect. There can, of course, be no evidence for this assumption since when we experience another person we do so within a context which is inseparable from the experience itself. We can never know another in himself since in the very act of knowing our presence creates the context on which knowledge depends. The data by which we describe character are the aggregate of our experience in a number of situations, relationships, contexts. Without these contexts the characters of others do not make sense for us. We can have what may be called intrinsic knowledge of ourselves; we can only have contextual knowledge of others.

It is tempting to draw parallels between our experience of life and of fictional characters. Thus it is ridiculous to isolate characters from a novel and discuss them as totally autonomous entities; the novel itself is nothing but a complicated structure of artificially formed contexts parallel to those within which we experience real people. But can we go further than this? Can we say that the author, however he may disguise himself, is to his characters what we are to other people—the one context that must exist if we are to experience anything at all? The answer here must be no; in this case the analogy is false. For the author is not to his characters as we are to other people; his relationship to them is not human but god-like. However invisible he may make himself, whatever narrative techniques he may use to conceal his exit from his fiction, the novelist is and must be both omnipotent and omniscient. The last word is, both literally and metaphorically, his alone.

This being so, the novelist may confer on us his god-like power and privilege; we, too, can see the fictional character in his private self, secret, entirely solitary. Life allows only intrinsic knowledge of self, contextual knowledge of others; fiction allows both intrinsic and contextual knowledge of others. Many modern critics, of course, have regarded this god-like vision as illegitimate, as something inimical to the truth of fiction.[1] These theoretical objections have their correlative in creative practice; the novelist's abdication of his god-like prerogatives is a central fact of modern fiction. While it may result from adherence to a philosophical theory or simply from a loss of nerve, this refusal to allow intrinsic knowledge of other characters merely creates a new kind of novel; it does not prove that this new kind is the *only* truthful sort of fiction. It is surely fair to say that the omniscient author of the classical novel destroys no necessary fictional illusion. On the contrary, he often creates a world which seems more real than many of those created by his more timid or more scrupulous successors. To say that because in real life we can only have contextual knowledge of others, therefore we can only be allowed a similar knowledge in fiction seems to me a naïve mistake. It is akin to the confusion of those neo-classical critics who demanded a strict adherence to the unities, lest the dramatic illusion be destroyed. The "suspension of disbelief" involved in reading what we *know* to be fiction seems to me to pose no special psychological difficulty; every day we make more daring and radical assumptions about other people in real life. Surely the fact that we are allowed intrinsic knowledge of other characters is a prime reason for our enjoyment of fiction; the imaginative release from our actual imprison-

[1] *Cf.* pp. 162–3.

ment within our own single point of view is one of the great consolations of art.

It is, however, on contextual knowledge of character that I wish to concentrate. Remarkably few great novelists have attempted a really prolonged revelation of a single centre of consciousness treated entirely as though from within. In most cases the mimetic richness of a novel derives from the writer showing us his characters functioning within a wide variety of contexts, situations, relationships. Early in *A Portrait of the Artist as a Young Man*, Stephen Dedalus turns to his geography book, on the flyleaf of which he has written:

> Stephen Dedalus
> Class of Elements
> Clongowes Wood College
> Sallins
> County Kildare
> Ireland
> Europe
> The World
> The Universe

This is an apt paradigm of the sense of plurality, of interlocking circles and multiple relationships, through which we move in our everyday lives. Reality in this sense is nothing but an incredibly complicated pattern of contexts, a pattern which moves in time and which ripples continuously outwards, as though from Stephen Dedalus to the Universe, until we can discern no pattern at all. Hence *any* formal limitation must be artificial and where to draw the line becomes a prime problem for the novelist. As Henry James puts it:

> Really, universally, relations stop nowhere, and the exquisite problem of the artist is eternally but to draw, by a geometry of his own, the circle within which they shall happily *appear* to do so. He is in the perpetual predicament that the continuity of things is the whole matter, for him, of comedy and tragedy; that this continuity is never, by the space of an instant or an inch, broken, and that, to do anything at all, he has at once intensely to consult and intensely to ignore it.[1]

[1] In the preface to *Roderick Hudson*.

c

Granted this, then one part of the truth of any novel will depend on the novelist's power of persuading us to accept these formal limitations. This he may do by working within some convention which, once accepted by the reader, permits him to concentrate intensely on the area of life thus circumscribed. The convention is, so to speak, a signal to the reader—"*This* is what you may accept. Pay *this* kind of attention."A simple example would, I suppose, be the "once upon a time" formula of the fairy-tale; a more sophisticated kind is the device of descriptive interchapters in Virginia Woolf's *The Waves*. Alternatively, the novelist may so disguise the frontiers of his fiction that we sense beyond the story the continuum of life itself. In this way the reader's experience of fiction merges imperceptibly into other, "real-life" experiences just as, in actuality, one context of our lives overlaps with another. This disguise, this effect of blurring the frontiers of fiction and life, is again the product of art, whether naïve or crafty. A crude example, I think, is the technique of montage used by Dos Passos in *U.S.A.*; we may contrast with this the author's addresses to the reader in *Tom Jones*. These may look simple minded when compared with modern technical experiments but are, I believe, sophisticated and designed to produce quite complicated effects upon the reader. At first sight they might seem to be conventional devices artificially delimiting the area of the novel. But they have the opposite effect, raising the novel to the magnitude of life itself and giving the fictional world a wonderful openness which is then played off against the formal intricacy of the plot.

III

To catalogue the various contexts which produce the density of relationships characterizing our everyday experience would be tedious and, since they constantly interact, misleading. We must risk both tedium and distortion, however, if we are to realize the extreme complexity of the problem. For what we are attempting is a descriptive analysis of the quality of experience and in such a task method and subject stand in much the same relationship as a chemical formula to the distinctive tang of a fruit on the palate. So much is fugitive, evanescent, dies under scrutiny; nevertheless we must labour, however clumsily, to follow the imaginative artist in his pursuit of experience. Let us start, at least, from relative simplicity by considering the least complex of human contexts—our relation, that is, to *things*, to the world of inanimate objects.

> "When you've lived as long as I you'll see that every human being has his shell and that you must take the shell into account. By the shell I mean the whole envelope of circumstances. There's no such thing as an isolated man or woman; we're each of us made up of some cluster of appurtenances. What shall we call our 'self'? Where does it begin? Where does it end? It overflows into everything that belongs to us—and then it flows back again. I know a large part of myself is in the clothes I choose to wear. I've a great respect for *things*! One's self—for other people—is one's expression of one's self; and one's house, one's furniture, one's garments, the books one reads, the company one keeps—these things are all expressive."
>
> (*The Portrait of A Lady*, Chapter 19)

Madame Merle's excursion into metaphysics raises a great many questions about the nature of character—indeed, more than character, for without her viewpoint what would become of our old thematic friend, Appearance and Reality? But she also states with finality the most obvious *function* in fiction of the various relationships assumed to exist between people and objects. This function is to create settings which, as Wellek and Warren observe, "may be viewed as metonymic, or metaphoric, expressions of character". This function has so often been the object of critical attention that I shall not discuss it further here. My concern is with some less obvious and more problematical aspects of the relations established between mind and things.

We may begin with a passage from the superb eleventh chapter of *Our Mutual Friend*, which describes a dinner party at the Podsnaps:

> Mr. and Mrs. Veneering, and Mr. and Mrs. Veneering's bran-new bride and bridegroom, were of the dinner company; but the Podsnap establishment had nothing else in

common with the Veneerings. Mr. Podsnap could tolerate taste in a mushroom man who stood in need of that sort of thing, but was far above it himself. Hideous solidity was the characteristic of the Podsnap plate. Everything was made to look as heavy as it could, and to take up as much room as possible. Everything said boastfully, "Here you have as much of me in my ugliness as if I were only lead; but I am so many ounces of precious metal worth so much an ounce;—wouldn't you like to melt me down?" A corpulent straddling epergne, blotched all over as if it had broken out in an eruption rather than been ornamented, delivered this address from an unsightly silver platform in the centre of the table. Four silver wine-coolers, each furnished with four staring heads, each head obtrusively carrying a big silver ring in each of its ears, conveyed the sentiment up and down the table, and handed it on to the pot-bellied silver salt-cellars. All the big silver spoons and forks widened the mouths of the company expressly for the purpose of thrusting the sentiment down their throats with every morsel they ate.

It is not enough to say that the dinner table is merely metonymic, that it simply reflects or symbolizes the qualities of Podsnappery. The passage may begin in that way but any sense of equivalence is soon overtaken by a livelier fantastication of the prose. The objects in a sense *become* Podsnap and his guests; in the sustained exuberance of the conceit salt-cellar and spoon live a life of their own far more intense than that of the assembled company, who suffer for a moment the unnatural reverse of becoming merely objects. All critics have remarked on Dickens's power of animating the inanimate world; none better than R. H. Horne who in an early essay compares him with Hogarth:

There is a profusion and prodigality of character in the works of these two artists. A man, woman, or child, cannot buy a morsel of pickled salmon, look at his shoe, or bring in a mug of ale; a solitary object cannot pass on the other side of the way; a boy cannot take a bite at a turnip or hold a horse; a by-stander cannot answer the simplest question; a dog cannot fall into a doze; a bird cannot whet his bill; a pony cannot have a peculiar nose, nor a pig one

ear, but out peeps the first germ of "a character". Nor
does the ruling tendency and seed-filled hand stop with
such as these; for inanimate objects become endowed with
consciousness and purpose, and mingle appropriately in
the background of the scene. Sometimes they even act as
principals, and efficient ones too. . . .[1]

The good thing about Horne's comment is the way in
which he connects two main characteristics of Dickens's
fictional world. The Dickensian qualities of abundance and
prodigality are such that, moving with him through his
imaginatively crowded world, we seem continually to be
bumping into things. This is a world of perpetual small
collisions. At a pinch, we might say that this was an objective quality of his age, that a Victorian drawing room, for
example, literally was crowded with objects. But it was also a
quality of his imagination since this dense world of things is
also alive; it has a comic or malign energy of its own.
Dickens's imagination is primitive, animistic. I think we misread him slightly if we take his quickening power as merely
conceit or metaphor or symbol; I believe this inanimate
world was, for him, literally alive. There is nothing very odd
in this; when a pencil breaks or we stub our toe in the dark
we often have, in a transient way, this primitive sense of
objects stubbornly leading a mysterious life of their own, a
life which sometimes thwarts or obtrudes into ours. Most of
us have vestigial terrors which are the feeble descendants of
a magical view of the world. This primitive, animistic sense
of things not just as "out-there", opaque, other-than-us, but
also as alive, hostile or benevolent, is only one end of a
whole scale of relationships between mind and the world of
objects. Up and down this scale the novelist may range at
will. Its centre—that which we take to be both norm and
normal—is surely represented in fiction by Tolstoy, in whose
work, as F. G. Steiner says, "Physical objects derive their
raison d'être and solidity from the human context." Mr.
Steiner at this point in his argument is contrasting Tolstoy's
humanistic attitude to the world of things with that of Flaubert; he quotes from *Madame Bovary* the famous description
of Charles's schoolboy cap:

[1] "Charles Dickens" in *A New Spirit of the Age* (1844).

It was a headgear of composite order, containing elements of an ordinary hat, a hussar's busby, a lancer's cap, a sealskin cap and a nightcap; one of those wretched things whose mute hideousness suggests unplumbed depths, like an idiot's face. Ovoid and stiffened with whalebone, it began with three convex strips; then followed alternating lozenges of velvet and rabbit's fur, separated by a red band; then came a kind of bag, terminating in a cardboard-lined polygon intricately decorated with braid. From this hung a long, excessively thin cord, ending in a kind of tassel of gold netting. The cap was new; its peak was shiny.[1]

The object here is more truly metonymic, but Mr. Steiner is surely right to dismiss those critics who load this passage with tremendous symbolic import. While it may throw *some* light on Charles's character it also communicates a kind of linguistic desperation in the face of a contingent and multitudinous world of objects—as though the author has said to himself, "At least I will pin *this* down in a definitive manner." By contrast, Tolstoy moves freely and confidently through his imagined world which seems denser, of greater plenitude, precisely because he does not lavish his attention on detail in the way that Flaubert does. Tolstoy is lord of creation—at least of his creation—and things retreat before him to their humble place in a centrally human world.

If we travel further down the scale of mind–thing relationships, from the primitive imagination of Dickens, through the human centrality of Tolstoy, past the desperation of Flaubert, then we arrive at something like this:

"We went back to look for Minta's brooch," he said, sitting down by her. "We"—that was enough. She knew from the effort, the rise in his voice to surmount a difficult word that it was the first time he had said "we". "We" did this, "we" did that. They'll say that all their lives, she thought, and an exquisite scent of olives and oil and juice rose from the great brown dish as Martha, with a little

[1] G. Steiner, *Tolstoy or Dostoevsky*, p. 50. London: Faber and Faber, 1960. The quotation from *Madame Bovary* is from the translation by Francis Steegmuller (New York, 1957).

flourish, took the cover off. The cook had spent three days over that dish. And she must take great care, Mrs. Ramsay thought, diving into the soft mass, to choose a specially tender piece for William Bankes. And she peered into the dish, with its shiny walls and its confusion of savoury brown and yellow meats, and its bay leaves and its wine, and thought: This will celebrate the occasion—a curious sense rising in her, at once freakish and tender, of celebrating a festival, as if two emotions were called up in her, one profound—for what could be more serious than the love of man for woman, what more commanding, more impressive, bearing in its bosom the seeds of death; at the same time these lovers, these people entering into illusion glittering eyed, must be danced round with mockery, decorated with garlands.

"It is a triumph," said Mr. Bankes, laying his knife down for a moment. He had eaten attentively. It was rich; it was tender. It was perfectly cooked.[1]

There is here, as in Flaubert, a desperation in face of the world of objects. But whereas Flaubert reacts by attempting to capture the thing in itself, objective, in all its bizarre detail, Virginia Woolf tries to pin the thing down at the moment when it deliquesces into the consciousness of her characters. The sensuous richness of so much of her prose is not, as it might at first seem, her tribute to a crowded world of autonomous objects since for her all things ultimately become mind-stuff, entering the glow of that "luminous halo" which is her metaphor for life itself. Virginia Woolf is perhaps too often a naïve Berkeleyan since *esse percipi est* is only one side of the equipoise between mind and the world of objects. The other side is our sense that objects *resist* our attention, that they remain opaque, stubbornly themselves. This sense is abundant in Dickens—it is a source of his metaphoric richness—but is deficient in Virginia Woolf. To dine with the Podsnaps is to surrender to a world of things sensed as living a life of its own; to dine with the Ramsays is to celebrate a triumph of mind over matter. For in the passage I have quoted from *To The Lighthouse*, the book as well as the dinner has been beautifully cooked.

[1] V. Woolf, *To The Lighthouse*, Part I, Section 17.

Behind the perfection of the Bœuf-en-Daube, with its subtle
blend of ingredients, is Mrs. Ramsay's triumph in blending
and reconciling the human ingredients of her dinner party;
Mr. Bankes pays tribute to both successes. And behind Mrs.
Ramsay, of course, stands Virginia Woolf triumphantly
blending the elements of life into her art. The extreme self-
consciousness of this process is evident—"this will celebrate
the occasion," Mrs. Ramsay thinks. This is one reason why
Virginia Woolf's novels, though containing many striking
and beautiful effects, are in the last analysis irritating. The
metaphoric vivacity of Dickens's prose only enhances the
independence of the objects described; Virginia Woolf, by
contrast, allows the external world too little freedom. The
sensibility of her characters too easily digests whatever it
encounters. We are left with facts of mind where sometimes
we hunger for simple, brute facts. Moreover—this is a
different but related complaint—the mind which thus trans-
mutes is far too limited, allowing little dramatic variety;
most of her characters metamorphose the world in strikingly
similar ways. The results achieved are rich but narrow; intensity is purchased at too great a cost. After so much Bœuf-
en-Daube one hungers for plain bread-and-cheese.

If we go still further in our scale of mind–thing relationships, beyond Virginia Woolf, then we encounter something
like Roquentin's famous confrontation with the chestnut
tree:

> Absurdity; another word; I struggle against words;
> down there I touched the thing. But I wanted to fix the
> absolute character of this absurdity here. A movement, an
> event in the tiny coloured world of men is only relatively
> absurd: by relation to the accompanying circumstances.
> A madman's ravings, for example, are absurd in relation
> to the situation in which he finds himself, but not in
> relation to his delirium. But a little while ago I made an
> experiment with the absolute or the absurd. This root—
> there was nothing in relation to which it was absurd. Oh,
> how can I put it in words? Absurd: in relation to the
> stones, the tufts of yellow grass, the dry mud, the tree, the
> sky, the green benches. Absurd, irreducible; nothing—
> not even a profound, secret upheaval of nature—could

explain it. Evidently I did not know everything, I had not seen the seeds sprout, or the tree grow. But faced with this great wrinkled paw, neither ignorance nor knowledge was important; the world of explanations and reasons is not the world of existence. A circle is not absurd, it is clearly explained by the rotation of a straight segment around one of its extremities. But neither does a circle exist. This root, on the other hand, existed in such a way that I could not explain it. Knotty, inert, nameless, it fascinated me, filled my eyes, brought me back unceasingly to its own existence. In vain to repeat: "This is a root"—it didn't work any more. I saw clearly that you could not pass from its function as a root, as a breathing pump, *to that*, to this hard and compact skin of a sea lion, to this oily, callous, headstrong look. The function explained nothing: it allowed you to understand generally that it was a root, but not *that one* at all. This root, with its colour, shape, its congealed movement, was . . . below all explanation. Each of its qualities escaped it a little, flowed out of it, half solidified, almost became a thing; each one was *in the way* in the root and the whole stump now gave me the impression of unwinding itself a little, denying its existence to lose itself in a frenzied excess. I scraped my heel against this black claw: I wanted to peel off some of the bark. For no reason at all, out of defiance, to make the bare pink appear absurd on the tanned leather; to *play* with the absurdity of the world. But, when I drew my heel back, I saw that the bark was still black.[1]

This passage, which perhaps suffers more than the others in being wrenched from its context, is really the extension of an insight which has come to Roquentin a few pages earlier, when he ponders the seat of a tramcar in which he is travelling:

Things are divorced from their names. They are there, grotesque, headstrong, gigantic and it seems ridiculous to call them seats or say anything at all about them: I am in the midst of things, nameless things. Alone, without words, defenceless, they surround me, are beneath me,

[1] J. P. Sartre, *Nausea (La Nausée)*, pp. 174-5. London: Hamish Hamilton, 1962.

behind me, above me. They demand nothing, they don't impose themselves; they are there.[1]

It is clear, even from these short extracts, that part of *La Nausée* is concerned with dramatizing the struggle of a mind to leap through the void that separates it from the world of things and to make sense of a totally senseless universe. The desperation of both the effort and the inevitable defeat is to be sensed in the language, particularly in its quality of powerful but slightly sinister metaphor. The thing, the tree-root, can be named, but the name is divorced from the thing; that its "absolute character" can never be fixed is shown by the drastic metamorphoses it undergoes—a breathing pump, a sea-lion, a black claw. The prose oscillates between that and a kind of abstraction—"a circle is not absurd"—which enacts, I suppose, the effort of the mind to come to terms with the vigour and plenitude of an external world totally subversive of all logic. Even to speak in these terms is to do the passage an injustice, since what appears as metaphorical is also, in a sense, literal. In a world where, as Roquentin says, "the essential thing is contingency", where no necessary or stable relationships are to be discerned, which is sensed primarily as a viscous flux, such metamorphoses are not impossible. Why, in this totally random world, should a root *not* become a black claw or the seat of a tramcar change into the upturned belly of a dead donkey? The prose does more than play with such questions; behind it is a serious and sophisticated philosophy. Yet, oddly enough, our scale of mind–thing relationships seems almost to be circular, with its extremes meeting; the philosophic imagination of Sartre seems much more akin to the primitive imagination of Dickens than to anything else we have encountered.

IV

Alienation has unfortunately become something of a cant word in many kinds of intellectual discourse, including literary criticism. But it is the right and inevitable word if we are to see the passages I have quoted as representative rather than arbitrary. Its primary connotations are, of course, social; it directs us to such topics as the replacement of

[1] J. P. Sartre, *Nausea* (*La Nausée*), p. 169.

community by mass or the breakdown in communication between the artist and any coherent audience. If its effects have been primarily social so, we may agree, was its cause; I see little to quarrel with in the Marxist thesis that alienation is a product of complex industrial and capitalist societies. But a contributary cause was certainly the decline of a theology in which man's relation to his world was given stability by being part of a divinely-ordered cosmos. We need not discuss how the breakdown of this world-view was related to social and economic changes. But we should notice that one of the series of correspondences supposed to exist between microcosm and macrocosm presupposed a stable relation between the world of things and man's mind,

> *that ocean where each kind*
> *Does streight its own resemblance find.*

At first the grandeur and order of the Newtonian universe buttressed the coherence and stability of this world view. But as the idea of rational man living in a rational universe crumbles, as scientific laws turn into mere high-order probabilities, as the possibility of certain knowledge dwindles and as the necessary turns into the contingent, so the novelist comes to inhabit an exciting but unstable world. I am not, of course, suggesting a simple relationship between intellectual cause and imaginative response; no doubt there is a cultural time-lag and no doubt diffusion means distortion. But gradually man's view of his world changes and gradually this affects the novelist's response; we move from confidence to uncertainty, from stability to flux, from the assurance that we know what is normal to Roquentin's sense of the absurd. The effects of this breakdown—of alienation—are discernible in every aspect of life, including man's relation to the world of things.

The breakdown usually takes one of two forms. There is the common Romantic nightmare—particularly acute in Coleridge—of the material world when the creative mind fails in its seminal function; a universe of little things, dry, disconnected, dead. But it is the second kind of alienation that I wish to stress, one denounced by Carlyle and Ruskin, not to speak of Marx himself. This is the view of man as victim of the cash-nexus and the industrial jungle; man as reduced to the status of a mere thing, an extension of the lever or the loom; man as an object to be manipulated and exploited.

Most novelists view with abhorrence this reduction of man to thing. This is partly because most of them write from within a liberal world view with its respect for people as autonomous beings, as ends-in-themselves. But this respect is also inherent in the nature of their craft; acutely aware of the dangers of creating puppets, they must strive to give at least the illusion of autonomy to their characters. Hence most of them react sharply to this aspect of alienation; manipulation of other people, the reduction of man to object, quickly become objects of attack in their fiction. This is certainly what happens in the extract quoted from *Our Mutual Friend*, constituting the important difference between Dickens and Sartre. For Dickens's primitive imagination of the world is given moral point and direction by a mind that is, in the last analysis, in confident control, whereas Sartre's protagonist is helpless in face of a totally contingent world of objects.

It is rare for the problems thus raised to be intellectually formulated by the novelist. Indeed, it is quite possible— witness most English novels—to rest in a kind of comfortable empiricism, to concern oneself with particular, limited human and social situations, and to be entirely unaware that any larger problem exists. Alienation most often manifests itself as a diffused and undefined pressure to which the novelist responds obliquely. As one might expect, an important set of responses is religious in nature; yet these produce surprisingly few really great novels. There is a kind of neo-Platonic response in which objects are placed and given significance by being the symbolic manifestation of a transcendental reality. This, of course, is the descendant of the traditional Christian metaphysic; what is new is that the god is veiled and ambiguous; reality may be divine or diabolic. Of this kind of reaction Melville and Kafka are perhaps the major representatives. As against this, by believing that the divine is also totally immanent, one may simultaneously celebrate God and life in all its particularity; parts of Tolstoy's work are here the best example. Finally, one can accept the entire contingency of the phenomenal world as it

is humanly experienced and leap, like Kierkegaard, across
the void between the breakdown of reason and the acceptance of faith. I cannot recall any great novel which dramatizes this position; Dostoievsky comes closest, I suppose, but
does not quite fit into this or into any other category.
Roquentin makes part of the journey and comes to the edge
of the void, to the absurd; but he can go no further since
God is absent from his universe. Sartre, to be sure, subsequently makes the leap to a total faith. But this is irrelevant
to his fiction; indeed, perhaps it killed him as a novelist.

The significant reaction, in fact, has not been so much
religious as aesthetic. One thinks, for example, of characters
like Mrs. Ramsay whose sensibility works on the raw data of
her experience in a typically aesthetic way, composing relationships into harmony, translating her gastronomic triumph
into a symbolic celebration of human love. One thinks of all
those novelists—the Mrs. Ramsays of that craft—who have
written novels exploring the preconditions necessary to the
writing of a novel. One thinks of the rise of the *bildungs-
roman*. Most significant of all, perhaps, one thinks of
Roquentin's faint hope of escape from the world of nausea;
he, too, however feebly, can rejoice, having to construct
something on which to rejoice. Why can Roquentin hope
that the writing of a novel will make some sense of his life?
Because the work of art—viewed as a self-sufficient artefact
—is a necessary and not a contingent thing. It is a thing
wrenched from the chaotic flux of the experienced world; it
has its own laws and its own firm structure of relationships;
it can, like a system of geometry, be held to be absolutely
true within its own conventionally established terms.

Many modern novelists have found consolation in this
view which has consequently affected their creative practice.
While few novels can be derived from it in any philosophically rigorous sense, it is clearly no accident that autonomy
theories of art have concurrently become dominant. Connected with these theories there is another kind of aesthetic
response to the fact of alienation which is important to the
substance and the implied values of many modern novels. In
an autonomy theory of art the cardinal sin is didacticism. By
this I mean any attempt on the part of either writer or reader
to *use* the work of art. On this theory the artefact both

arouses and completes emotion; the aesthetic state is one of stasis. Kinetic responses—those which carry over from the artefact to life—are at best irrelevant and at worst vitiating since the work of art is a sufficient end in itself, containing its own values. In the post-Kantian, liberal ethic endorsed by most novelists, the human being has much the same status as that accorded the work of art by this type of aesthetic. Man is an end in himself; we must respond to him as an autonomous being; the cardinal sin is to use or to manipulate him, to reduce him to a mere thing. The fields of aesthetics and ethics have a common frontier; thus one may easily understand how many novelists will therefore dramatize the moral substance of their novels in aesthetic terms. Aesthetic value becomes a metaphor for moral value; if man, in his alienated state, is reduced to a thing, then the novelist responds by asserting that he is at any rate a very special *kind* of thing—a work of art. Ethical discrimination merges into aesthetic discrimination; good taste becomes nearly synonymous with good sense and right feeling.

Here again, Virginia Woolf is a relevant example, especially if one sees her as sharing an ethos derived from G. E. Moore:

> By far the most valuable things, which we know or can imagine, are certain states of consciousness, which may be roughly described as the pleasures of human intercourse, and the enjoyment of beautiful objects. No one, probably, who has asked himself the question, has ever doubted that personal affection and the appreciation of what is beautiful in Art or Nature, are good in themselves; nor, if we consider strictly what things are worth having *purely for their own sakes*, does it appear probable that any one will think that anything else has nearly so great a value as the things which are included under these two heads.[1]

But it is probably Henry James who has most consistently, richly and subtly exploited this interplay between aesthetics and ethics. Let us examine briefly, therefore, some aspects of *The Portrait of A Lady*.

---

[1] G. E. Moore, *Principia Ethica*, pp. 188–9. Cambridge University Press, 1959.

v

In the education of Isabel Archer no lesson is more bitter
or more important than this recognition of what Osmond
and Madame Merle have done to her:

> She saw, in the crude light of that revelation which had
> already become a part of experience and to which the
> very frailty of the vessel in which it had been offered her
> only gave an intrinsic price, the dry staring fact that she
> had been an applied handled hung-up tool, as senseless
> and convenient as mere shaped wood and iron.
>
> (Chapter 52)

This perfect example of the sin against human autonomy
—of use and exploitation, of the person reduced to a thing—
gains part of its force from a context of imagery which per-
sistently renders human experience in aesthetic terms. This
is particularly true when applied to Isabel herself; thus,
early in the novel, her cousin Ralph thinks of her:

> "A character like that," he said to himself—"a real
> little passionate force to see at play is the finest thing in
> nature. It's finer than the finest work of art—than a
> Greek bas-relief, than a great Titian, than a Gothic
> cathedral. It's very pleasant to be so well treated where
> one had least looked for it. I had never been more blue,
> more bored, than for a week before she came; I had
> never expected less that anything pleasant would happen.
> Suddenly I receive a Titian, by the post, to hang on my
> wall—a Greek bas-relief to stick over my chimney-piece.
> The key of a beautiful edifice is thrust into my hand, and
> I'm told to walk in and admire." (7)

As Isabel is seen in aesthetic terms, so she sees others;
thus Lord Warburton is "a hero of romance" (7) and in
Caspar Goodwood "she saw the different fitted parts of him
as she had seen, in museums and portraits, the different
fitted parts of armoured warriors—in plates of steel hand-
somely inlaid with gold" (13). So her moral life, too, is defined in these terms; of her relation with Madame Merle,
"it was as if she had given to a comparative stranger the key
to her cabinet of jewels. These spiritual gems were the only

ones of any magnitude that Isabel possessed" (19). The notion of the key is, of course, recurrent and related to the persistent image of the house, both conveying the basic themes of independence, invasion and possession. Similarly when Ralph tells Isabel, "Don't question your conscience so much—it will get out of tune like a strummed piano" (21), his simile perhaps gains a resonance from the literal, emphasized fact of Madame Merle's skill at the piano; she *plays* on Isabel as well.

This brings us to Madame Merle and Osmond, and to one of the central problems confronting James in this novel. Madame Merle and Osmond must be made to *seem* fine and impressive, at least in Isabel's eyes; otherwise her sensibility will be coarsened and her value as moral agent diminished. If she is to be deceived then at least she must be taken in by a very good imitation of the real thing. But she *is* deceived; Madame Merle and Osmond must be seen by the reader only as *seeming* what Isabel actually takes them to be. James's major techniques for solving this problem are not relevant here, but clearly the problem *is* closely related to the view of human beings as aesthetic objects. Thus many critics have noticed the limiting qualification in James's description of Madame Merle: "Of painting she was devotedly fond, and made no more of brushing in a sketch than of pulling off her gloves" (19). Similarly, Osmond *appears* a fine aesthetic object:

> He suggested, fine coin as he was, no stamp nor emblem of the common mintage that provides for general circulation; he was the elegant complicated medal struck off for a special occasion. (22)

But the fine coin proves to have too great an admixture of base alloy; Osmond is like the precious coffee-cup flawed by a minute crack (49). The human failure is suggested in aesthetic terms; thus Madame Merle admits that "his painting's pretty bad" (19); thus Rosier (whose testimony we tend to trust since he sacrifices Art for Life by selling his bibelots) thinks that much of Osmond's taste is bad (37); Ralph, while allowing to Isabel that Osmond is "the incarnation of taste", comes as near as he can to savagery by telling her, "you were meant for something better than to

keep guard over the sensibilities of a sterile dilettante"(34).
Osmond himself reveals his human-aesthetic flaw. He dismisses Madame Merle thus; "Oh, the imagination of
women! It's always vulgar, at bottom. You talk of revenge
like a third-rate novelist" (49). Yet within a few pages he too
becomes the third-rate novelist:

> Osmond turned slightly pale; he gave a cold smile.
> "That's why you must go then? Not to see your cousin,
> but to take a revenge on me."
> "I know nothing about revenge."
> "I do," said Osmond. "Don't give me an occasion."
> (51)

Naturally these two predators regard Isabel in similar
terms:

> What could be a happier gift in a companion than a
> quick, fanciful mind which saved one repetitions and re-
> flected one's thought on a polished, elegant surface?
> Osmond hated to see his thought reproduced literally—
> that made it look stale and stupid; he preferred it to be
> freshened in the reproduction even as "words" by music.
> His egotism had never taken the crude form of desiring a
> dull wife; this lady's intelligence was to be a silver plate,
> not an earthen one—a plate that he might heap up with
> rich fruits, to which it would give a decorative value, so
> that talk might become for him a sort of served dessert.
> He found the silver quality in this perfection in Isabel; he
> could tap her imagination with his knuckle and make it
> ring. (35)

Even before this Isabel has conceived of herself in a like
way:

> She only felt older—ever so much, and as if she were
> "worth more" for it, like some curious piece in an anti-
> quary's collection. (32)

This, of course, is precisely what she is destined to become; part of the tragedy of her relationship with Osmond is
in the metamorphosis from "silver plate" to "an applied
handled hung-up tool, as senseless and convenient as mere
shaped wood and iron".

D

The examples I have quoted in this brief analysis are not isolated; such imagery is dense in *The Portrait of A Lady*. It is a concern, moreover, which persists through much of James's work; one thinks of *The Princess Casamassima* and *The Tragic Muse*. From it James derives many of his most beautiful effects; I can think of few more lyrical passages in his work than his description of Strether's walk through the French countryside in the eleventh book of *The Ambassadors*. Yet in the margins of this translation of human experience into aesthetic terms there remains a faint question mark. How adequate, after all, to the complexity of life is this view of human relationships as a matter of connoisseurship? If Osmond regards Isabel as a work of art, so do Ralph and Lord Warburton; if Osmond regards his daughter thus, so does Rosier. But unlike them, Osmond has a base and improper aesthetic sense; unlike them, he wants to *use* the work of art. It is precisely in these terms that James achieves the desired moral discrimination and, in doing so, achieves also a masterpiece. Nevertheless, the question remains; the balance between aesthetic vehicle and moral tenor is a precarious one; the traffic between the two areas is often equivocal and ambiguous. This is the reason, surely, why the attitude of the Ververs to their captive Prince has caused so much critical debate.

For a symbol of this mingled strength and weakness, this combination on the reader's part of admiration and marginal doubt, we may turn to another novelist. Aschenbach in *Death In Venice* is truly representative of many writers whose dilemma and response I have tried to describe. His artistic life has been dedicated to the wrenching of a classic order out of the delirium and flux of life. Yet behind the order lies the dream of a Dionysiac revel; life reasserts itself, fascinating, corrupt, chaotic, a jungle. In face of this, "his art, his moral sense, what were they in the balance beside the boons that chaos might confer? ... Knowledge is all-knowing, understanding, forgiving; it takes up no position, sets no store by form. It has compassion with the abyss—it *is* the abyss."

Yet before he plunges into the abyss of life, immersing himself for the last time in the destructive element, Aschenbach once more asserts his identity and dignity as an artist, "and fashioned his little essay after the model Tadzio's beauty set; that page and a half of choicest prose, so chaste, so lofty, so poignant with feeling, which would shortly be the wonder and admiration of the multitude".

It is a heroic stance, compelling respect and compassion. The artist for the last time tames the multitudinous seas, before breaking his magic staff and drowning into life. Yet even here we hear the whisper of our marginal doubt. Do we ever really believe in that page and a half of exquisite prose? Is the purity of the aesthetic response ever adequate to the challenge of a corrupt, contingent, chaotic world? Can a last-ditch defence ever become a proper base for further explanation?

CHAPTER III

The Human Context

THE last chapter will at least have demonstrated the complexities inherent in even the simplest of human relationships. It would be tedious to analyse many contexts in such detail; cumulatively they support the point made by Kenneth Burke in an essay called *Four Master Tropes*:

> It is customary to think that objective reality is dissolved by such relativity of terms as we get through the shifting of perspectives (the perception of one character in terms of many diverse characters). But on the contrary, it is by the approach through a variety of perspectives that we establish a character's reality.[1]

Burke is here writing of metaphor and the word *character* has a special meaning for him; but if we reinterpret this passage to suit our own interest it still remains relevant and stimulating. For if we compile a list of all those relationships which make up our contextual knowledge of others and if we then try to recreate our sense of these relationships overlapping, interacting and developing in time, what we achieve is precisely that "variety of perspectives" whereby "we establish a character's reality". It is precisely because the novel can establish a greater range and variety of perspectives than any other art-form—indeed, a greater variety of viewpoints than we usually have of most other people in actual life—that we may legitimately talk of the reality of fictional characters.

By far the most important of contexts is the web of human relationships in which any single character must be enmeshed. So much of what we are can only be defined in terms of our relations with other people; indeed, if we wish to be rigorous, we can say with the philosophers that other people must exist if only to show us what we ourselves are not. Thus, for example, one aspect of Strether's reality for us in *The Ambassadors* lies in his relation to Waymarsh. Waymarsh

[1] K. Burke, *A Grammar of Motives*, p. 504. New York: Prentice Hall, 1945.

represents one possible line of development, or rather regression, for Strether. Again, little Bilham is not simply the
Complete European displayed for the benefit of the American visitor, nor yet simply a politely uncomprehending
audience for Strether's mature views on life; he also illumi-
nates aspects of Strether not directly revealed in the book
but which we feel as part, perhaps, of Strether's past and
as such, which we can check against James's recapitulation
of Strether's history. Of course, what these characters do
not share is more important than what they have in common
and equally there are some alternatives for Strether which we
feel are just not possible. Thus he might *just* become a kind
of Waymarsh but we feel he could *never* become a Jim
Pocock.

The first thing to notice about this network of relationships—obviously very simplified in my account of *The
Ambassadors*—is that *we* perceive it, not any of the characters. They may be more or less perceptive, and again we
distinguish them as such, but none of them can aspire to our
wholeness of vision. What we are offered is an exercise in
contrast and comparison, a variation on the old theme of
unity in variety, of similitude in dissimilitude, which is one
of the major formal pleasures of art. But the pleasure is more
than merely formal; we are also aware of a real analogy
between our responses as readers of fiction and the process
whereby in actual life we establish a person's reality by considering his many relationships, by viewing him through
many perspectives. The only difference is that the fictional
character offers a challenge that is perhaps more clear-cut,
disciplined and subtle. If he offers no such challenge what
do we call him? Probably an unreal stereotype; we can all
think of creative failures which render such a verdict just.
But we should also realize that too often we live by standards
we condemn in art. In real life our perspectives are often
extremely artificial and limited; for example, we often impose
our own created stereotypes on others because we are too
tired or too timid for anything else. This man is a bore, that
man a hypocrite, we say—as though that were the whole
truth of the matter. The bore bores us, the hypocrite disgusts
us—life is that simple. But in fiction the bore delights us,
the hypocrite fascinates us; for in fiction they become inter-

esting and complex characters. A good novel, by its various strategies, breaks down our stereotypes and enforces its own perspectives. If we read well we shall attend to these; the effort of so attending—which implies understanding, sympathizing, judging, etc.—is a *real* effort, a real psychological adjustment on our part. This effort on our part we impute, by a confusion of cause and effect, to the characters themselves; thereby we call them real.

The variety of perspectives thus established by fiction depends upon a double awareness on our part:

(*a*) Our awareness that the world is humanly diverse and abundant. This I shall take for granted; the range of individual variety is an obvious criterion by which we judge the greatness of most great novels. Even where experience is concentrated and focused by the lens of a single consciousness—a Tristram Shandy, a David Copperfield, even a Stephen Dedalus—we are still as much interested in the various human worlds thus revealed, however distorted or partial they may be, as in the consciousness itself.

(*b*) Our awareness that we experience the world in differing degrees of depth, that the quality of our various relationships depends especially on the degree of intimacy, insight and knowledge in our contact for others. For example with some people we communicate well, with others badly. Generally it is probably fair to say that in real life we transmit or receive on pretty insensitive instruments, covering a wide and blurred waveband; there is always plenty of static, plenty of merely human *noise*, against which our messages sometimes emerge loud and clear, sometimes as a jumbled code. A good novelist will generally pay tribute to this variety in the quality of our human communication; perfect communication if prolonged is implausible. Some of James's characters, for example—those who perceive every nuance, every implication, who read brilliantly not only the lines but between the lines—sometimes irritate us on this account. Of course James, like most great novelists, can exploit miscommunication between characters, and of course miscommunication between characters may often be part of the author's strategy in communicating to the reader. The important point to stress is the variety of quality in human relationships. Thus this person we know almost as well as ourselves, that one is interesting or intriguing but elusive and shadowy, a third only occasionally impinges on us so that we can fit him into one of those stereotyped categories by means of which, as I have said, we simplify and make convenient our lives.

Granted this, we can discover two sets of perspectives in fiction. This first set we may call perspectives of range and these derive from the greater knowledge bestowed on us as readers; thus we can make connections inaccessible to individual characters, we can spot motives hidden from them, we may even know the future towards which they move in their dramatic present. Anything that we label "dramatic irony" derives from this kind of perspective. But there is a second kind—we may call it the perspective of depth—in which certain characters become important because they stand out from, or are immersed in, a world of other human beings seen briefly, shallowly or in fragments. This kind of perspective corresponds to the varying quality of our relationships in the real world and like them, it is fluid and unstable. A face that is no more than a blur in the crowd may for a moment be focused sharply and significantly before fading away again; a stranger briefly met and almost totally unknown may illuminate a new possibility of life for us. So also in fiction; a background figure, a mere stereotype, may be granted a moment of dramatic intensity in which he achieves fullness as a human being. Dostoievsky and Proust are supreme in their mastery of this technique whereby we are suddenly plunged from shallows to depths, but the trick is not uncommon. This brief illumination of an otherwise sketchily realized character is one of the many ways in which the novelist legitimately provokes the reader to speculate about, and thereby give substance to the character; what we are offered, so to speak, is only one arc of the circle that if fully drawn would make up the rounded character. But the arc is so curved that we can, if we wish, extend it full-circle in our imagination.

This kind of perspective in depth, then, is a fluid and shifting affair in art as well as in life. Some characters stand in a full light, others remain shadowy, still others advance and retreat in our consciousness as readers. Nevertheless, for convenience we can group most characters into three categories. The most important are clearly the protagonists—those characters whose motivation and history are most fully established, who conflict and change as the story progresses, who engage our responses more fully and steadily, in a way more complex though not necessarily more vivid than other characters. They are the vehicles by which all the most interesting questions are raised; they evoke our beliefs, sympathies, revulsions; they incarnate the moral vision of the world inherent in the total novel. In a sense they are end-products; they are what the novel exists for; it exists to reveal them. Because of this it is unwise to generalize about them; each exists as an individual case and demands special consideration.

At the other end of the scale are those many different kinds of creation we may lump together as "background" characters. These may, as I have said, be allowed a moment of intensity and depth, but equally they may be almost entirely anonymous, voices rather than individualized characters. Singly they may be merely useful cogs in the mechanism of the plot, collectively they may establish themselves as a chorus to the main action—one thinks, for example, of Hardy's rustics—or may exist simply to establish the density of society in which the protagonists must move if they are to have any depth of realization. Clearly this social setting is one of the most important of all human contexts, and while the novelist can do a great deal by way of direct description and analysis, society must also be seen as a complex web of *individual* relationships. This is most economically achieved by establishing a range of background characters whose individuality need be no more than is adequate to typify social trends or pressures; without them society will tend to become hopelessly abstract and external. One thinks, for instance, of the weakness of those inter-chapters in *The Grapes of Wrath* in which Steinbeck attempts to convey the vast impersonal forces of a complex society determining the destinies of the Joad family. When he works in the opposite direction and allows us to take the family as the representative focus of a particular kind of society, he is much more successful.

So much, of course, depends on the society to be depicted. With a relatively simple and static world the novelist may easily convey a sense of the whole community in action— the village of Hayslope, for example, in *Adam Bede*. The same holds true of any society which is isolated or artificially delimited and which lives according to a traditional code of its own—one thinks of the ships' crews in *Moby Dick* or *The Nigger of the Narcissus* or the isolated communities, white and Indian, of a novel like *The Prairie*. In a more complex society the problems are correspondingly greater but in either case human relationships must be felt to merge into social relationships without too abrupt a change from dramatic realization to external analysis and commentary.

Indeed, one can think of remarkably few novels in which the protagonists achieve reality while remaining isolated from some social context. On the other hand, many novels may approach if not achieve greatness by realizing through a host of background characters a sense of society in action. *Germinal* is here a relevant example. Surely there is no single character in this novel who remains powerfully in the mind as an individual. Étienne is a mere dummy with the same status, say, as Felix Holt. Souvarine's inadequacy can be seen by contrasting him with his equivalent in *The Possessed*. Perhaps the character nearest to achieving individual status —and even this is peripheral—is the tormented Hennebeau. This lack prevents *Germinal* from being a truly great novel but it is still a very good one. What, then, does one remember as the source of the novel's power? First, there are individual *gestures* as distinct from individual characters— Moquette flaunting her bum in derision. Then there are superbly melodramatic scenes—Chaval's corpse bumping against Étienne and Catherine in the flooded mine. Above all there is the symbolic power of the book—the mine, for example, seen as an animal, finally wounded and collapsing in its death throes; counterpointing this, the miners seen as animals, the human figure almost being submerged into the natural. The symbolism is gross, face-slapping; the delicate tools of critical analysis would be as out of place here as a pick and shovel in a surgery. All these things derive from Zola's control of the mass; nowhere is he finer than in his mob scenes, where he is only equalled by Dickens at his best.

Here is a community in action; the coarse vigour of the book is appropriately channelled through a number of characters who hardly ever achieve more than a background status; indeed, more complex characterization or greater psychological subtlety would have compelled a different kind of interest, quite fatal to the book's distinctive achievement.

Between the protagonists and the background characters fall a wide variety of intermediate figures; I wish to concentrate on two of them. The first we may call, after James, the ficelle, the character who while more fully delineated and individualized than any background character, exists in the novel primarily to serve some function. Unlike the protagonist he is ultimately a means to an end rather than an end in himself; the novelist's success in treating him will often reside in the function being so disguised that it may be performed unobtrusively. But before I consider the various functions of the ficelle, I wish to consider another type of intermediate creation—the Card, the character who is a "character".

II

One fairly common use of the word *character* occurs in a phrase like "What a character!" When we describe a person in such terms we often have at the back of our minds the notion that life may here be imitating art, that such a person is "larger than life" or is distinguished by some fiction-like idiosyncrasy. Of course, in a sense we all know that life is weirder and richer than fiction, that what seems phantasmagoric may often turn out to be sober and even underplayed realism. Los Angeles is *in fact* stranger than anything in *The Loved One*; most English universities are *in fact* much odder than anything in *Lucky Jim*. Of course, the oddness of real life is diluted with a good deal of dreary ordinariness. And, of course, one must have been a don or have lived in Los Angeles to know the difference; the fictional representation of these states and places seems cardish only to outsiders. Can we say, then, that what seems odd is the result of our limited view, that if we lived inside the situation the sense of strangeness, the "larger than life" quality, would erode and crumble? Are characters who are Cards merely the result of the novelist forcing us to take an outside, objective view of them? Mary McCarthy would seem to think so; I quote at some length from a characteristically provocative essay of hers. She has just pointed out that the "real people" in novels tend not to be the "straight" characters, the heroes and heroines, but rather the minor and comic characters:

In what does this "reality" consist? In the incorrigibility and changelessness of the figure. Villains may reform, heroes and heroines may learn their lesson, like Emma or Elizabeth or Mr. Darcy, or grow into the author, like Stephen Dedalus and David Copperfield, but a Lady Catherine de Bourgh or a Molly Bloom or a Mr. Dedalus, regardless of resolutions, cannot reform or change, cannot be other than they are. . . . Real characterization, I think, is seldom accomplished outside of comedy or without the fixative of comedy: the stubborn pride of Mr. Darcy, the prejudice of Elizabeth, the headstrongness of Emma. A comic character, contrary to accepted belief, is likely to be more complicated and enigmatic than a hero or a heroine, fuller of surprises and turnabouts; Mr. Micawber, for instance, can find the most unexpected ways of being himself; so can Mr. Woodhouse or the Master of the Marshalsea. It is a sort of resourcefulness. . . . The comic element is the incorrigible element in every human being; the capacity to learn, from experience or instruction, is what is forbidden to all comic creations and to what is comic in you and me. The capacity to learn is the prerogative of the hero or the heroine: Prince Hal as opposed to Falstaff. The principle of growth in human beings is as real, of course (though possibly not so common) as the principle of eternity or inertia represented by the comic; it is the subjective as opposed to the objective. When we identify ourselves with the hero of a story, we are following him with all our hopes, i.e., with our subjective conviction of human freedom; on the comic characters we look with despair, in which, though, there is a queer kind of admiration—we really, I believe, admire the comic characters *more* than we do the hero or the heroine, because of their obstinate power to do-it-again, combined with a total lack of self-consciousness or shame.[1]

This account, which has much in common with an existentialist conception of character and human relationships, raises some important points. But it is full of semantic dodges; some characters, like Emma or Mr. Darcy, figure on both sides of the ledger; *subjective* and *objective* are notoriously tricky words, while to say that such characters are more complicated and enigmatic than most protagonists is simply to use a common set of terms to describe two very different sets of phenomena. Nevertheless I feel that the truth is on Miss McCarthy's side rather than, for example, on the side of Chesterton and Santayana when they try to defend Dickens's card-like characters. Chesterton and Santayana maintain that such characters are in fact realistic and true to life, that the reader mistakes them for flat caricatures only because he has such a limited and stereotyped view of reality. In other words, this is the life-is-richer-than-art theory all over again. One cannot prove Chesterton and Santayana to be wrong; indeed one knows that their root proposition is true and I have already invoked it in this chapter. Yet the effect of their argument is to assimilate very different kinds of characters—Pip and Wemmick, for example—into one kind of realism and this one knows to be wrong. Pip and Wemmick *are* both "real"; yes, but in different senses of the word. Whether or not one agrees entirely with Miss McCarthy, she at least perceives a distinction does exist. Can we do more to clarify the ambiguities lurking in the word *real*, when applied to card-like characters? Let me start with some simple assertions:

(*a*) Most Cards—however large they bulk in the reader's imagination—are not the nominal heroes of the novels that contain them. Few novels make the Card a protagonist and these few, although they may be very good, do not approach real greatness. Most of them stay on the level, say, of *Oblomov* or *Babbit*. The one possible exception to this—though I am doubtful whether any category can possibly contain the example—is *Don Quixote*.

[1] M. McCarthy, "Characters in Fiction", *On the Contrary*, pp. 288–9. London: Heinemann, 1962.

(*b*) The distinguishing feature of the Card—we may agree with Miss McCarthy—is his relative changelessness, combined with a peculiar kind of freedom; the joker is always wild. The Card is triumphantly himself; he is like the child's toy, its base filled with lead, which always bobs upright no matter how far it is pushed over. Part of the joy of these characters lies in their immunity to the knocks and buffets doled out to them, in their ultimate reassertion of their own natures. This is not a truth of the world as we know it in terms of sober, everyday realism; but it *is* a truth of the imagination. Man dreams of freedom from time and the world of circumstance, he dreams of innocence, integrity, invulnerability. Such a dream, such a holiday from existence as is incarnate in the Card, is no less real than our sad, open-eyed recognition of our manifold limitations. It is a part of empirical reality, part of the total complex of hopes, fears, desires, decisions that make us what we are.

(*c*) But, given this, the Card is not necessarily simple; in particular, he is not simply comic. He is often comic and pathetic at the same time or—as so often in Dickens—comic and sinister. If he is pictured as a fool then we know also that the fool can speak wisdom. Krook, Quilp, Miss Flite, Miss Mowcher—they all arouse mingled responses. But such complexity exists only in the reader's response; the character himself is not aware of it. This is one of the prime differences between the Card and the protagonist who shares in our common knowledge of internal conflict. This is why Ahab, for all his concentration and singleness of will, is a protagonist and not a Card; he has locked himself in his own monomania and he knows it; sometimes we can feel him beating his fists against the walls of his prison.

(*d*) Moreover, the Card's freedom is only relative. Here, I think, I disagree with Miss McCarthy. Cards are not absolutely immune from change and growth; of the examples she quotes, even if we discount Micawber's Australian career, we are still left with Mr. Dorrit. Dorrit's freedom as a card-like character coincides with his imprisonment in the Marshalsea; when he is offered the very different freedom of the world he begins to change. Such change presents very tricky problems for the novelist. The reader is reluctant to forego the peculiar consolation he finds in this kind of character; he wants Don Quixote to continue in his dream. So, very often, does the novelist. An interesting example is Denry Machin, hero of Bennett's *The Card*. In the first few chapters of the sequel to this novel, *The Regent*, Bennett seems to be nerving himself to break down his hero and make him vulnerable to the world; he comes near to creating an anti-hero. And although he changes his mind and Denry continues his triumphant antics, something has gone wrong; the balloon of invention sags a little and the sequel has nothing of the original's élan and buoyancy.

Nevertheless, although the sharp demarcation between the Card and the protagonist may sometimes be blurred, the essential distinction remains. And because the Card is free in his captivity—or equally, captured in his freedom—the novelist can frequently release through him a vividness, an energy, an abundance that would submerge and obscure the more intricate contours of the protagonist. Card-like characters are, so to speak, chemically pure; that is why they are so often tonic, even intoxicating. Their realism is one of intensity, singleness, vivacity; the realism of the protagonist is that of dilution, complexity and process. Who is to say that one or other of these is the "really real"? Fiction—and indeed, life—would be impoverished if the critic sought to pass an Act of Exclusion.

III

At first glance the Card and the ficelle might seem to be diametrically opposed types of character. Despite the Card's difference from the protagonist, he too is an end-in-himself in the novel; any function he serves is a by-product. The danger of allowing a Card into a novel is that so exuberant is he in his autonomy, so sheerly gratuitous and in excess of what the theme or vision of the novel may demand, that he is liable to grow out of all proportion, become mutinous and anarchic in his creator's hands and destroy the structure of the total work. Beside a Charlus or a Micawber it may seem that Marcel or David Copperfield are dwarfed and dim; we may forget that it is only in the story of the pale narrator that ultimately these vivid characters have any significance. The danger of the ficelle, on the other hand, is that he may seem merely a function, serving his purpose without that margin of gratuitous life which changes a schematic figure into an interesting character. Only the greatest novelists can fuse these two types, can so blend freedom and discipline that the categories no longer apply.

The ficelle has many functions, some of which are too obvious to merit much discussion. Like the background character he too may serve a purely mechanical role in the plot or act as chorus. He may become a transitional agent between protagonist and society; he may afford relief and contrast of the simplest kind. Like the Card he may allow us the pleasurable relaxation of recognizing the limited and familiar after our struggle with the involvements or complexities of the protagonist. In innumerable ways he may act as foil to the protagonist, creating what I have called the perspectives of depth. By his misunderstanding and partial view he may focus the protagonist's dilemma more clearly. Alternatively, by a flash of insight or simply by being the spokesman of sober reality and common sense, he may illuminate the protagonist's blindness and folly. He may stand as a possible alternative to the protagonist, incarnating what the character might have been—so stands Banquo to Macbeth. Or he may embody in a simpler form some analogue, positive or negative, to the hero's experience—so stands Gloucester to Lear. He may be the moral touchstone by which we judge the aberrations of others; he may, by being simple and static, become the point of reference by which we measure change and growth elsewhere. Examples of these, and no doubt of many other functions, will readily occur to the reader; I will isolate only two typical points for more detailed discussion.

The more exceptional the experience embodied in the protagonist the greater become the problems of mimetic adequacy and hence the more important are the mediating and choric functions of the ficelle. He becomes, so to speak, the spring-board from which we launch ourselves into the turbid depths of the central figure. *Exceptional* can here mean one of two things. The experience may be remote from the reader because it is beyond the range of his normal experience—the protagonist, for example, who happens to be a saint or an artistic genius. Alternatively, the experience may be within the range of the reader but beyond his depth. That is, the reader may discover analogues for the experience within himself, but it may still be exceptional by reason of its extreme intensity and purity. We have all sinned and felt guilt, but we are still a long way from being Macbeth.

A single illustration of exceptional experience will suffice. One of the distinguishing features of much modern fiction is its concern with the epiphany, the Wordsworthian "spot of time", the moment of intense vision which yields a significance far beyond the mundane world of common experience. In different forms we find it in Forster, Joyce, Proust, Lawrence, Virginia Woolf and many other novelists. It is an essentially post-Romantic concern and—with the possible exception of Proust—quite different from the Aristotelian moment of anagnorisis or self-recognition which we should normally expect as a climax of any interesting moral process. But clearly it will, like anagorisis, have implications for the creation of character; to put it at its crudest, some characters will be capable of the moments of vision, others not. This capability is indeed often made the basis of moral judgment and discrimination.

As I say, a similar concern is central to Romantic poetry. If the visionary moment is expressed quintessentially, asserted as a value of its own, it may properly form the basis of a lyric poem. But the epiphany cannot thus be isolated in a novel; it must in one way or another be related to a context of life stretching before and after. Such also is the concern of many Romantic poets, notably of Wordsworth in *Tintern Abbey* and *The Prelude*. How is the epiphany to be related to the ordinary, day-to-day concerns of the moral life; how, in Wordsworth's formulation, is the moment when:

> *We are laid asleep*
> *In body, and become a living soul:*
> *While with an eye made quiet by the power*
> *Of harmony, and the deep power of joy,*
> *We see into the life of things.*

How, precisely, do we connect this moment with "the din/ Of towns and cities", so that it becomes for us,

The anchor of my purest thoughts, the nurse,
The guide, the guardian of my heart, and soul
Of all my moral being?

The problem of bridging the gap, of modulating without
obvious strain or incongruity from the intense to the relaxed,
the exceptional to the mundane, might seem to be primarily
one of style. And here poetry scores; the language of prose
which might seem more flexible and various is in fact in
serious danger of achieving no more than an isolated purple
patch when it attempts to render the intensity of the epiphany. In the novel, therefore, modulation must be in terms
of structure and particularly in terms of character relationships. Take, for example, Mrs. Moore's epiphany in the
Marabar Caves; a moment, as it happens, of negative
vision:

> If they reached the big pocket of caves, they would be
> away nearly an hour. She took out her writing-pad, and
> began, "Dear Stella, Dear Ralph," then stopped, and
> looked at the queer valley and their feeble invasion of it.
> Even the elephant had become a nobody. Her eye rose
> from it to the entrance tunnel. No, she did not wish to
> repeat that experience. The more she thought over it, the
> more disagreeable and frightening it became. She minded
> it much more now than at the time. The crush and the
> smells she could forget, but the echo began in some in-
> describable way to undermine her hold on life. Coming
> at a moment when she chanced to be fatigued, it had man-
> aged to murmur, "Pathos, piety, courage—they exist, but
> are identical, and so is filth. Everything exists, nothing
> has value." If one had spoken vileness in that place, or
> quoted lofty poetry, the comment would have been the
> same—"ou-boum". If one had spoken with the tongues
> of angels and pleaded for all the unhappiness and mis-
> understanding in the world, past, present, and to come,
> for all the misery men must undergo whatever their
> opinion and position, and however much they dodge or
> bluff—it would amount to the same, the serpent would
> descend and return to the ceiling. Devils are of the North,
> and poems can be written about them, but no one could
> romanticize the Marabar because it robbed infinity and

E

eternity of their vastness, the only quality that accommodates them to mankind.[1]

To relate the radical negation of this moment to the multifarious concerns of the novel, to show its effects radiating through time until it results if not in affirmation—for Godbole is the only character who can face and contain Mrs. Moore's vision in his own—then at least in the tentative note of the novel's ending; all this requires that the moment diffuses itself through many characters and many relationships. It is quite possibly this fact that dictates Mrs. Moore's departure and death; for had she lived she would have had to work out the consequences of her vision in her own terms and this might well have thrown the rest of the novel out of balance. The moment itself must be gradually connected with the disparate and commonplace concerns of everyday life, through a careful gradation of characters from those who are able in greater or lesser degree to comprehend Mrs. Moore's experience to those who, all unknowing, are brushed by the events which stem from the scene in the Marabar Caves. The moment and the subsequent events are refracted, echoed, distorted through a range of characters from Godbole to Dr. Panna Lal and the punkah-louvre wallah; together they form the complex prism which breaks up the pure light of this remote epiphany into the various and interesting colours of a human world which we can share and understand.

In this process a crucial role is obviously played by Adela Quested. On my reading of the novel she shares Mrs. Moore's vision in the caves, but unlike Mrs. Moore she cannot realize it for what it is. In Eliot's phrase she, like most of human kind, "cannot bear very much reality"; consequently she retreats to an explanation which is false but which at least can be comprehended and endured in terms of the everyday world. In Eliot's play, *Murder In The Cathedral*, one of the Four Knights (corresponding to the Fourth Tempter?) tempts the audience into believing that Becket's martyrdom can be explained away in terms of a death-wish leading to suicide. We are asked to accommodate the intense moment of truth to our own more comfortable and familiar

[1] E. M. Forster, *A Passage to India*, Chapter 14.

categories. This is what Miss Quested initially tries to do. In other words her experience of the inhuman and the absolute in the Caves is transmuted into a moral process which reaches its climax in her recantation at the trial of Aziz.

But Miss Quested is not the only agent of modulation; she is backed by many other intermediate characters who play a humble but important part. They are *our* representatives, members of the ordinary, bread-and-butter life in which the otherwise remote experience of the novel is set. The Marabar Caves and what happens there are extraordinary—Forster hammers home this point—but we can only judge how extraordinary by being planted vicariously in the ordinary life of Chandrapore. Sometimes this spectrum of human understanding assumes the structure of a formal hierarchy; thus Melville in *Moby Dick* makes use of the chain of command of a ship's crew. Starbuck, Flask and Tragg, according to their rank, have almost ritualistically a greater or lesser degree of insight into Ahab's passion. Sometimes the spectrum is less schematic but even more important; thus it is only through the limited narration of the foppish Lockwood and the earthbound Nelly Dean that we can grasp and measure the transcendental relation of Heathcliff and Cathy.

Because he is, so to speak, the reader's delegate within the story, the ficelle can often take on a generalized and representative value. He is so often a type because the reader needs precisely the comfortable recognition of the typical. Because of this the ficelle may often bear the weight of a good deal of symbolic value which can in various ways extend the story of the protagonist. To load the protagonist with a great deal of generalized, representative value is always a tricky business since what we attend to in his story is the individual, the unique and particular case. It is *his* story and his alone; we can easily think of alternative equivalents for Starbuck but change Ahab and the whole of *Moby Dick* is changed. We quickly feel uneasy if the protagonist is made to stand for something general and diffused; the more he *stands for* the less he *is* and we may soon end up with an allegorical figure, an Everyman. Of course, many protagonists are in a sense Everyman but only because they are in the first instance a particular man; if the protagonist is in some way a universal value or meaning, he is primarily a *concrete* universal. Consequently the intermediate character can usefully act not just as a foil, creating perspective, but also as a buttress, supporting and extending the central meaning. Behind the type we can easily sense a representative mass; thus Isabel Archer can say of Henrietta Stackpole:

> "She's a kind of emanation of the great democracy—of the continent, the country, the nation. I don't say that she sums it all up, that would be too much to ask of her. But she suggests it, she vividly figures it."

Thus Millicent in *The Princess Casamassima* is "the muse of Cockneydom" and Mrs. Lowder in *The Wings of The Dove* is the "Britannia of the Market Place—Britannia unmistakeable, but with a pen in her ear."

These we can accept where we would worry about the same technique being employed on Isabel Archer or Hyacinth Robinson or Milly Theale. To load them so would be to detract from their individuality, and it is an important part of that reality that we should feel them simply to be there, autonomous and unique. The ficelle is a chief means to this end; on him can be loaded the weight of the typical and the representative; through him the world in which the protagonist gains his individual contours can be given the necessary mass and density, that "solidity of specification" which James felt was so essential to successful representation.

IV

These categories—protagonist, background, Card, ficelle —are, of course, only approximate; they must be, in so far as the novelist captures the fluidity of what I have called perspectives of depth. These are linked to one further important difference between fiction and life which is the source of many critical difficulties. If I maintain that a fictional character is functionally flat or stereotyped, what answer can I give the critic who argues that on the contrary, such a character is the result not of deliberation but of the failure to create a "rounded" protagonist? While we cannot appeal to the author's intention and while, of course, each case must be argued on its merits, it is surely true that any argument will include an appeal to the whole work, as a structure of relationships. Here fiction differs from life in that consideration of the aesthetic strength—that is, the successful realization—of any one character will involve consideration of the aesthetic strength of other characters with whom he is brought into relation. For example, in *Middlemarch* Dorothea is a much more successful creation when seen in relation to Casaubon, another strongly realized character, than she is when linked to the relatively sketchy figure of Will Ladislaw. Again, the reality of Isabel Archer depends vitally on the reality of Osmond. If one examines *The Portrait of A Lady* with care one realizes that Osmond's charm and attraction for Isabel, and the whole process of seducing her into marriage, is asserted rather than dramatically realized. If this relationship were shown in isolation I believe we should feel a gap or blur in the developing human spectrum at this point. The gap is partly closed by James's stressing those points of Isabel's character which make her vulnerable to attack, and partly by his evocation of the diffused glamour of Italy. But more important, Osmond— and James—find a ready ally in Madame Merle; her success as a strongly realized character conceals and compensates for a lacuna in the total human pattern. So one could go on, complicating this network of relationships, until the whole was encompassed.

The human context, then, is primarily a web of relationships; the characters do not develop along single and linear roads of destiny but are, so to speak, human cross-roads. It is within this pattern, this meshing together of individualities, that they preserve their autonomy, yet through our perception of the pattern their significance extends beyond themselves into a general comment on the world. No one has illustrated the point better or more succinctly than Germaine Brée in her study of Proust:

> No Proustian character is isolated or unique. Each is bound to other characters who surround him, and who reflect certain aspects of his personality. But these families of characters are as numerous for each individual as are the

aspects of his own character, so that none is ever enclosed within a "type". A secondary character like Legrandin, for example, takes his place with the Proustian "snobs", a pale reflection of Swann, of the narrator, of Bloch, and of so many others; through his homosexuality he joins Saint-Loup whom he resembles outwardly, the Baron de Charlus, and indeed, a whole Proustian population; through his literary vocation he is part of a whole company of would-be artists who are failures, or incomplete artists; Ski, the baron, Swann. Each principal character is thus doubled, tripled, quadrupled by a whole series of secondary Legrandins, as well as many others paler than he. . . . This play with mirrors gives for each character a series of reflections, each a little distorted, which are variations of his own species. In this way the individual goes beyond his own individuality, and is related to a general type. But he is never merely an example of that type, for he always evokes in addition a multitude of other characteristics. Charlus is not the prototype of the homosexual. He is the Baron de Charlus, a great lord like his brother, the Duc de Guermantes, or like Monsieur, the brother of Louis XIV; he is a scholar and an artist, like Swann. No Proustian character entirely exemplifies one species. He suggests several, and Proust gathers about him other individuals of the various species to which he belongs, who again are never simply doubles. Each character has infinite possibilities; he remains enigmatic and complex by virtue of all the ties which link him, quite humanly, to a great many other people. The Proustian vision is determined here by Proust's marked conviction that in every individual there exists a general humanness which is greater than he, but of which he is a unique specimen.[1]

Within such a pattern the characters themselves may make or mistake connections; but the pattern itself is the result of a real process in the reader's response. His knowledge and insight encompass those of any single character; hence because of his greater range and lucidity, all the effects of dramatic irony. And hence, as I have already said, because

[1] G. Brée, *Marcel Proust and Deliverance from Time*, pp. 242–3. London: Chatto and Windus, 1956.

the reader does the work, reality is imputed to the raw material on which the work has been done.

In doing the work the reader enriches his knowledge of the world; that is his reward. He begins, as he probably does in life, by assimilating what is familiar to him; this he then uses as a base from which to explore the unknown. In many cases he will never complete his exploration; there will still remain a heart of darkness in the character, a central mystery which is never quite penetrated. In aesthetic terms this is often what we mean when we praise the inexhaustibility of great art; but it is also a truth of life which may form part of the mimetic substance of the novel. There are dangers in the reader's lucidity becoming *too* great; we all know the novel which is suspiciously neat and satisfying in the way it clicks together. Dramatic irony, for example, easily becomes oppressive, obvious or over-schematic. Such irony results from the reciprocal ignorance of the characters; they are opaque to each other as we are to each other in real life. But to some extent, perhaps, they should also retain a core which remains opaque to the reader as well? Several of Dickens's characters, for example, have been condemned as melo-dramatic stereotypes; yet they have an excess of energy which suggests a residual heart of darkness far more pro-found than the merely queer or sinister. I am thinking here of such figures as Carker or Tulkinghorn. However well one gets to know them, however much Dickens explains them, they remain ultimately concealed and mysterious. Since we cannot explain them we often explain them away. But per-haps it is part of any character's mimetic adequacy that he should resist the encroaching lucidity of the reader. One of the novelist's greatest problems is thus to reconcile trans-parency and density.

The fascination of this problem is one reason, I believe, for much of the characteristic ambiguity of modern fiction. No man is an island; yet no man is to be thoroughly explored and charted. How is the novelist to convey this sense that there will always remain an unknown factor in the human equation? Dramatic irony, we have seen, results from the reader's superior perspective, but there are many other kinds of irony which involve and attack the reader himself so that he, too, is asked to recognize his fallibility and limitations.

The reader will forgive me if I offer an unashamedly subjective example, but where the novel implicates each one
of us as individuals, all testimony must be personal and
variable.

My example is *Death In Venice* and I am concerned here
not so much with the meaning of the novel as with the process of getting to understand it; my point, of course, is that
this process is part of the meaning. How we travel determines our destination. Even a first, naïve reading of *Death
In Venice* cannot but reveal the obvious nature of its extreme
artifice—the accumulation of symbols, the reverberation of
echoes, the parallelisms, contrasts and anticipations. The
artifice is quite overt; it is not concealed but is so deliberately
emphasized that one soon feels it become oppressively
schematic. This, for some time, was my own judgment of
the novella; a clever—indeed, over-clever—piece of work,
the explicator's paradise, but ultimately claustrophobic and
repugnant. A further reading contradicted this initial impression by offering the explanation that the oppressively
schematic nature of the work is deliberately expressive of its
theme. The theme now becomes a paradox; here is a novella
which conquers life into order to show, through Aschenbach,
that art can never conquer life; *Death In Venice* thus becomes
a work of art devoted to destroying its own claims. This
realization is then merged in a final paradox; *Death In
Venice*, *because* it is successful, denies its self-destructive assertion *at the same time* that it affirms it. Art can never subdue
life; this is what the novella says while it is engaged in the
very process of subjugation. We can put it this way; *Death
In Venice* is a story about Aschenbach *by* Aschenbach—but
with a difference. Aschenbach tries to assimilate his experience of chaos and fails, whereas disorder in the novella is
successfully given form. The extreme artifice of the work is
now explained; it is expressive ultimately of the immense
effort needed to control the jungle and the abyss into which
Aschenbach plunges to destruction. And the difference
between Aschenbach and the controlling narrator is this—
that Aschenbach rejects irony whereas the novella depends
upon it. But this irony is not simple dramatic irony; it
derives rather from the complicated interplay of the reader's
mind as the work impels him through some such developing

process of perception and adjustment as I have tried to describe.

This process is also the reason why we can grant reality to a work which is, in one sense, so obviously contrived and artificial. For we are made not merely to understand the work but also to understand ourselves in relation to the work. It has forced us to the effort of self-exploration and if we deny its reality, then we deny our own. In this process the role of the narrator is clearly crucial. The narrator—and behind the narrator, the author himself—is clearly part of the total network of relationships between character and reader which make up the human context. So important is he, indeed, that he deserves a chapter to himself.

CHAPTER IV

Character and Narration

DISCUSSION of the part played by the narrator in creating the human context is made much easier by the existence of Wayne Booth's classic study of the narrative art, *The Rhetoric of Fiction*.[1] I make no apology for depending on such a monumental survey; what I have taken from it is warped, of course, not only by compression but also by my particular interest and, no doubt, by my limited understanding of all its implications. Any reader interested in the present survey who has not read Professor Booth's work is urged to check my account against his full exposition.

Most discussions of the problem begin with an elementary distinction between omniscient narration and various methods of indirect narration which aim, in one way or another, at the elimination of the omniscient author. This distinction is unsatisfactory since, as Professor Booth shows, in *every* novel, omniscient or indirect, there is present an implied author, the novelist's "second self". The novelist may have silenced the omniscient voice but we are still left with the question, "Why has he chosen *this* mode of indirection rather than that? Why has he selected *this* for emphasis, ordered things in *this* sequence?" No novelist can escape such choices and in making them he reveals, directly or obliquely, a view of the world which, however disguised, is ultimately his alone.

In place of the omniscient–indirect categories, Professor Booth proposes a distinction between reliable and unreliable narrators. Reliable narrators are the trustworthy spokesmen of the particular reality presented in the world of any novel; their view of the world, although it may not be precisely our own, is still reckoned by us to be sane, decent, candid, mature. Unreliable narrators may be of various kinds but they all have in common the fact that the reader needs to introduce a correcting factor of his own into the narrative, to check or counterbalance some particular bias or blind

[1] W. Booth, *The Rhetoric of Fiction*, University of Chicago Press, 1961.

spot. Thus one sort of narrator may be honest and decent, telling the truth as he best sees it, and limited only by ignorance or by partial understanding of events—Conrad's Marlow, for example. Or the narrator may be unreliable because he is a fool or a liar or profoundly self-deceived. Many novels—particularly modern novels—depend for their distinctive effect upon such narrators and the ambiguities they create. I will instance, briefly, four typical examples to illustrate the range of problems involved.

Reliable narrators, I have said, are the spokesmen of reality—not the reality of our world but the reality as it figures in the world of the novel. Suppose, however, that the aim of the novel is to create a convincing illusion of an illusion—what then? Is not reality dissolved in the subjective viewpoint of the narrator? Take, for example, the role of Marcel in *À La Recherche Du Temps Perdu*. On the whole we trust Marcel because, although he is often mistaken or blind to reality, he admits to this and shows, retrospectively, his growth from blindness to insight. But how are we to be sure that the vantage point from which he surveys time past is real, that Marcel has not merely progressed *within* an illusion? Surely because Proust's second self in the novel is not to be identified with Marcel? Thus Proust so orders the narrative as to create analogues—the Swann–Odette relationship, for instance—which the reader and *not* the narrator will transfer to the Marcel–Albertine situation. Marcel may perceive *some* connections but by no means all; in other words, Proust creates for the reader a perspective and a context larger than that of the nominal narrator, within which the reader may test the veracity of Marcel's account. Paradoxically, because his limitations are thus obliquely acknowledged, we take him on trust within these limitations.

In extremer cases the ambiguity deepens. What of the novel which aims to create a convincing illusion of a deluded world—Dostoievsky's *The Double*, for example? Most of the novel is a brilliantly ordered account of disorder, of hallucination seen from within. But the real world is there in an apparently omniscient narrator who deals, for example, with the schizophrenic state by distinguishing between Golyadkin Senior and Golyadkin Junior. We soon recognize, however, a powerful satiric element in the novel; the "real"

world of the story, the society which Golyadkin sees as so
distorted and threatening, is in fact flat, insipid and entirely
conventional. But are we meant therefore to conclude that
society is as "unreal" as Golyadkin's imagination of it? Is
Dostoievsky here attempting, as he so often does, a subversive attack on the reader, tempting him to acquiesce in
the norms of this society and then betraying him to the
radically disrupted viewpoint of Golyadkin? And where does
the narrator stand in all this; does he, too, merely belong to
the real–unreal world of society? There is a kind of grue-
some archness and whimsicality in his treatment of Golyadkin which suggests that we should be profoundly mistaken
in identifying him with Dostoievsky—but the novel itself
provides no sure answer to such questions.

Again, are we to take Clamence, the narrator of Camus's
The Fall, at his own word? Is he what he declares himself to
be or is the reader meant to go behind the character and see
his most extreme attempt at honest self-revelation as only
another, subtler example of existential bad faith? What is
the relation of such unreliable narrators to the implied author
and thence ultimately to the actual author? Are we to take
Stephen's exposition of his aesthetic in *A Portrait of The
Artist As A Young Man* as Joyce's own and to see the novel
as written out of that aesthetic, or are we to see the theory as
a dramatic index of Stephen's still limited and immature
outlook? Such questions raise vertiginous possibilities of
infinite regression; where, and by what criteria, is the critic
to draw the line? And such are the questions prompted by
Professor Booth's book; our immediate problem is their
relevance to the notion of "real" characters.

We should notice first that the distinction between reliable
and unreliable narrators cuts clean across the categories of
omniscient and indirect narration. We may often judge an
omniscient narrator unreliable; thus, as I have argued elsewhere, George Eliot's treatment of Hetty in *Adam Bede* is
vitiated by the intrusion of some unacknowledged personal
bias. "Never trust the artist. Trust the tale"—D. H.
Lawrence's prescription sounds fine but it is really too
simple when the artist is also deeply involved in the teller
who tells the tale. Moreover, as I have said, if we turn the
problem upside down, many indirect narrators are as reliable

as any imperfect human testimony can be; an instance of this will be examined later in the chapter.

Clearly linked with the mode of narration is the author's control of aesthetic distance; here I quote Professor Booth:

> In 1912 Edward Bullough formulated the problem of what he called "psychic distance" as that of making sure that a work is neither "over-distanced" nor "under-distanced". If it is over-distanced, it will seem, he said, improbable, artificial, empty, or absurd, and we will not respond to it. Yet if it is under-distanced, the work becomes too personal and cannot be enjoyed as art. For example, if a man who believes that he has reason to be jealous of his wife attends *Othello*, he will be moved too deeply and in a manner not properly aesthetic. . . . The emphasis on the need for control of distance is obviously sound. But the novelist will find himself in difficulties if he tries to discover some ideal distance that all works ought to seek. "Aesthetic distance" is in fact many different effects, some of them quite inappropriate to some kinds of works. More important, distance is never an end in itself; distance along one axis is sought for the sake of increasing the reader's involvement on some other axis. . . . Every literary work of any power—whether or not its author composed it with his audience in mind—is in fact an elaborate system of controls over the reader's involvement and detachment along *various* lines of interest. The author is limited only by the range of human interests.[1]

The advantages of omniscient narration in controlling aesthetic distance are those of economy and flexibility; the dangers are those of over-distancing leading to remoteness, lack of reader's involvement and therefore frigidity; or of varying the degree of distance in too abrupt and clumsy a manner. The advantages of indirect narration, particularly where the narrator is deeply involved in the story he is telling, are the ease and speed of the reader's involvement. As Professor Booth says, "perhaps the most important effect of travelling with a narrator who is unaccompanied by a helpful author is that of decreasing emotional distance". And this is

[1] Booth, *op. cit.*, pp. 122–3.

true, he thinks, even when the narrator turns out to be unreliable: "generally speaking, the deeper the plunge, the more unreliability we will accept without loss of sympathy".[1] I am sure this is true, though we should note that a novelist may easily limit both involvement and sympathy with an unreliable narrator—witness Emily Bronte's treatment of Lockwood in the opening pages of *Wuthering Heights*. But the point I wish to make is that with an unreliable narrator, a novelist can quickly create in us a conflict between the impulse to decrease aesthetic distance and the impulse to increase it by our making an objective judgment on the degree of unreliability. To put it crudely, it is a clash between sympathy and detachment; we are impelled both to engage and to withdraw ourselves. With an indirect narrator, this clash of responses may create interest and a sense of complexity which leads to our imputing reality to the character. But where such a clash occurs in an omniscient narration, it is destructive of this sense of reality in so far as we tend much more simply to quarrel with the author. We will not be anything like so tolerant of *his* dishonesty as that of his characters. Nevertheless many novelists working in the omniscient mode have felt it necessary to take such risks in order to evoke such a clash of responses about their characters; such work raises interesting problems with which I wish to deal before turning to the sense of reality evoked by reliable narration.

II

The problem is again one of irony, though not the kind briefly analysed at the end of the last chapter nor yet the classic mode of dramatic irony defined by Allen Tate as "that arrangement of experience, either premeditated by art or accidentally appearing in the affairs of men, which permits to the spectator an insight superior to that of the actor".[2] It derives rather from the author's attempt to create in the reader a response which will pay full tribute to the richness and complexity of the imagined human situation, which will discriminate, qualify and ponder carefully the balance of one element against another.

---

[1] Booth, *op. cit.*, p. 164.
[2] Quote by K. Burke, *op. cit.*, pp. 513–14.

Let us consider first the case of Isabel Archer. She has provoked a wide variety of responses which might be interpreted either as a tribute to the success of her realization or as evidence simply of the critic's perversity. At one extreme it seems to me that Dr. Leavis is demonstrably wrong when he writes of her that:

> Beyond any question we are invited to share a valuation of Isabel that is incompatible with a really critical irony. We can't even say that James makes an implicit critical comment on the background of American idealism that fostered her romantic confidence in life and in her ability to choose: he admires her so much, and demands for her such admiration and homage, that he can't be credited with "placing" the conditions that, as an admirable American girl, she represents.[1]

At the other extreme, the view of Isabel which I have also seen expressed, as a pert young American miss who richly deserved her fate, is even more distorted; the truth, as usual, surely lies somewhere in between. But where, precisely? Consider these two sets of descriptive phrases which I have abstracted from the first few chapters of *The Portrait of A Lady* and strung together. On the one hand, according to the narrator, Isabel shows "clear perception . . . high spirit . . . comprehensiveness of observation . . . independence. . . love of knowledge . . . strong imagination . . . immense curiosity about life . . . a strong will and high temper . . . a natural taste . . . nobleness of imagination". But on the other hand she is "theoretic . . . innocent . . . liable to the sin of self-esteem"; she has an "unquenchable desire to please" and "the faculty of seeing without judging"; her imagination is "ridiculously active" while "the unpleasant had been ever too absent from her knowledge".

Clearly, in our developing experience of Isabel, we do not place these two sets of characteristics in opposition; the whole drift of the novel is to destroy the validity of this crude kind of ethical calculus which functions, for example, in Mrs. Touchett. For one thing, these two sets are closely interrelated; the strength, the attractiveness, the piquancy

[1] F. R. Leavis, *The Great Tradition*, p. iii. London: Chatto and Windus, 1948.

of the one depends upon its being rooted in the other. But viewing them abstractly for the moment, we may see that these two sets serve a clear function in the novel. The second set lays the necessary ground for Isabel's error, preparing us for the ease with which she is snared by Madame Merle and Osmond; while the first set ensures that she is a sufficiently interesting and valuable case for us to bother whether or not she is so ensnared. But beyond this, by so intimately relating the strength and weakness of Isabel, James ensures that she evokes in us that blend of sympathy and detached observation which is such an important factor in her successful realization. This blend finds its structural correlative, of course, in James's manipulation of us so that we are constantly shifting from direct contact with Isabel's dramatized consciousness through the various perspectives afforded by the other characters' perception of her to a reasonably unobtrusive but still insistent omniscient narration. By such means James controls aesthetic distance.

It is with this blend of sympathy and detachment that irony enters. Such irony derives from James's scrupulous effort never to assert the value of Isabel without careful qualification; never to assert to her quality without hedging it round with an *if* or a *but* or a *however*. The attempt to preserve this poise is not without strain. James successfully avoids the pitfalls of idealization; the danger is rather the opposite, that in the effort to avoid idealization the irony will seem so persuasive that it will entirely subvert our sense of the genuine value embodied in Isabel. The narrator is driven to confess that "meanwhile her errors and delusions were frequently such as a biographer interested in preserving the dignity of his subject must shrink from specifying". How carefully and how precariously this poise is maintained can be seen from the fact that these two impulses—the impulse to value highly, closely, sympathetically and the impulse to a cool, objective scrutiny—are sometimes syntactically intermingled within the same sentence.

Altogether, with her meagre knowledge, her inflated ideals, her confidence at once innocent and dogmatic, her temper at once exacting and indulgent, her mixture of curiosity and fastidiousness, of vivacity and indifference, her desire to look very well and to be if possible even better, her determination to see, to try, to know, her combination of the delicate, desultory, flame-like spirit and the eager and personal creature of conditions: she would be an easy victim of scientific criticism if she were not intended to awaken on the reader's part an impulse more tender and more purely expectant. (Chapter 6)

Surely our attention here is directed not just at Isabel but also at the narrator's embarrassment at his Agag-like posture. Do we not feel James reddening a little at the strain of having to walk the tightrope of our sympathies? But though he wobbles, he never falls off; Isabel Archer is by and large a successful exercise in the control of aesthetic distance.

For a failure in this aspect of narrative art we must turn to *The Princess Casamassima*. Very roughly we can say that this novel is built upon a pun which James himself almost makes explicit when he writes of his hero in the preface to the novel that "what was essential with this was that he should have a social—not less than a socialist—connexion, find a door somehow open to him into the appeased and civilized state, into that warmer glow of things he is precisely to help to undermine". The word *social*, then, in one direction leads off to *socialite* and the Princess, in another to *socialist* and Paul Muniment. Trapped in this pun is the hero, Hyacinth Robinson. As he emerges in the book he is a somewhat feeble and pathetic character, less agent than patient; it is this that constitutes the major problem of the novel. In order to give reality to Hyacinth's conflict, James must give full weight to both the aristocratic and the revolutionary poles of the social scale. While a certain amount of this can be done by direct description or commentary it is the characters who must bear the main weight of general value. Their significance must be more than purely individual; they must also be indices of the social scene and of the various drives—political, aesthetic and moral—which govern the book.

As I have said in a previous chapter, it is usually the secondary characters who can most conveniently carry the burden of this generalized value; an example of this in *The Princess Casamassima* is Millicent, the embodiment of a

F

shrewd, sharp-tongued, vulgar but warm-hearted Cockney-dom. But it is with the greater detail and complexity of characters like Paul Muniment and the Princess that James's difficulties begin.

One would expect James to succeed with the Princess. On the surface she is a type well-known to him; she comes, too, from a social milieu in which he is very much at home and in so far as he uses that milieu, positively or negatively, to endow her with general value he is successful. But the Princess is complicated by the problems of aesthetic distance and irony; for what James bestows on her, he must also take away. Hyacinth's view of the Princess must be shown to be mistaken; the reader must be prepared by successive qualifications for the Princess's ultimate betrayal of the hero.

Thus James's predicament is that on the one hand he must show the Princess, not merely as superficially attractive, but as possessing a genuine value; to do otherwise would be to coarsen the quality of Hyacinth's response where the whole novel assumes his sensitivity and fineness of perception. On the other hand James must, by ironic qualification, pare away and subvert the value of the Princess; she is, ultimately, a sham and a seducer, standing in a similar relation to Hyacinth as Osmond to Isabel Archer.

We may examine this process of ironic qualification in greater detail. James begins the process in a most delicate manner—entirely by way of nuance, suggestion, overtone—but he also begins firmly at the beginning, with the first meeting of Hyacinth and the Princess at the theatre. This conversation piece—in Chapter 13—is a beautifully poised piece of economy, conveying at least four things simultaneously. As regards Hyacinth, it conveys both his personal ingenuousness, his confusion at the unexpected social situation into which he is pitchforked, and also his political ingenuousness which expresses itself in enthusiastic rhetoric and cloudy abstraction. As regards the Princess, the scene allows her a genuine value but also starts off the train of ironic qualification. This James achieves in various ways; first, by unobtrusive omniscient comment. Consider, for example, the deflation that occurs with the word *convenient* in this:

The Princess Casamassima had a clear faculty of completely ignoring things of which she wished to take no account; it was not in the least the air of contempt, but thoughtful, tranquil, convenient absence, after which she came back to the point where she wished to be.

Even more subtly, James creates an ironic overtone by means of the Princess's own conversation. It is hardly perceptible, but it is there—a faint resonance of which the Princess herself is of course entirely unaware:

"Oh this country—there's a great deal to be said about it and a great deal to be done, as you of course understood better than anyone. But I want to know London, the people and all their sufferings and passions; not Park Lane and Bond Street. Perhaps you can help me—it would be a great kindness; that's what I want to know men like you for."

This is a note which the Princess often strikes—the desire for the real, the need to be on the inside. This hunger for reality causes her to commit the sin against human autonomy, to leech on to people who may give her reality. She doesn't like people—she uses them as she will use Hyacinth and then drop him when Paul Muniment seems more useful. In this very scene we can see something of the kind in the casual, off-hand way she dismisses Captain Sholto. Of course, as many critics have pointed out, the Princess is appropriately punished. She is in turn used by others; moreover her appetite for the real is ultimately frustrated; the revolutionary movement uses her money but does not trust her; she is never admitted to the inner circle to which she aspires.

The process so delicately begun in the theatre scene deepens throughout the novel. It is indeed a double process, working in different ways for Hyacinth and the reader. The reader is always kept just slightly ahead of the character; he always knows a little more about the Princess than Hyacinth, though very rarely, except for a few crucial chapters, does he desert Hyacinth's point of view. The double focus that results—by which, so to speak, we look at her at once through his eyes and over his shoulder—is most deftly done. The chronology of it is tricky to work out and need not concern us here, but its results are vital to our sense of reality in the novel. In the first place, this ironic process qualifies not only the Princess but also Hyacinth—so that the reader, from his wider perspective, perceives also the hero's limitations and blind spots. In the second place, Hyacinth's final judgment of the Princess is likely to differ radically from that of the reader, thus involving James in tricky problems of aesthetic distance.

When Hyacinth visits the Princess at her country-house, for example, delicate irony broadens into something like comedy. Chapter 22 is crucial here; one may note in passing how James enforces by the structure of his narrative the tensions existing in his key-word, *society*. The country-house society of Medley is immediately juxtaposed with the revolutionary proletariat of the *Sun and Moon* in the preceding chapter. Moreover, in both societies Hyacinth forfeits his freedom; in the revolutionary world by his oath to the anarchist, Hoffendahl, while in the world of Medley he is captured by the Princess who refuses to accept the fact that he must return to his job and takes him on as her pet bookbinder. She has, says James, "an extraordinary way of taking things for granted, of ignoring difficulties, of assuming that her preferences might be translated into fact". Ironic comedy flourishes, for example, with the Princess's disappointment when Hyacinth appears at Medley without his working clothes; these would make him a more interesting, more piquant "case". Again, there is her chagrin at learning that Hyacinth already knows a member of the aristocracy, Lady Aurora, whose humble and awkward but genuine philanthropy will, later in the novel, place and qualify the Princess's intellectual slumming. The Princess tells Hyacinth that she is sorry:

> "I mean for my not being the first—what is it you call them?—noble lady you've encountered."
> "I don't see what difference that makes. You needn't be afraid you don't make an impression on me."
> "I wasn't thinking of that. I was thinking you might be less fresh than I first thought."

One notes here the concealed insolence and vulgarity of her interjection—"What is it you call them?"—a vulgarity which shades off into something positively unpleasant with the idea of Hyacinth being less "fresh" than he might be—as though he were some succulent dish to be served up for her delectation (which in a sense, of course, is just what he is).

So the process continues, with James's demonstration of her bad faith in taking up residence in the shabbiness of Paddington, until it deepens into something sinister and near-evil, when she joins forces with Paul Muniment. The scenes between these two are little masterpieces of conspiratorial complicity, a most subtle mixture of the political and the sexual. As I have said, the chronology and results of this process are different for Hyacinth and the reader; a fine example of aesthetic distance controlled by the varying of perspectives. Hyacinth's eyes, of course, are gradually opened; he perceives, for example, that when the Princess goes slumming with him, "her behaviour, after all, was more addressed to relieving herself than to relieving others". But this disillusionment hardly makes any difference to him.

To ask himself if she were in earnest was now an old story to him, and indeed the conviction he might arrive at in this head had ceased to have any high importance. It was just as she was, superficial or profound, that she held him.

This may serve well enough for Hyacinth, but it will hardly do for the reader. Where, then, are we to "place" the Princess, what status are we to allow her? It is not enough, as I have said, to see her as being given value only by Hyacinth's limited and diseased viewpoint; there is plenty of evidence in the book that James intends her to have a genuine value as well. Yet one must ask whether James has not made the process of ironic qualification too effective, whether it doesn't subvert her status entirely? The crux of this problem occurs at the very end of the novel when the Princess, having learnt from Paul Muniment that Hyacinth has at last received his orders to kill, declares that she will release him from his oath by herself assuming the task of assassination. In the context of ironic pressure already built up, how can one take this as having any weight at all, as being anything more than a final gesture, a merely dramatic flourish which completes that quiet but consistent chain of theatrical imagery by which the Princess has been characterized?

James, then, is caught between the impulse to dignify and the impulse to demolish the Princess. The two cannot be reconciled and yet the novel demands that James should try. In the attempt he resorts to a certain amount of quite blatant faking, the sort in which the reader should never be able to catch the novelist out. A particularly clear example occurs in Chapter 37, in which Mr. Vetch visits the Princess to beg her to influence Hyacinth away from his revolutionary activities. Receiving no satisfaction from her, Mr. Vetch declares that he will try Paul Muniment and the chapter ends thus:

> The Princess rang for her maid to usher Mr. Vetch out, but at the moment he laid his hand on the door of the room, she checked him with a quick gesture. "Now that I think of it don't go, please, to Mr. Muniment. It will be better to leave him quiet. Leave him to me," she added with a softer smile.
>
> "Why not, why not?" he pleaded. And as she couldn't tell him on the instant why not he asked, "Doesn't he know?"
>
> "No, he doesn't know; he has nothing to do with it." She suddenly found herself desiring to protect Paul Muniment from the imputation that was in Mr. Vetch's mind—the imputation of an ugly responsibility; and though she was not a person who took the trouble to tell fibs, this repudiation on his behalf issued from her lips before she could stay it. It was a result of the same desire, though also an inconsequence, that she added: "Don't do that—you'll spoil everything!" She went to him, suddenly eager, she herself opened the door for him. "Leave him to me—leave him to me," she continued persuasively, while the fiddler gazing at her, dazzled and submissive, allowed himself to be wafted away.

There are at least two pieces of outrageous faking here. The first is the sudden capitulation of Mr. Vetch. Knowing what we do of his character and remembering the unsatisfactory interview he has just had, it is impossible that he should suddenly be "dazzled and submissive". It is far too arbitrary, far too obviously contrived for the novelist's convenience. Even more serious is James's omniscient description of the Princess just after she has given the lie direct to Mr. Vetch. "She was not a person who took the trouble to tell fibs," says James; yet during the whole interview she has been doing little else. There are two kinds of mimetic failure here; the first—Mr. Vetch's capitulation—is a failure of internal consistency and reality; what he does is incoherent with what he is. In the second place, there is a clear contradiction between the dramatic presentation of the Princess and James's direct evaluation of her, a contradiction which points to the ambiguity and uncertainty of his treatment of her in the whole novel.

Paul Muniment is a simpler problem than the Princess and is, I think, more obviously a failure. With the Princess, James at least had a good many initial advantages; she comes from a familiar world and he can create value for her. But James doesn't *know* Paul Muniment or his world: consequently he can do little more than suggest or assert the values attached to him. There is relatively little dramatic presentation; Paul Muniment isn't sufficiently there in the novel as a human being for us to take very seriously the kind of value Hyacinth finds in him. There is a clear gap between intention and achievement. We can see well enough what sort of person Paul Muniment is meant to be—cold, clear-headed, entirely realistic—the man who gains political strength by forfeiting certain human values. But in fact this doesn't come off. Muniment is meant to be invested with a certain kind of political authority but there is nothing in him, as shown in the novel, which persuades us to grant him such authority.

In this the individual character is related to the whole political milieu; the novel fails to establish certain vital contexts. One political insight James does amply demonstrate; namely, the extent to which political ideology is intertwined with purely personal drives and motives. The Princess's revolutionary idealism is in part a revulsion from her mercenary marriage to a clodhopping Italian aristocrat; Hyacinth's from his bastardy; Lady Aurora's from the fact that she is ugly and awkward in her own social circle. This is acceptable as far as it goes, but it doesn't compensate for the fact that James simply doesn't know enough about the political underworld he depicts. In his preface he tries, indeed, to suggest one escape route when he suggests the subterranean world of politics should be kept suggestively obscure; "the value I wished most to render and the effect I wished most to produce were precisely those of our not knowing; of society's not knowing, but only guessing and suspecting and trying to ignore what 'goes on' irreconcilably, subversively, beneath the vast smug surface." But we can hardly accept this disclaimer since Hyacinth and Muniment are already *below* the vast smug surface, so that any presentation of them can't simply be a matter of suspecting and guessing.

Historians of nineteenth-century anarchism assure us that it wasn't in the least like the authoritarian conspiracy depicted by James. That kind of deficient realism doesn't matter very much; it doesn't, for example, impair the achievement of Conrad in *The Secret Agent*. The serious mimetic failure, as with Mr. Vetch, is one of internal coherence—the discrepancy between Paul Muniment and his milieu. If he is as realistic and politically adept as James wants us to think him, then would he be likely to affiliate himself with such a bunch of frustrated cranks and secret assassins as James depicts? Historical hindsight shows us that the future was with Marx and not with Bakunin, that the anarchist movement in England was interesting but entirely peripheral. We may allow that James has no such advantage of historical perspective; we do not demand that he be a political prophet and we may grant that a terrified imagination bred out of ignorance may be a sufficient creative force. And yet the facts, as James gives them to us, don't add up. Even so—if Paul Muniment is what James wishes us to think him—would he have wasted his time with Hoffendahl, Schinkel, Poupin and the rest; would he not rather have moved with coolness and assurance towards the channels of real political power then open to him?

The failure, then, is one of internal coherence. But in the last analysis, I believe, this rests on a further and truly mimetic failure; that is, James fails in his heroic attempt to extend his imaginative insight into a world of which he has inadequate knowledge. The failure is ultimately one of correspondence with reality; James did not know enough. Perhaps the scene in which he comes closest to an adequate presentation of Paul Muniment is in Chapter 35, in which he and Hyacinth go on an outing to Greenwich. There, lying on the grassy bank of the park, they "watched the young of both sexes, hilarious and red in the face, roll in promiscuous accouplement over the slopes".

That, in its way, is one of my favourite Jamesian phrases. But it does reveal how far he is from the full body of experience and insight necessary to the success of the novel. The comment of a writer who really knew the working classes— D. H. Lawrence, say—on this "promiscuous accouplement" would probably be a much more curt and pungent summary of the criticism I have been trying to make.

III

One way of stating the failure of *The Princess Casamassima* would be to say that James is no Dickens, while this is the most Dickensian of his novels. And it is to Dickens and *Bleak House* that we may finally turn to examine a quite different set of problems involved in the relation of character to narrator.

Dickens has often been likened to a Jacobean dramatist both for his vivid, exuberant, "poetic" use of language and for his methods of characterization. There is a third point of likeness. Critics frequently discuss Jacobean plays in terms of "episodic intensification". By this they mean the impulse to exploit to the full possibilities of any particular scene, situation or action without too much regard for the relevance of such local intensities to the total work of art. Clearly much of Dickens's fiction is of the same order. To admit this is to risk the displeasure of much modern criticism of fiction which, largely deriving from James, lays great stress on the organic unity of the novel and demands that no part shall be allowed autonomy if this threatens the integrity of the whole.

We can defend in four ways the novel of episodic intensification from such criticism. First, we may admit that in some cases the work may fail as a whole while succeeding in some part. The result may be a dead or crippled work which yet intermittently achieves the vigour of a masterpiece. We may admire what we can and regret the waste of so much

else. This, I think, is true of *Barnaby Rudge*. Second, we may
deny the fiat of organic unity and maintain that in *some* cases
a novel achieves no more than episodic intensification and
yet possesses so much vitality that we are content simply to
accept its greatness. In James's terms there must be room in
the house of fiction for such "loose, baggy monsters". With
much less certainty I would place *Pickwick Papers* in this
category. Third, we may accept the idea of organic unity
and yet maintain that by its standards Dickens's novels are
entirely successful. Sometimes he achieves an economy,
firmness, and clean-cut clarity of control that can only be
called classical. This is surely true of *Great Expectations*.
Finally, we may accept the idea of organic unity but argue
that the criteria by which we judge its presence or absence
have been too narrowly conceived and that there exist conventions and methods of organization which are non-
Jamesian but still appropriate and effective. (James, unlike
some more recent critics, admitted as much.) *Bleak House* is
here a relevant example. Indeed, I would say that one of the
reasons for its greatness is the extreme tension set up between the centrifugal vigour of its parts and the centripetal
demands of the whole. It is a tension between the impulse
to intensify each local detail or particular episode and the
impulse to subordinate, arrange and discipline. The final
impression is one of immense and potentially anarchic
energy being brought—but only just—under control. The
fact that the equipoise between part and whole is so precariously maintained is in itself a tribute to the energy here
being harnessed.

How well does an examination of the novel's structure
support this general view? *Bleak House* is for Dickens a
unique and elaborate experiment in narration and plot
composition. It is divided into two intermingled and roughly
concurrent stories; Esther Summerson's first-person narrative and an omniscient narrative told consistently in the his-
toric present. The latter takes up thirty-four chapters;
Esther has one less. Her story, however, occupies a good
deal more than half the novel. The reader who checks the
distribution of these two narratives against the original part
issues will hardly discern any significant pattern or correla-
tion. Most parts contain a mixture of the two stories; one

part is narrated entirely by Esther and five parts entirely by the omniscient author. Such a check does, however, support the view that Dickens did not, as is sometimes supposed, use serial publication in the interest of crude suspense. A sensational novelist, for example, might well have ended a part issue with Chapter 31; Dickens subdues the drama by adding another chapter to the number. The obvious exception to this only proves the rule; in the final double number the suspense of Bucket's search for Lady Dedlock is heightened by cutting back to the omniscient narrative and the stricken Sir Leicester. In general, however, Dickens's control of the double narrative is far richer and subtler than this. Through this technique, as I shall try to show, he controls the immense, turbulent and potentially confusing material of his novel. Indeed, the narrative method seems to me to be part of the very substance of *Bleak House*, expressive of what, in the widest and deepest sense, the novel is about.

Let us first examine the structural functions of Esther Summerson and her narrative. Esther has generally been dismissed as insipid, one of Dickens's flat, non-comic good characters, innocent of imaginative life, more of a moral signpost than a person. Even if we accept this general judgment we may still find good reasons why Dickens had necessarily to sacrifice vitality or complexity here in order to elaborate or intensify other parts of his novel. If Dickens, far from failing to create a lively Esther, is deliberately suppressing his natural exuberance in order to create a flat Esther, then we may properly consider one of Esther's functions to be that of a brake, controlling the runaway tendency of Dickens's imagination—controlling, in other words, the impulse to episodic intensification.

Can we possibly accept this view? The contrasting styles of the two narratives, while they offer the reader relief and variety, also seem to me evidence of Dickens's control in making Esther what she is, even at the risk of insipidity and dullness. The omniscient style has all the liveliness, fantastication and poetic density of texture that we typically associate with Dickens. Esther's narrative is plain, matter-of-fact, conscientiously plodding. Only very rarely does her style slip and allow us to glimpse Dickens guiding her pen—as

when, for instance, she observes "Mr. Kenge, standing
with his back to the fire, and casting his eyes over the dusty
hearthrug as if it were Mrs. Jellyby's biography" (Chapter
4), or when, as Turveydrop bows to her, she could "almost
believe I saw creases come into the white of his eyes"
(Chapter 14). Here one may glimpse Dickens chafing at his
self-imposed discipline. Such moments apart, any stylistic
vivacity or idiosyncrasy in Esther's prose comes from the
oddities and foibles of other characters. Dickens imagines
them; Esther merely reports them. Even when, at moments
of emotional stress, her prose strays into the purple patch,
one still feels that this is the rhetoric of an amateur, not to
be compared, for instance, with the controlled crescendo
of Jo's death. Similarly, whenever the straightforward flow of
Esther's narratives falters—as in her over-casual mention of
Allan Woodcourt at the end of Chapter 14—we prefer to
see this as appropriate to her character rather than to spot
Dickens signalling a new relationship to us behind her back.
That, of course, is precisely what he is doing, but the disguise of style persuades us to focus on Esther and not on her
creator. (There is, I think, a corresponding and quite remarkable impersonality about the omniscient narrative. The
general impression is of a vast, collective choric voice brilliantly mimicking the varied life it describes, yet able to
generalize and comment without lapsing into the idiom of
one man, of Dickens himself. Obviously the style exploits
and manipulates our sympathies; yet surprisingly rarely do
we feel that Dickens is directly buttonholing us.)

As I have said, the two narratives are *roughly* concurrent.
Deliberately so; Dickens juggles the two chronologies by
keeping the details sufficiently vague. Only rarely do we feel
any awkwardness in this temporal matching together and
any obvious discontinuity generally has a specific narrative
or dramatic point. Esther's tale, taken in isolation, plods
forward in the simplest kind of sequence. Yet, being auto-
biographical, it is retrospective and was written, so we are
told, at the very end, seven years after the main events. This
simplicity is rarely disturbed; only occasionally does Esther
sound the note of "If I had known then what I know now";
only occasionally does she throw an anticipatory light forward into the shadowy future of her tale as, for example, she

does at the end of Chapter 37. The reason is that, despite the retrospective nature of her story, Esther must *seem* to be living in a dramatic present, ignorant of the plot's ramifications. Dickens is *really* omniscient in the other narrative; god-like he surveys time as though it were an eternal present and Esther must seem to belong to that present. It is a convention most readers readily accept.

In what ways does Esther's tale throw light on its teller? During his later period Dickens showed considerable interest in the possibilities of the first-person narrative. In some cases—*David Copperfield, Great Expectations*—the adult narrator judges, implicitly or explicitly, his growth towards maturity. Esther is clearly not in this category; she swiftly advances from child to woman and scarcely changes at all. We feel that she was "born old"—a feeling reflected in the nicknames given her, though in fact she is little older than Ada Clare. On the other hand, she cannot be classed with Miss Wade, of *Little Dorrit*, whose story is taken by some critics as an early exercise in that kind of point-of-view technique which dramatizes a limited or crippled consciousness so that what is conveyed to the reader differs radically from the intention of the narrator. Clearly, we are meant to take Esther on trust. If what she tells us is wrong or limited this signifies no moral blindspot in her, no flaw in her sensibility but only her necessary innocence of the full ramifications of the plot. Dickens's treatment of Esther is devoid of irony. We have only to imagine what narrative would have resulted if the teller had been Skimpole—or even Richard Carstone—to see that Esther's responses, attitudes, and actions are never qualified or criticized. She is, in short, thoroughly idealized.

One result of the idealizing process is the static nature of Esther's character, the essentials of which we quickly come to know. These never change; her story merely exhibits them in a variety of situations in which she is generally the patient rather than the agent. That is, Esther *does* very little in the sense of initiating a chain of actions by a deliberate choice. Things are done to her or because of her rather than by her. Devastating things happen to Esther from the moment of her birth, but she generally emerges with her usual placidity and acceptance of duty. Indeed, at times

Dickens takes care to subdue the effect on the reader of these crises through which Esther as patient must pass. The chapter which deals, for example, with the recognition scene between Esther and her mother closes in fact with Esther's reunion with Ada. The curious thing is the feelings aroused by the Esther–Ada relationship seem more intense —and intensely rendered—than those aroused by the Esther–Lady Dedlock encounter.

Esther then is static, consistent, passive. She is also good. The difficulties of combining these qualities to produce a compelling character are so immense that we should wonder not that Dickens fails, but that his failure is so slight. Still, he does fail. The exigencies of the narrative force him to reveal Esther's goodness in a coy and repellent manner; she is, for instance, continually imputing to others qualities which the author transparently wishes us to transfer to her. Esther's goodness is most acceptable when she is least conscious of its effects radiating out to impinge on others. Similarly, her narrative is most acceptable when she is pushed from the centre of the stage by the typical inhabitants of the Dickens world. Happily, this is usually so. In other words, Dickens has to reconcile in Esther the demands of a narrator and a main character and he chooses to subdue Esther as a character in the interests of her narrative function. We do not, so to speak, look *at* Esther; we look *through* her at the teeming Dickensian world. This viewpoint is no Jamesian dramatization of a particular consciousness; Esther is as lucid and neutral as a clear window. We look through at a human landscape but we are not, as with James, constantly aware that the window is limited by its frame or that it has a scratch here and an opaque spot there. The penalty Dickens pays for this is the insipidity of Esther's character. But then, *Bleak House* is a thickly populated novel; each character claims his own share of attention and all are connected by a complicated series of interlocking actions. There is no single centre, no Jamesian *disponsible*; rather we have a complex field of force, of interacting stresses and strains. Given this complication it would be too much to ask of the reader that he concentrate on the perceiver as well as the perceived. Were Esther to be complicated the novel would have to be correspondingly simplified and the

Dickens world depopulated. Who would wish it so? If the real subject-matter of a novel is a subtly dramatized consciousness then the objects of that consciousness will tend to the sparse refinements of the closet drama. Dickens is the opposite of this; he is to Shakespeare as James is to Racine.

While this, I hope, explains the necessary limitations of Esther's character, it only pushes the real problem one stage further back. Why was it necessary to have a narrator of this kind at all? Any adequate answer must also take into account the omniscient narrative as well. The two narratives are the systole and diastole of the novel and between them they produce the distinctive effect of *Bleak House*; something that I can only call, in a crudely impressionistic manner, the effect of *pulsation*, of constant expansion and contraction, radiation and convergence.

The famous first chapter of *Bleak House* has had more than its fair share of critical attention; at the risk of tedium, therefore, I wish to isolate two striking features of Dickens's method. The omniscient eye which surveys the scene is like the lens of a film camera in its mobility. It may encompass a large panoramic view or, within a sentence, it may swoop down to a close scrutiny of some character or local detail. Closely related to this mobility is the constant expansion and contraction from the omniscient eye to Esther's single viewpoint. Closely related again is the constant expansion and contraction of the total narrative; now concentrating at great length on some episode, now hustling the plot along with a rapid parade of characters. Dickens's narrative skill is nowhere more evident than in his control of tempo.

All this I mean by *pulsation*. But Chapter 1 displays yet another related effect. The scene contracts to the Court of Chancery at the heart of the fog, but suddenly this process is reversed; Chancery monstrously expands to encompass the whole country:

> "This is the Court of Chancery; which has its decaying houses and its blighted lands in every shire; which has its worn-out lunatic in every madhouse, and its dead in every churchyard. . . ."

The heart of Chancery in this respect is Tom All Alone's the breeding-ground of disease (again the radiation of infection). The two are appropriately linked, for Chancery *is* a disease and is constantly described in these terms.

This theme is, of course, abundantly worked out in the novel—in Miss Flite, in Gridley, and above all, in Richard Carstone. The idea of corruption radiating out from a rotten centre (Chancery *and* Tom All Alone's) is reflected, in geographical terms, in the constant to-and-fro movement between London, Bleak House, and Chesney Wold. But this idea is counterpointed, in plot terms, by the sense one has of convergence, especially the sense of something closing-in on Lady Dedlock. Geography and plot coalesce in the final constriction of the chase and the discovery of Lady Dedlock dead near her lover's tomb.

This pulsation, this interaction of radiation and convergence, is also temporal. The case of Jarndyce and Jarndyce does not merely fan out in the present to enmesh innocent and remote people; it also has a terrible history:

> Innumerable children have been born into the cause; innumerable young people have married into it; innumerable old people have died out of it. Scores of persons have deliriously found themselves made parties in Jarndyce and Jarndyce, without knowing how or why; whole families have inherited legendary hatreds with the suit.

Diverse pressures from the past converge to mould the present; Jarndyce and Jarndyce bears down on Richard Carstone; the past catches up with Esther and finally with her mother. This temporal convergence is reflected in the structure of the novel as a whole and locally, in its parts. Thus the first chapter given to Esther (Chapter 3) quickly brings us from her childhood back to the dramatic present already described in the omniscient first chapter. Sometimes the dramatic present is illuminated by a shaft driven back into the past; thus both Boythorn and Miss Barbary are in some sense enlarged by the revelation of their abortive love long ago. Or again, the dramatic present will be left unexplained until time has passed and many pages have been turned; thus, on a small scale, the mystery of Jo's disappearance from Bleak House or, on a large scale, Bucket's uncovering of Tulkinghorn's murderess.

Granted the extremely complicated tangle of effects I have labelled *pulsation*, the desirability of a simple, lucid, straightforward narrative such as Esther's should be obvious. It offers us stability, a point of rest in a flickering and bewildering world, the promise of some guidance through the labyrinth. The usual novel may be compared to a pebble thrown into a pool; we watch the ripples spread. But in *Bleak House* Dickens has thrown in a whole handful of pebbles and what we have to discern is the immensely complicated tracery of half-a-dozen circles expanding, meeting, interacting. Esther—to change the metaphor—has the stability of a gyroscope; by her we chart our way.

She is, of course, much more than this. She is, as well, a moral touchstone; her judgments are rarely emphatic but we accept them. She can see Richard more clearly than Ada; through her Skimpole is revealed in his true colours and the Growlery becomes a sign of Jarndyce's obtuseness. She is also the known constant by which we judge all the other variables of character. Through her we can see the horrifyingly vivid notation of decay and infection that signals the slow process of Richard's destruction. (Among other things, the intertwining of the two narratives enables Dickens, drastically to foreshorten and mould the *apparent* time sequence here.) Again, by her consistency Esther contributes to the wonderfully skilful characterization of Sir Leicester and Guppy, who change by fits and starts throughout the novel. Because these characters demand very different reactions from us at different times we impute complexity and development to them. In fact they are not so much complex as discontinuous. Dickens's art lies in masking this discontinuity and Esther in large part provides a convincing façade; because she is a simple unity we are conjured into believing that the heterogenuity of Guppy or Sir Leicester is a unified complexity.

Finally—and perhaps most important—by intertwining the two narratives Dickens compels us to a double vision of the teeming, fantastic world of *Bleak House*. We—and Esther—are within; we—and the omniscient author—are outside. This double perspective forces us as readers to make connections which as I have said, because *we* make them have more validity than if Dickens had made them for us. The most crucial instance is Esther's ignorance of so much that surrounds her. What she sees she sees clearly; but she cannot see more than a fraction of the whole. In this she is not alone; one of the triumphs of the novel is the delicacy with which Dickens handles the knowledge, suspicions, guesses, and mistakes of the various characters. Some of them are limited to one or other of the narrative streams; Esther is never seen by the omniscient eye, nor does Tulkinghorn ever appear personally in Esther's narrative. This corresponds to their limited knowledge; Tulkinghorn, for all his plotting, never knows of Esther's relation to Lady Dedlock while there is no substantial evidence that Esther knows anything of her father until after her mother's death.

Granted this, the opportunities for dramatic irony are clearly enormous and it is to Dickens's credit as an artist that with great tact he refuses many of the chances for irony offered by the interlocking narratives. How close—all unknowing—is Esther to meeting her father during her first visit to Krook's? Yet we scarcely perceive this, even on a re-reading of the novel. A lesser artist would have wrung dry the irony of such an incident, but Dickens is sound in his refusal to do so. For the novel, as it stands, is so taut, so potentially explosive, that to expatiate on, or to underline, its implications would make it quite intolerable. Of course the irony is there but it is kept latent and, so to speak, sub-critical; it does not explode in the reader's conscious attention. In this, of course, its effect is almost the opposite of that which I tried to analyse in *Death In Venice*. Mann's story depends largely on its insistently schematic nature, whereas Dickens's problem—like that of most novelists—is to avoid over-schematization, to control the complex and manifold life of the novel without drawing too much attention to the art involved. In this he is again helped by his chosen mode of narration. Through the double narrative Dickens refracts, reflects, varies, distorts, reiterates his major themes, and the disturbing resonance thus set up is expressive of his deepest sense of what life is like. *Bleak House* is so dense with examples of this process that I will quote only one, very minor example. In Chapter 25, Mrs. Snagsby is suspicious:

Mrs. Snagsby screws a watchful glance on Jo, as he is brought into the little drawing-room by Guster. He looks at Mr. Snagsby the moment he comes in. Aha! Why does he look at Mr. Snagsby? Mr. Snagsby looks at him. Why should he do that, but that Mrs. Snagsby sees it all? Why else should that look pass between them; why else should Mr. Snagsby be confused, and cough a signal cough behind his hand. It is as clear as crystal that Mr. Snagsby is that boy's father.

Mrs. Snagsby's magnificent illogicality is a comic analogue, a parody of the dominant atmosphere of the book, that of hints, guesses, suspicions, conspiracies. It is also a distorted echo of one of the novel's major themes, that of parents and children. Even here, in an insignificant corner of the book, its major concerns are repeated and echoed in a different key; this abundance of doubling, paralleling, contrasting, this constant modulation from sinister to pathetic or comic, serves to create a density of life providing a context for those vivid scenes of episodic intensification. We accept these, take them on trust as more than brilliant but isolated moments, because we know they mesh with that complicated web of human affairs which entangles all the characters, even the most trivial. We weave this web, this pattern, as the tale shuttles to and fro between its two tellers and, of course, it is a pattern which gradually and continuously develops and emerges. It is to the novel as an essentially temporal product that we must now turn.

CHAPTER V

Time and Identity

A<small>N</small> unusual emphasis on the thematic importance of time is one of the distinguishing features of modern literature. Proust and Eliot spring to mind as obvious examples, but I wish to make my starting point a passage from another profound and subtle meditation on the theme, Thomas Mann's *The Magic Mountain*. Like *A La Recherche Du Temps Perdu* and *Four Quartets* this is a work about time which constantly draws the reader's attention to its own temporal nature; thus at the beginning of Chapter 7, entitled "By the Ocean of Time", the narrator writes:

Can one tell—that is to say, narrate—time, time itself, as such, for its own sake? That would surely be an absurd undertaking. A story which read: "Time passed, it ran on, the time flowed onward" and so forth—no one in his senses could consider that a narrative. It would be as though one held a single note or chord for a whole hour, and called it music. For narration resembles music in this, that it *fills up* the time. It "fills it in" and "breaks it up", so that "there's something to it", "something going on"—to quote, with due and mournful piety, those casual phrases of our departed Joachim, all echo of which so long ago died away. So long ago, indeed, that we wonder if the reader is clear how long ago it was. For time is the medium of narration, as it is the medium of life. Both are inextricably bound up with it, as inextricably as are bodies in space. Similarly, time is the medium of music; music divides, measures, articulates time, and can shorten it, yet enhance its value, both at once. Thus music and narration are alike, in that they can only present themselves as a flowing, as a succession in time, as one thing after another; and both differ from the plastic arts, which are complete in the present, and unrelated to time save as all bodies are, whereas narration—like music—even if it should try to be completely present at any given moment, would need time to do it in.

So much is clear. But it is just as clear that we have also a difference to deal with. For the time element in music is single. Into a section of mortal time music pours itself, thereby inexpressibly enhancing and ennobling what it fills. But a narrative must have two kinds of time; first its own, like music, actual time, conditioning its presentation and course; and second, the time of its content, which is relative, so extremely relative that the imaginary time of the narrative can either coincide nearly or completely with the actual, or musical, time, or can be a world away. A piece of music called a "Five-minute Waltz" lasts five minutes, and this is its sole relation to the time element. But a narrative which concerned itself with the events of five minutes, might, by extraordinary conscientiousness in the telling, take up a thousand times five minutes, and even then seem very short, though long in relation to its imaginary time. On the other hand, the contentual time of a story can shrink its actual time out of all measure.

It is in terms of the distinction here made by Mann that this chapter will develop. Any discussion of realism soon dissolves its subject into many kinds of realism, the basic division being, I suppose, between a realism of substance and a realism of treatment. In many ways this is a tricky and unfortunate division, one which at the risk of confusion I have tried to avoid in this book. Nevertheless we may first regard time as part of a novel's substance—what Mann calls its imaginary or contentual time. Here the question then becomes of correspondence between the view of time portrayed or implicit in any novel and our own experience of what it is like to live in a world of sequence and change. From this we may progress to narrative or musical time, to the novel as a distinctively temporal product and thence to time as a factor in the reader's aesthetic response to fiction.

II

In one way time certainly fulfils the criteria previously laid down both for a constitutive category and for an adequate mimetic frame of reference. It is something very close to the pith and particularity of our experience, without which it would become a dangerously abstract critical concept. As Hans Meyerhoff says:

> Time, as Kant and others have observed, is the most characteristic mode of our experience. It is more general than space, because it applies to the inner world of impressions, emotions, and ideas for which no spatial order can be given. It is also more directly and immediately given than space or any other general concept such as causality or substance. The blooming, buzzing confusion of experience seems to convey an immediate awareness that certain elements succeed each other, change or endure. Succession, flux, change, therefore, seem to belong to the most immediate and primitive data of our experience; and they are aspects of time. There is no experience, as it were, which does not have a temporal index attached to it.[1]

But granted its particularity, we may still ask whether the concept of time has even the relative stability which was postulated as necessary to any reasonably adequate mimetic theory. We may discount the nature of time as it is experienced in remote cultural contexts. But even within that part of the historical continuum relevant to the growth of the novel, is there still not a great change in our conception of time? Consider these five views:

(1) Time *sub species aeternitatis*—that is, human history seen as having a distinct beginning and end, an end moreover which may not be very far in the future; in other words, what was the predominantly Christian view of time during a very long historical period. One aspect of this Christian view especially relevant to any consideration of character or mimesis is noted by Mann in *The Magic Mountain*:

> The schoolmen of the Middle Ages would have it that time is an illusion; that its flow in sequence and causality is only the result of a sensory device, and the real existence of things is an abiding present.

Clearly the artist who believes that he is imitating illusion will have a different view of character from the artist who

---

[1] H. Meyerhoff, *Time in Literature*, p. 1. University of California Press, 1955.

believes that he is imitating reality. He may, for example, desert the faithful delineation of the individual, preferring the typical as being closer to the essential reality that lurks behind particulars; he will certainly feel more free to distort the natural in the interests of the symbolic.

(2) Time viewed as a cyclical repetition.

(3) Time viewed pessimistically as linear; that is, a view of the world as growing more and more corrupt as man plunges further and further into the consequences of the Original Fall.

(4) Time viewed optimistically as linear; that is, a largely secular view of history as the record of man's progress—often slow and interrupted—from the barbarous dark to the civilized light.

(5) Time viewed as none of these, but felt as a mere chaotic welter and flux.

On the whole, it might seem fair to say that the classical traditions of the novel have flourished within the fourth of these categories and that the first, at least, has had relatively little impact on fiction. In fact few men or ages have held any one of these categories with any purity; they have intermingled and to a greater or lesser degree have all impinged on the novel. In their interaction they clearly create a wide range of temporal "realities" and thus a considerable degree of mimetic variation. How, then, can we find a stable frame of reference?

It may, of course, be argued that such categories view time on a large scale; that they are, in fact, Ideas of History. The novel, it may be maintained, is usually much more concerned with time as a day-to-day continuum, as a small-scale condition of human experience. Yet clearly even the kind of small-scale continuum is conditioned by its existence within one or other of these larger categories. Moreover, even within the range of our mundane experience there is great variation in the ways in which time may be experienced. Where we live and how we live determine our sense of time; the child's temporal world differs from the adult's, the man on holiday differs from the man at work, the farmer inhabits a different temporal world from the industrial artisan. Even within an apparently tight, insulated world such a factor as social status may change the quality of our experience of time; one remembers that in *Adam Bede* the Poysers' clock literally keeps a different time from that of Squire Donnithorne.

Most of us, I imagine, would by and large agree with Lewis Mumford in his description of this range and variety of our experience of time; he is concerned here with the effect on it of technological change, particularly with the impact of the clock:

> The clock, moreover, is a piece of power-machinery whose "product" is seconds and minutes: by its essential nature it dissociated time from human events and helped create the belief in an independent world of mathematically measurable sequences: the special world of science. There is relatively little foundation for this belief in common human experience: throughout the year the days are of uneven duration, and not merely does the relation between day and night steadily change, but a slight journey from East to West alters astronomical time by a certain number of minutes. In terms of the human organism itself, mechanical time is even more foreign: while human life has regularities of its own, the beat of the pulse, the breathing of the lungs, these change from hour to hour with mood and action, and in the longer span of days, time is measured not by the calendar but by the events that occupy it. The shepherd measures from the time the ewes lambed; the farmer measures back to the day of sowing or forward to the harvest: if growth has its own duration and regularities, behind it are not simply matter and motion but the facts of development: in short, history. And while mechanical time is strung out in a succession of mathematically isolated instants, organic time—what Bergson calls duration—is cumulative in its effects. Though mechanical time can, in a sense, be speeded up or run backward, like the hands of a clock or the images of a moving picture, organic time moves in only one direction —through the cycle of birth, growth, development, decay, and death—and the past that is already dead remains present in the future that has still to be born.[1]

[1] L. Mumford, *Technics and Civilization*, pp. 15–16. London: Routledge, 1947.

Is it not precisely here that some kind of mimetic stability may be found? However our experience of time varies— whether as individuals or as prisoners of a particular historical epoch—we are alike and constant in this duality. On the one hand we know with Auden that

> *All our intuitions mock*
> *The formal logic of the clock.*[1]

We are aware of the richness and freedom of our subjective experience, liberated from time by memory and imagination; yet we are also aware, in some sense, of this freedom as contained in an objective or organic time, which manifests itself in the larger rhythms of life and nature and which bears us irreversibly in one direction towards one final end. If we confuse the two and really try, like Gatsby, to put the clock back, then we end in disaster.

It is with this duality, this commonplace of the human condition, that time, as an overt theme, enters *The Magic Mountain*:

> "You say 'actually'," Hans Castorp answered. He sat with one leg flung over the balustrade, and his eyes looked bloodshot. "But, after all, time *isn't* 'actual'. When it seems long to you, then it *is* long; when it seems short, why, then it is short. But how long, or how short, it actually is, that nobody knows." He was unaccustomed to philosophize, yet somehow felt an impulse to do so.
>
> Joachim gainsaid him. "How so?—we do measure it. We have watches and calendars for the purpose; and when a month is *up*, why, then up it is, for you, and for me, and for all of us."

Some balance, then, must be struck between time experienced subjectively and natural or objective time. I know of no important novel which overemphasizes objective time; presumably its faults would be those of simple dullness and monotony. It is the opposite disbalance, the overstressing of subjective time, which is the more tempting and dangerous; one would not wish for a great many novels to aspire to the status of *Tristram Shandy*. This danger is particularly present in much modern fiction. It is interesting to

[1] W. H. Auden, *New Year Letter*, Lines 440–1. London: Faber and Faber, 1941.

notice that the more centrally a novel is located in a subjective consciousness, then the more the novelist has to compensate by stressing not objective, natural time (the passing of the seasons, the organic rhythms of growth and decay, etc.), but simple mechanical time. Thus Joyce is concerned throughout *Ulysses* to emphasize "the dance of the hours"; thus Big Ben booms throughout *Mrs Dalloway*; thus Roquentin's story is cast in the form of a diary.

Again, *The Magic Mountain* offers an interesting illustration of this point. Throughout the novel Mann stresses, as a condition of the inhabitants' life at the Berghof, how radically their experience of time differs from that of "flatland". Here the unit of time is not the hour of the day but the month; a year ago is only yesterday; even "the perception of time tends, through periods of unbroken uniformity, to fall away". And, because of the climatic conditions of the mountains, even the most obvious example of natural time is distorted; at any moment the calendar of the landscape may be blotted out by the neutral snow. November seems to follow May; the seasons jostle and fluctuate as abnormally as the irregularities of the fever chart. But natural time, however disturbed, is not completely expelled from the consciousness:

> Yet, looking closer, there were the wild flowers, speaking, though softly, yet to the same effect; the meadow orchis, the bushy aquilegia were no longer in bloom, only the gentian and the lowly autumn crocus, bearing witness to the inner sharpness of the superficially heated air, that could pierce one to the bone as one sat, like a chill in fever, though one glowed outwardly from the ardour of the sun.
>
> Hans Castorp did not keep inward count of the time, as does the man who husbands it, notes its passing, divides and tells and labels its units. He had not heeded the silent entry of the tenth month, but he was arrested by its appeal to the senses, this glowing heat that concealed the frost within and beneath it.

Moreover, "Time, however weakened the subjective perception of it has become, has objective reality in that it brings things to pass." Even at the Berghof patients die, newly arrive, depart cured or still diseased; while beyond the mountains the thunder-clouds of Europe gather to discharge in war.

In maintaining this balance between the two poles of our temporal experience, Mann stresses one further truth about the nature of subjective time; namely, its elasticity, its power to expand or to dwindle, depending on the richness of experience present to the consciousness. This he does in the simplest of ways, by regulating the proportions of his novel and thus controlling its "musical" or reading time. Mann himself makes the point quite explicit at the opening of Chapter 5:

> And now we are confronted by a phenomenon upon which the author himself may well comment, lest the reader do so in his stead. Our account of the first three weeks of Hans Castorp's story with "those up here"— twenty-one midsummer days, to which his visit, so far as human eye could see, should have been confined—has consumed in the telling an amount of time and space only too well confirming the author's half-confessed expectations; while our narrative of his next three weeks will scarcely cost as many lines, or even words and minutes, as the earlier three did pages, quires, hours and working-days. We apprehend that these next three weeks will be over and done with in the twinkling of an eye.
>
> Which is perhaps surprising; yet quite in order, and conformable to the laws that govern the telling of stories and the listening to them.

Hans Castorp stays seven years at the Sanatorium, yet this record of his first three weeks—up to the point where he changes from visitor to patient—takes, in my edition, 182 pages or just over one quarter of the whole book. Even within this first section there is considerable variety; thus his first week occupies 131 pages, his second 30 pages and his third only 21 pages. The illusion of length and slowness of time in the first week is achieved by the simple trick of inserting a lengthy flashback devoted to the hero's early history; the reader tends to forget the greater amount of content involved and simply transfers the amount of reading time to the dramatic present of Hans's arrival at the Sanatorium.

There is, of course, no simple or single explanation of this proportioning. One reason undoubtedly is the simple need for detailed and leisurely exposition, the introduction and establishment of the characters, and so forth. Moreover, despite all the other precautions he takes, Mann needs time and the illusion of gradualness if we are to assent to the probability of Hans's sickness, if the change from visitor to patient is not to seem abrupt and coincidental. But the way in which our reading time is structured, the gradual increase of tempo, also serve to indicate the progression of the hero from the values of "flatland"—where mechanical time dominates the routine of life—to the timeless world of the Berghof. At first this is a new world for Hans Castorp; his experience is therefore rich and time goes slowly, each day being heavily freighted with new knowledge and impressions. But as he is gradually absorbed into the life of the community so the pace and the proportions of the novel begin to even out. The structure of the book—particularly the discrepancy created between its "musical" or reading time and its "contentual" time—thus enforces a truth both about the particular world of the novel and also about our actual experience of time. The perception of such discrepancies immediately raises the problem of time as a factor in the reader's experience of fiction and it is to this that we must now turn.

III

Reading time—time as a constituent of aesthetic response —is a by-product of a novel's mass and proportions. Remarkably few critics have pondered the implications of simple *length*; we have not progressed much beyond the Aristotelian distinction between drama and epic. Because of its greater length, says Aristotle;

> In epic poetry the narrative form makes it possible for one to describe a number of simultaneous incidents; and these, if germane to the subject, increase the body of the poem. This then is a gain to the Epic, tending to give it

grandeur, and also variety of interest and room for episodes of diverse kinds.[1]

Yet even Aristotle misses the crucial distinction when he says of the epic:

> As to its length, the limit already suggested will suffice: it must be possible for the beginning and end of the work to be taken in in one view.[2]

Must it? Surely, it is not merely that a long work allows for a greater range of characters, the interaction of many plots, the minutely detailed depiction of a world, the greater variation of tempo—it is also that the mere length of reading time determines whether or not certain effects are possible. F. G. Steiner, one of the few critics to have written well on this subject, points out that:

> Constantly, the leisures of prose, the fact that we *read* a novel, put it aside, and pick it up in a different mood (none of which occurs in the theatre) imperil the sense of a continuous action and unflagging tension on which a dramatic formula such as Dostoevsky's relies.[3]

We may certainly lose compression, intensity, the sense of an experience lived through in its entirety; but we may gain certain other things. Our response depends vitally on whether we can encompass in one act the work as a unity within our imagination or whether we are forced to break our attention into a number of roughly sequential but separated units. (I say *roughly* sequential because we may go back and re-read certain parts of a novel.) Certain effects are thus possible in *Death In Venice* or *The Great Gatsby* which are excluded from *Clarissa* or *War and Peace*; and vice versa. Some modern works, I think—*Ulysses* or *Dr. Faustus*— derive part of their distinctive quality from the fact that they are very long works designed to be read as though they were very short and could be grasped as unities by a single act of attention.

Let us consider one possible effect of varying length or mass. We all know that as readers we are variables; that is,

[1] Aristotle, *Poetics* (trans. Bywater), p. 82. O.U.P., 1947.
[2] *Ibid.*, p. 81.   [3] G. Steiner, *Tolstoy or Dostoevsky*, p. 182.

we read the same work in different ways at different times in our lives. But the author of a short work can assume that *at a single reading* the reader is a constant confronted by variables; that is, by the different characters presented to him which he will hold together within a unified act of attention. Let us suppose, however, that a massive novel enforces a prolonged and probably interrupted reading. To this extent the reader is himself much less a fixity and much more a variable; the variety of his responses to the novel, therefore, will be much greater. The act of reading, after all, is not a special event, nor time out of our lives, but runs concurrent with our everyday existence. Thus with a prolonged reading our lives will, so to speak, run alongside our imaginative response and the fact of our changing, multiple viewpoints in actuality may confer a greater density and reality on the world of fiction. In most cases, of course, this will be accidental and fortuitous, a chance by-product of the massive work of art on which the novelist cannot count. But it need not always be accidental; the writer *may* be able to manipulate and control to some extent this prolonged interaction of life and art.

Let us first consider a very crude example of this—the T.V. soap-opera, particularly the kind which aims at a simple kind of realism rather than at weekly injections of fantasy; *Coronation Street*, for example. I imagine that most people who saw only one instalment of this working-class saga would dismiss it not only as insignificant but also as obviously spurious in its claims to realism. On the other hand most people, if they were entirely honest, would report a change in the quality of their response after faithfully watching the series for weeks or months; the illusion of reality comes gradually, working like a drug. How does this change work? It is partly mere repetition and familiarity, no doubt; partly the fact that the substance of the soap-opera is given a chance to extend itself. But it is more than this. I am inclined to locate the growing illusion in the fact that regular doses of the drug become part of our actual lives so that we assign them a place in our own routine; the everyday concerns of the fictional characters run parallel with the everyday concerns of our own world. More important, the two begin to intermingle; the important agent here is surely memory. Time builds up parallel memories of life and fiction in which the barriers between the two worlds are lowered since a memory, whether of life or fiction, has the same degree of real psychic existence.

Surely this same process may work in our reading of massive novels? The most obvious point of comparison occurs with works designed for serialization. If the reading of a novel were a regular process lasting months or years, then our memory of the fictional world would surely be more likely to merge imperceptibly into our memory of the real world? There is plenty of evidence that both writers and readers of Victorian serial-novels felt a peculiar reality and intimacy in this prolonged concurrence of fictional characters with their own lives. And surely, to a lesser degree, the same may hold for single but massive novels; in a sense we do not merely read *War and Peace* or *À La Recherche Du Temps Perdu*, we also live with them and the work in some way draws substance from our own lives.

I stress this otherwise minor point since the special reality of remembered experience is also the basis of our accepting a much greater elasticity of time in fiction than in life. Flashback, anticipation, digression, sudden accelerations of tempo—all the discrepancies between reading time and contentual time we accept without question because we have an analogue for this in the rich, free play of our own minds over past and future. Memory may be arbitrary and capricious or it may yield to the discipline of deliberate recollection—in either case it affords a basis in reality for the artifice of the novelist. We object only when the disturbance of time is too obviously schematic, when the past is too easily distorted or dragooned into a pattern. One remembers the facile juxtapositions of *Eyeless in Gaza*, or more subtly, Chapter 4 of *Anglo-Saxon Attitudes* in which, by a simple association of phrases, the memories of the protagonist are mechanically marshalled into a neat retrogression for the purposes of economical exposition. Proust uses much the same mechanism of association but is careful to disguise his effects by conveying also the random and wilful way of the mind. Our criteria for reality are not excessive in the matter of disturbed chronology; all we generally demand is a minimum illusion of the chance and untidiness we know to be characteristic of our own memories. Chance and untidiness derive from the incredibly complex nature of our associational processes and we accept elasticity of time when, as in *Ulysses* or in *À La Recherche Du Temps Perdu*, the author pays sufficient homage to this complexity. It is only when association is over-simplified—to ease narration, to point a moral or for a thousand other purposes—that we object.

Two further points arise from considering time as a factor in the reader's response rather than as a quality of the dramatized substance of the novel. One is the relation of the temporal nature of our reading to what are commonly called spatial readings of the novel; that is, our perception, in surveying the total unity of the work, of themes or patterns which in a sense exist beyond time, as independent wholes in our minds. Since I have discussed this problem elsewhere I shall not deal with it in detail here.[1] I would now agree more wholeheartedly with those critics who stress the inescapably sequential nature of our experience of fiction. Spatial readings are critical constructs which themselves can only exist in time and the organized patterns to which they point contain time as a factor in that organization; to be organized at all they must be ordered in time, must follow a certain sequence. Of course our memory of the whole book is greater than that of any single character; of course we can anticipate and connect where the characters cannot; this greater freedom creates one of the most inclusive of those perspectives through which, as we have seen, we establish a character's reality. Nevertheless this freedom to create spatial patterns is a freedom dependent on time; were the events of any particular novel structured in a different sequence then the resulting spatial patterns would also be different. This is particularly obvious if we consider the foreknowledge we bring to a book on rereading it; the sequence is still the same but its meaning, because we know the end of it all, is totally different. Yet our rereading is none the less temporal; we have merely added to the sequential process another time element—a very peculiar one, it is true—that of remembering what is still in the future. It is not an experi-

1 W. J. Harvey, *The Art of George Eliot*, pp. 90–108. London: Chatto and Windus, 1961.

ence we can ever have in life but it is nevertheless still temporal and if it detracts from the existential, moment-by-moment living through the story with the characters, it adds to them by compensation a lucidity of meaning which then becomes part of their reality for us.

My second point in a sense illustrates this; certainly it shows our primary dependence on a sequential ordering of experience. One of the obviously interesting things about a protagonist is the process of change and growth (or decay) which he undergoes during the course of the novel, changes of which he—lacking our privilege of varied perspectives—is often unaware. Simple change is not a difficult achievement for the novelist but growth is a more complicated process. What I have in mind here is, for example, the triumphant progression of a novel like *The Ambassadors*. Strether does not merely make a simple moral journey in the novel; when we take our farewell of him we can see how he has changed, but we can also see the lineaments of the old Strether in him still, in his final rejection of Maria Gostrey. He carries the past with him into his dramatic present. The same thing, at least as a possibility, happens with Chad; we are left uncertain how well he has learnt the lessons of Paris and Madame de Vionnet. There is still the tragic chance that he is basically the same provincial oaf whose apparent metamorphosis so surprised Strether at their first meeting.

Thus far, no complications appear; what we have here in the novel is a parallel to the situation in real life when we meet a friend we haven't seen for years and say simply, "My God, how he's changed!", without bothering to push the question further. But sometimes we are also aware of a change in ourselves as complicating our recognition of change in others. It is very difficult, perhaps impossible, for the novelist to convey this feeling, since the reader is much more a fixity and since the novel in relation to life is short and packed, the relevant time-span measuring not so many years lived but so many pages read. Hence the form is not amenable to evoking this reciprocal process; even in a relatively massive novel like *The Ambassadors*, we see Strether change while we ourselves stand still. How, then, can the novelist come closest to giving the reader the sense

H

that he is not standing still but that he, too, is involved as a changing observer of a world of change?

One way is by deliberate misdirection of the reader, by attacking the assumptions he has built up while reading the novel, by disappointing his aroused expectations and by forcing him to make a sudden and kaleidoscopic change of perspective. We may discover false clues laid for the purpose of arousing a crude plot suspense; there are many other kinds of misdirection which the novelist can use for a great variety of purposes. Let us consider briefly four examples, of increasing complexity. At the end of Chapter 17 of *Bleak House* Mr. Jarndyce tells Esther what he knows of her past history; in the course of the conversation she "blesses the Guardian who is a father to her":

> At the word Father, I saw his former trouble come into his face. He subdued it as before, and it was gone in an instant; but, it had been there, and it had come so swiftly upon my words that I felt as if they had given him a shock. I again inwardly repeated, wondering, "That *I* could readily understand. None that *I* could readily understand!" No, it was true. I did not understand it. Not for many and many a day.

Despite this last sentence, Dickens is here doing much more than creating suspense or laying a false trail. Esther, of course, wonders if Jarndyce is not her father; she has done this before, in Chapter 6. In fact, Jarndyce—though we do not yet know it—wishes to marry her and his troubled reaction is caused by the paternal role he is obliged to adopt; he does not wish Esther to think of him as a father. What we have, then, is a paradigm of that whole foggy world of cross-purposes, misunderstandings, hints, guesses, suspicions that fills *Bleak House*. That Jarndyce *may* be Esther's father is left dangling as a possibility but it is only one of many as Dickens dramatizes Esther's plight—the plight of us all, as we stand uncommitted before a dark and open future. This is a relatively simple effect and one used in different ways by various novelists; James, for example, constantly forces us to read between the lines and simultaneously to question our own readings. In each case the novelist alerts us to hold our judgment in check; he shakes our confidence

in the rightness of our interpretation so that we leave ourselves open, tentative, ready to change course with every
ripple of the narrative.

Consider now the opening chapters of *The Scarlet Letter*.
When John Wilson tells Hester that Dimmesdale will address her, "knowing your natural temper better than I";
when he tells Dimmesdale that "the responsibility of this
woman's soul lies greatly with you" or when Dimmesdale
tells Hester, "thou hearest what this good man says, and
seest the accountability under which I labour"—the irony of
such remarks is obvious to the reader who knows the full
story. But this irony is only tolerable because we read *back*
into the opening scenes our knowledge of the whole; were
Hawthorne to make the Dimmesdale–Hester relationship
explicit from the start, then the irony would seem heavily
obvious and cheaply earned. Consequently Hawthorne
draws our attention away from this relationship by introducing the mysterious stranger, Chillingworth. The reader
easily guesses *his* secret, is satisfied that the mystery is solved
and thus, at an initial reading, looks no further. In other
words, Hawthorne misdirects us so that we shall, in retro-
spect, have to revise our judgment of these early scenes; in
doing so we savour the irony for what it is worth without any
sense of points being scored or dice being loaded by the
author.

Misdirection can sometimes lend greater reality to a process not fully shown in a novel, or at least can disguise the
gap by diverting our attention elsewhere. Consider *The
Portrait of A Lady*. There is little doubt from the general
drift of the novel that Isabel will marry Osmond. Madame
Merle prepares us for this and we have seen how the art
imagery attached to Isabel—so that she becomes a collector's
item—prepares us too. Indeed, the mere fact that she has
previously rejected two proposals of marriage serves the
same function; we feel that she simply can't keep this up.
At the same time we have seen what a difficult problem
Osmond—that first-rate imitation of a second-rate thing—
poses for James and we have noticed how little of the courtship is actually shown. But if Isabel's disillusionment—
treated with full dramatic detail—is to have its proper effect,
then it must be balanced by the illusion at least of charm and

real value in Osmond before the marriage. Hence James's art—his superb faking—must be directed to covering up a discontinuity in the middle of their developing relationship; the final stages, that is, of their putative courtship. At the end of Chapter 31, James has deliberately heightened our expectations; hence the real narrative surprise of the following chapter when we expect Isabel to meet Osmond and instead she meets Caspar Goodwood. The first mention of her forthcoming marriage is then obliquely slipped into the conversation, thus bridging the gap of events not shown, but our capacity for surprise has already been satisfied by the appearance of Caspar so that we are in part numbed by the time this real surprise occurs. We are thus more ready to accept it. This extremely obvious piece of strategy does not occur in isolation. The shock of Chapter 32 is prepared for by the previous minor surprise of Chapter 27, of Isabel meeting not Osmond but Lord Warburton at Rome. If we examine our reactions I believe we shall find ourselves saying, "Surely James won't pull *this* trick twice"—and, of course, he does precisely that. It is a fine example of a narrative double-cross which by creating one set of reactions—those of local surprise—renders immune any doubts we may have about the adequate realization of the central process of courtship.

Finally we have the case of a novel which by misdirection tempts us into errors of judgment. Our recovery from these is so doubtful and tentative that the novel virtually manoeuvres us into the task, not merely of exploring the characters in greater depth, but also of exploring ourselves. Such is *Lord Jim*. It is, for example, only on these grounds that the tripartite narrative structure of the novel makes sense. We start with a few chapters of omniscient narration which slide, with the Court of Inquiry, into Marlow's tale. This is surely a clear warning that Marlow, although reliable and honest, is still a partial and limited point of view, one we should not easily take on trust. But take him on trust we do, at least until the second shift in narration, from the after-dinner anecdote to Marlow's letter to his friend recounting the final events. This checks and in part reverses the judgments we have already made; we realize that Marlow himself was ignorant of Jim's fate and we have, retrospectively, to make

the appropriate adjustments. In doing so we change as much
of the characters; their development depends on our development.

Within this overall narrative scheme there is a more complicated pattern of misdirection. Jim's desertion of the *Patna*
and his subsequent determination to face the music at the
Court of Inquiry are, morally speaking, relatively clear-cut
events. He is, or is not, "one of us" and we do not yet pause
to ask what ethos is implied in that "us". We condemn and
approve humanely but with fair certainty, since these actions
take place within a moral code—the duty of an officer and a
gentleman—which is absolute and which cuts clean across
the indefinable nuances of human reality, across blind panic,
moral inertia at the capacity to imagine catastrophe. So far,
so good. But Conrad, as many critics have pointed out, is
concerned to draw very detailed parallels between the *Patna*
episode and the subsequent events in Patusan. Jim himself,
consciously or unconsciously does so; so does Marlow. This
formal structuring thus tempts us to see moral equivalences
between the two events, between Jim's desertion of the ship
and the death of Dain Waris at the hands of Gentleman
Brown. Jim himself feels that he has betrayed the natives as
he betrayed the passengers, and ends his life by attempting a
parallel act of expiation. The reader, too, is tempted to
transfer the moral certainties of the one situation to the other.
But in fact the situations are quite different. No comparable
ethos is relevant and the death of Dain Waris is largely
accidental and totally unforeseeable; thus moral rigidity is
quite inappropriate. From this point of view, Jim's expiation
is nothing but a fine and useless gesture, an act of immature
romanticism. What, then, is the right final judgment—what,
for example, do *we* mean by *immature* or *romantic*? We turn
for answers not to Jim or even to Marlow's view of Jim; we
can only turn to ourselves. Thus the problem of the book
becomes a *real* moral problem and the process of correcting
the narrative misdirection becomes a recreation of character.
Marlow himself recognizes the final ambiguity; Jim's exit
from the novel is appropriately in terms of a pun—"he passes
away under a cloud".

Thus by indirection we find direction out; what narrative
control at its best can do is so to complicate the process of

reading and response as to create in us an unfathomable sense of reality.

> *On a huge hill,*
> *Cragged, and steep, Truth stands, and he that will*
> *Reach her, about must, and about must go.*

So writes Donne, and this is a truth that fiction can recognize and enforce. Reality lies as much in the journey as in the goal, and the art of fiction lies in making each one of us, alone, attempt that circuitous route.

I V

The connection between time and identity has been most succinctly stated by Professor Meyerhoff:

> Time is particularly significant to man because it is inseparable from the concept of the self. We are conscious of our own organic and psychological growth in time. What we call the self, person, or individual is experienced and known only against the background of the succession of temporal moments and changes constituting his biography. But how can that which constantly changes be called the same person or an identical self? How can man be "for himself" if he always experiences himself as different and if he is always known as different from moment to moment in time? What is man, if he is nothing but a victim of temporal succession and change? What, if anything, endures throughout the constantly changing stream of consciousness of the individual? The question, what is man, therefore invariably refers to the question of what is time. The quest for a clarification of the self leads to a *récherche du temps perdu*. And the more seriously human beings become engaged in this quest, the more they become preoccupied and concerned with the consciousness of time and its meaning for human life.[1]

I think it is fair to say that in common, unreflective experience we evade or ignore most of these questions. And although novelists have always been concerned with the consequences of such questions, the questions themselves have not, until recently, provoked very radical answers in

---

[1] Meyerhoff, *op. cit.*, pp. 1-2.

most fiction. As I said in an earlier chapter, one aspect of our notion of identity lies in our sense that the self is discrete, isolate, unique; to this we may add the common assumption that it is a constant, stable thing. Most great novelists have inverted the Sartrean dictum and written on the assumption that essence precedes existence. Such a notion is, no doubt, philosophically unsound yet, most pre-twentieth-century novelists take it more or less for granted, particularly in so far as their interest in character has been moral rather than psychological. This distinction is naturally one of emphasis rather than of substance; an example will perhaps clarify the point.

No one would deny that George Eliot takes a dominantly moral interest in her characters; she is, more than anything, interested in the sequence of motive, act and consequence—above all, in the consequence. No one has been a finer analyst of what an existentialist would call "bad faith", the twists and turns of the corrupted self as it seeks to evade truth and responsibility. In particular, she is concerned with bad faith as it stems from various kinds of egoism. Yet egoism, bad faith, moral analysis—all these imply for her a central, stable core of character.[1] Of course this central ego depends on time, since consequences can only be analysed in time; indeed, it is always a symptom of moral degeneration in her characters that they lose their grip on past, present and future, that their sense of time is weakened and confused by hopes, fears, desires or evasive rationalizations. But she never questions the assumption that moral responsibility depends on a survival of personal identity; the moral problems confronting the hero of William Golding's *Free Fall*, for example, do not concern her. Her characters may ask themselves, "Where or why did I go wrong in the past?" But they do not ask the prior questions, "Who was that 'I' which went wrong in the past? How is that 'I' related to the present 'I' which asks the question? How far is the present 'I'

[1] George Eliot knows as well as Mr. Farebrother that "character is not cut in marble—it is not something solid and unalterable. It is something living and changing" (*Middlemarch*, Chapter 72). It is on these grounds, for example, that Sartre in *Existentialism and Humanism* can claim Maggie Tulliver as a type of existentialist heroine. But beneath this is George Eliot's conviction that "even while we rave on the heights" we "behold the wide plain where *our persistent self* pauses and awaits us" (*Middlemarch*, Chapter 15).

responsible for what that totally different past 'I' did?"
Of course, this is not to say that George Eliot—or any great
classical novelist—denies the facts of change and development. But change is still reconciled to the idea of a stable
ego; one's identity lies precisely in the unique pattern of past
changes which constitutes one's individuality. And this
pattern also involves the future to the extent that it allows
for some possibilities of development and excludes others.
This can be seen if we look at those Victorian novels which
involve precisely the search for identity; narrators like Pip
or David Copperfield clearly change and recognize the fact,
but they never deny their past, however strange, as belong-
ing to them and, in a sense, *being* them. Moreover, they view
it from a stable vantage point of retrospection which itself
implies a certain constancy of self.

One further point may be made about this commonsensical, unanguished, philosophically unsophisticated
notion of the self. We come fairly soon, I believe, to imagine
the nature of experience in terms of a basic polarity. This is
the opposition, tension, balance, interaction—call it what
you will—between the perceiver and the perceived, subject
and object, I and Thou. On the one hand we are aware of
identity, of ourselves; on the other hand, of all that which is
stubbornly and mysteriously itself, other than us. This
duality of what, for convenience, I shall call the Self and the
World varies enormously in its intellectual formulations;
hence the philosopher's fascination with epistemology. But
few of us—and few novelists—would, I believe, seriously
deny this sense of duality; there is no great solipsistic novel.
There is one important exception to this traditional sense of
Self and World which I shall consider in a moment, but
generally it holds good as a commonly accepted assumption.
Even if it is a false belief it still conditions action and therefore becomes part of the novelist's empirical data. The
notion of an 'I' set against a 'Thou' and surviving within the
succession of time may sometimes be thought of as a single,
central ego, or it may be thought of as a multiplicity of
selves which together form a unique pattern of identity; we
may admit, under pressure, that it is a fiction but we must
also admit that such "fictions" form a substantial part of
"reality".

The significant thing is that such notions of identity have been constantly subverted and corroded by much modern fiction. Generally the attack has been oblique, intermittent and unformulated, revealing itself in such things as the various stream of consciousness techniques; the most formidably organized attack, the existentialist, will be considered in a later chapter. But we may take as a fair symbol of this process of demolition the famous letter from D. H. Lawrence to Edward Garnett. After saying that he is no longer interested in:

> The old-fashioned human element—which causes one to conceive a character in a certain moral scheme and make him consistent. The certain moral scheme is what I object to. In Turgenev, and in Tolstoi, and in Dostoievsky, the moral scheme into which all the characters fit—and it is nearly the same scheme—is, whatever the extraordinariness of the characters themselves, dull, old, dead.

Lawrence continues:

> You mustn't look in my novel for the old stable *ego* of the character. There is another *ego*, according to whose action the individual is unrecognisable, and passes through, as it were, allotropic states which it needs a deeper sense than any we've been used to exercise, to discover are states of the same single radically unchanged element. (Like as diamond and coal are the pure single element of carbon. The ordinary novel would trace the history of the diamond—but I say, Diamond, what! This is carbon! And my diamond might be coal or soot, and my theme is carbon.)[1]

Clearly such a view of identity has drastic consequences for the creation of fictional characters. Most of these are peculiar to the modern novel; the one modification of "the old stable ego" that I wish to discuss, however, has its roots far back in the classical tradition.

v

I have said that one aspect of the common notion of identity stems from the sense we share of a duality between

[1] D. H. Lawrence, *Letters* (edited by Aldous Huxley), pp. 197-8. London: Heinemann, 1932.

Self and the World, I and Thou. What happens if this assumption is denied? It is perfectly legitimate to point out that my own argument, with its assumptions, is itself the result of cultural determination and that when I speak of *we* or of *sharing*, I am speaking from an outlook which is historically limited and mutable. It is not a sufficient answer to reply that this particular cultural or historical frame of reference is also precisely that which has produced the novel as its distinctive art form; though I believe, by and large, this to be true. We may agree that there may well have been cultures in which the duality between Self and World was not assumed. But such cultures, I think, would generally tend to be primitive, whereas the novel, historically considered, arises in an age of considerable sociological complexity and sophistication.

Yet it is also true that many novelists have shown a strong atavistic strain; their imaginations have been coloured by a primitive drive which tends to break down the duality of Self and World, and hence to blur and make more fluid the contours of individual identity. Dickens and Dostoievski are probably the greatest examples of this and we must in a moment consider the consequences of such an imaginative habit for the creation of their fictional characters. Moreover, I would accept that such an atavistic strain exists as a vestigial but nevertheless real element in the experience of most of us—so that at some time we do feel moments of unusual union or communion, when our own identities seem to merge with the forms of nature or with the feelings of another individual. This "oceanic" impulse, as Freud terms it, is part of empirical reality with which novelists may deal; it matters little whether we accept Freud's attempt to trace it back to infantile origins or whether, as I prefer to believe, it is the dim reflection in us of some remote cultural inheritance. It is enough to say that it is *there* and therefore exists as a proper subject for artistic treatment. We can value it as an end in itself or we can rationalize it by relating it to some metaphysic we happen to believe in; unless we are willing to do one of these we shall miss a great deal in, say, the poetry of Wordsworth or the novels of Lawrence. In the novel I believe it is exceptional rather than general and we may grant it an extra value on precisely this ground—that it counterbalances what I have taken to be a dominant strain in fiction, the ever-increasing stress on the isolation and alienation of the individual.

The sort of effect I have in mind when I speak of an atavistic or primitive imagination is best conveyed by Dorothy van Ghent, who in an essay on *Great Expectations*, describes the fictional world of Dickens as:

> A universe that is nervous throughout, a universe in which nervous ganglion stretch through both people and their external environment. . . . Dickens uses a kind of montage in *Great Expectations*, a superimposing of one image upon another, with an immediate effect of hallucination, that is but one more way of representing his vision of a purely nervous and moral organization. . . . This device, of doubling one image over another, is paralleled in the handling of character. In the sense that one implies the other, the glittering frosty girl Estella, and the decayed and false old woman, Miss Havisham, are not two characters but a single one, or a single essence with dual aspects, as if composed by montage—a spiritual continuum, so to speak. The boy Pip and the criminal Magwitch form another such continuum. The relationship between Joe Gargery, saintly simpleton of the folk, and Orlick, dark beast of the Teutonic marshes . . . has a somewhat different dynamics, though they too form a spiritual continuum. Joe and Orlick are related not as two aspects of a single moral identity, but as the opposite extremes of spiritual possibility—the one unqualified love, the other unqualified hate—and they form a frame within which the actions of the others have their ultimate meaning. A commonplace of criticism is that, as Edmund Wilson puts it, Dickens was usually unable to "get the good and bad together in one character". The criticism might be valid if Dickens' were a naturalistic world, but it is not very relevant to Dickens' daemonically organized world. In a naturalistic world, obeying mechanical laws, each character is organically discrete from every other, and presumably each contains a representative mixture of "the good and the bad". But in Dickens' thoroughly nervous world, that does not know the laws of mechanics

but knows only spiritual law, one simple or "flat" character can be superimposed upon another so that together
they form the representative human complexity of good-
in-evil and evil-in-good.[1]

It is possible to qualify or to quarrel with Mrs. Van
Ghent's analysis in matters of detail; thus one might wish
to lay greater stress on the obscure but potent psychic
intimacy that exists between Pip and Orlick. But as a general
picture of the kind of world inhabited by Dickens's characters, her statement seems to me extraordinarily fine and
complete. This process, wherein our sense of duality between Self and World is diminished and in which discrete
identities merge into the unity of a larger spiritual continuum, we may call psychic decomposition. By this I mean
that process whereby an artist's vision of the world is such
that it decomposes and splits into various attributes which
then form the substance of disparate characters. But the
relative solidity of individual characterization does not quite
conceal the fluidity of the original vision, so that characters
exist not merely in the context of normal human relationships but also unite in their common reference back to the
single imaginative vision from which they emerged and
which, so to speak, still envelops and overflows their individual outlines. The process is perhaps commoner in poetry
than in fiction; a particularly clear example is *The Waste
Land*, as Eliot indicates in one of his notes to the poem:

> Tiresias, although a mere spectator and not indeed a
> "character", is yet the most important personage in the
> poem, uniting all the rest. Just as the one-eyed merchant,
> seller of currants, melts into the Phoenician Sailor, and the
> latter is not wholly distinct from Ferdinand Prince of
> Naples, so all the women are one woman, and the two
> sexes meet in Tiresias. What Tiresias *sees*, in fact, is the
> substance of the poem.

What we are now exploring is by nature a shadowy and
ambiguous area of the psyche and our vocabulary, based so
much on the assumption of discrete identity, is inadequate to

[1] D. van Ghent, *The English Novel; Form and Function*, pp. 132–4. New York:
Rinehart, 1953.

deal with it. Consequently we must draw some careful distinctions. Certainly the effects of psychic decomposition are quite different from those produced by the web of relationships I termed the human context. What they can both equally well render, however, is the sense that we are all one life, all members one of another; the point expressed, for example, by Ishmael in Chapter 72 of *Moby Dick*, in which he is wedded to Queequeg by the monkey-rope:

> I seemed distinctly to perceive that my own individuality was now merged in a joint stock company of two; that my free will had received a mortal wound . . . I saw that this situation of mine was the precise situation of every mortal that breathes; only, in most cases he, one way or other, has this Siamese connection with a plurality of other mortals. If your banker breaks, you snap; if your apothecary by mistake sends you poison in your pills, you die.

What prevents Ishmael's reflections from being an example of psychic decomposition—though there is certainly more in his relationship with Queequeg than he is aware of—is his somewhat whimsical self-consciousness. If two characters are bound together in one psychological continuum they are precluded from being more than obscurely aware of the connection. Even an outside narrator, even the reader himself, should not be too aware of the relation. Thus we come much closer to the process when we see through Ishmael—and through suggestion by imagery rather than statement—the peculiar relation of Ahab and Fedallah. Thus:

> And Ahab chanced so to stand, that the Parsee occupied his shadow; while, if the Parsee's shadow was there at all it seemed only to blend with, and lengthen Ahab's. (Chapter 73)

or again:

> At times, for longest hours, without a single hail, they stood far parted in the starlight; Ahab in his scuttle, the Parsee by the mainmast; but still fixedly gazing upon each other; as if in the Parsee Ahab saw his forethrown shadow, in Ahab the Parsee his abandoned substance.

And yet, somehow, did Ahab—in his proper self, as daily, hourly, and every instant, commandingly revealed to his subordinates—Ahab seemed an independent lord; the Parsee but his slave. Still again both seemed yoked together, and an unseen tyrant driving them; the lean shade siding the solid rib. For be this Parsee what he may, all rib and keel was solid Ahab. (Chapter 130)

This is certainly much more effective than the explicit and intellectual formulation of Jack Burden, the narrator of Robert Penn Warren's *All The King's Men*:

Tiny Duffy became, in a crazy kind of way, the other self of Willie Stark, and all the contempt and insult which Willie Stark was to heap on Tiny Duffy was nothing but what one self of Willie Stark did to the other self because of a blind inward necessity. (Chapter 2)

What is intuitively grasped and imaginatively rendered by Melville has become a theoretical exposition for the modern novelist; the relationship withers in such clarity of statement.

Ahab and Fedallah may be regarded as an instance of character doubling or of what Mrs. Van Ghent calls montage; one aspect or attribute of Ahab is distilled, so to speak, from his total psyche and objectified in other figure. Fedallah is hardly a character at all in his own right; he exists rather as a presence, a shadow which falls across the multifarious concerns of the crew. Nevertheless, Ahab is not diminished by this extension of himself; Melville avoids the great danger inherent in most literary doubles or doppelgangers. In such instances the novelist generally splits a personality in order to objectify some internal moral struggle; the danger is that a crude and simple allegory may result in which the characters are little more than personifications of spiritual or psychological forces. Dr. Jekyll and Mr. Hyde come closer to this; a more subtle effect is achieved by Dickens in *Our Mutual Friend*. In this novel, Boffin is little more than a type, a piece of benevolent machinery, but by adopting the dramatic role of miser he breeds an antitype which is much more vivid and powerful than his own self. Dickens triumphantly has his cake and eats it too; greed and avarice hover around the fringes of the benevolent Boffin as a pos-

sibility which gives the character unusual depth and resonance.

The causes and nature of psychic decomposition are very
complex. It may be the result of some emotional nexus outside the book which is too painful to be brought into the
novel in a pure state; Edgar Johnson plausibly suggests that
this may be the case for the range of real and surrogate
parents in *David Copperfield*. They may well be an objectifi-
cation of Dickens's ambivalent feelings towards his parents;
this may account, too, for David's attitude to his half-brother
who dies as a baby:

> The mother who lay in the grave, was the mother of my
> infancy; the little creature in her arms, was myself, as I
> had once been, hushed for ever on her bosom. (Chapter 9)

Again, decomposition may result from the novelist's
attempt to render passional states of unusual depth and intensity, moments of union when one's identity is merged in
another's. This, I believe, is what Lawrence was pointing to
in his distinction between the diamond (the old-fashioned
"individualized" character) and the basic carbon (the deep
flow of drives and appetites which he shares with all human-
ity). *The Rainbow*, and particularly the chapter "Anna
Victrix", contains some fine dramatizations of those "allo-
tropic states". Another good example of the process occurs
in *Wuthering Heights*. One notices here that although the
metaphor differs, the substance of Cathy's passionate
declaration is very similar to the distinction drawn by
Lawrence in his letter to Garnett. Linton belongs to the
world of diamond, Heathcliff to the world of carbon:

> "I cannot express it; but surely you and everybody
> have a notion that there is or should be an existence of
> yours beyond you. What were the use of my creation,
> if I were entirely contained here? My great miseries in this
> world have been Heathcliff's miseries, and I watched and
> felt each from the beginning; my great thought in living
> is himself. If all else perished, and *he* remained, I should
> still continue to be; and if all else remained, and he were
> annihilated, the universe would turn to a mighty stranger:
> I should not seem a part of it. My love for Linton is like
> the foliage in the woods; time will change it, I'm well

aware, as winter changes the trees. My love for Heathcliff resembles the eternal rocks beneath: a source of little visible delight, but necessary. Nelly, I *am* Heathcliff! He's always, always in my mind: not as a pleasure, any more than I am always a pleasure to myself, but as my own being." (Chapter 9)

At the deepest level, psychic decomposition may be part of the novelist's vision of the world; I agree with Mrs. Van Ghent that this is so with *Great Expectations*. It also seems to me true of *Moby Dick*; the crew of the Pequod may be regarded collectively as Melville's view of the total range of man's possibilities when faced with the voyage of his destiny. In particular, as Leslie Fiedler and other critics have pointed out, the role of Ishmael may be seen as a dramatization of Melville's simultaneous complicity in, and detachment from, what he took to be a diabolic vision; the narrative structure of the book, as it fluctuates between epic and dramatic modes of presentation, thus being the formal correlative of theme. Again, do we not feel that the Karamazov family exist in a single psychological or spiritual continuum, so that without detracting from their individuality or without straying into allegory, Dostoievski is saying something not just about men—Aloysha, Ivan, Dmitri—but also about Man?

We must retreat from such clouded and speculative depths; the problem is, of its nature, one destroyed by the light of logical analysis.

> Tragedy, [Yeats wrote] must always be a drowning and breaking of the dykes that separate man from man, and . . . it is upon those dykes that comedy keeps house . . . behind the momentary self, which acts and lives in the world, and is subject to the judgement of the world, there is that which cannot be called before any mortal judgement seat. . . . We may not find either mood in its purity, but in mainly tragic art one distinguishes devices to exclude or lessen character, to diminish the power of that daily mood, to cheat or blind its too clear perception.[1]

[1] This is a conflation of many passages from Yeats, usefully gathered together in T. Parkinson's *W. B. Yeats: Self-Critic*, p. 51 ff. Berkeley: University of California Press, 1951.

Yeats's definitions of tragedy and comedy are idiosyncratic but we may apply his distinction to the process I have been trying to describe. In his terms the usual world of the novel is comic (Lawrence's world of diamond); that is, it depends on our perception of what separates man from man, and what gives man a distinctive, discrete identity. But in some novels we may also feel the presence of what Yeats calls tragedy (Lawrence's world of carbon); beneath the superstructure of the individualized character, we may sense those depths in which identity is submerged and united within a greater whole. And with the very greatest novels one feels that the individual character is thereby immeasurably enriched, that he is not obliterated, or dehumanized into allegory or symbol, but filled with an inexhaustible reservoir of meaning so that he becomes, as it were, a shaft of light defining the greater darkness which surrounds him. My metaphors are mixed but I trust my meaning is plain, for it points to a sense of human life, a dimension of reality, without which we should all be impoverished.

I

CHAPTER VI

Freedom and Causality

THE objects of imitation, says Aristotle, "are actions, with agents who are necessarily either good men or bad—the diversities of human character being nearly always derivative from this primary distinction".[1] But Aristotle's "primary distinction" rests upon an even more primary assumption about the nature of action. No account of man's actual or latent powers would be adequate without a parallel account of his limitations; what we cannot do defines us as much as what we can. In any given situation our powers and limitations, the *can* and *cannot* of our being, must rest in large part on our capacity to choose, our sense of whether or not we are free agents. The mimetic adequacy of any novel will therefore depend on the novelist's ability to create the sense of man as simultaneously both agent and patient, free and not free, capable of choice yet limited in innumerable ways.

The problem of freedom is clearly related to that basic duality between Self and the World which I discussed in the preceding chapter. Most of us, no doubt in a commonsensical and philosophically inarticulate way, take up some middle ground between the two hypothetical extremes of complete freedom or non-freedom of the Self. Few of us can imagine, let alone maintain that we exist in, a state of complete freedom and most of us would resist the notion that we are completely governed by a necessity—genetic, economic, psychological or metaphysical—that denies us all freedom. Indeed, should anyone wish to maintain that our sense of freedom is an illusion, the argument remains largely unaffected, since the illusion of freedom then becomes part of the reality we live by, part of the data of experience with which the novelist deals. Of course, this illusion of freedom may figure as part of the novelist's subject-matter in the sense that a character may think himself more free than he actually is. Many great works of art in this sense probe and explore the illusion of freedom—*Macbeth*, for example, or *The Portrait of A Lady*.

[1] Aristotle, *op. cit.*, pp. 25–6.

But this process takes place within our larger sense of the truth (or fiction) that we ourselves are free.

Most of us would say that freedom abides in our ability to choose; this, of course, entails the possibility of there being something in the World for the Self to choose from. It is for this reason that a state of complete freedom is unimaginable. All choices are acts of exclusion; even if we limit ourselves freely, the fact that we *have* always to limit ourselves is a compelling fact of the human situation which precludes the notion of complete freedom. Moreover, each choice has a history of previous choices which determines it; in turn, it determines future choices. In this sense, then, of course we are determined and many great novels are precisely concerned with relating what seems to be an inexorable history of choices, a causally linked sequence of decisions. But this inexorability appears only to the reader; the freedom—or the illusion of freedom—for the character *within* the sequence is preserved, since for him the future appears indeterminate and at each stage his decision opens up new possibilities from which he is free to choose. Precisely the same is true for us in real life. Indeed, without this history of choice behind us we would not exist as individuals to choose at all, since our sense of identity is in part defined by the *kind* of choices we have made in the past. It is on the basis of such history that we make predictions of the form, "He is the sort of chap who will do such-and-such."

We may sum this up by saying that we live in a world of the conditional, a world of relative freedom. Few of us, I imagine, would find much to quarrel with in Ishmael's reflections on the human situation, as in Chapter 47 of *Moby Dick* he sits, mat-making with Queequeg:

There lay the fixed threads of the warp subject to but one single, ever returning, unchanging vibration, and that vibration merely enough to admit of the crosswise interblending of other threads with its own. This warp seemed necessity; and here, thought I, with my own hand I ply my own shuttle, and weave my own destiny into these unalterable threads. Meantime, Queequeg's impulsive, indifferent sword, sometimes hitting the woof slantingly, or crookedly, or strongly, or weakly, as the case might be;

and by this difference in the concluding blow producing a corresponding contrast in the final aspect of the completed fabric; this savage's sword, thought I, which thus finally shapes and fashions both warp and woof; this easy, indifferent sword must be chance—aye chance, free will, and necessity—no wise incompatible—all interweavingly working together. The straight warp of necessity, not to be swerved from its ultimate course—its every alternating vibration, indeed, only tending to that; free will still free to ply her shuttle between given threads; and chance, though restrained in its play within the right lines of necessity, and sideways in its motions directed by free will, though thus prescribed to by both, chance by turns rules either, and has the last featuring blow at events.

It is the interplay of these three factors that creates our sense of conditional freedom. We cannot imagine that we are so many pieces on a chessboard. Although the pieces are limited by the size of the board and the conventions of the game, the permutations of movement are so innumerable that we, were we pawns, would seem to be so free that to all intents and purposes we would in fact be free. Few of us, I believe, would subscribe to a metaphysic which postulated some invisible, omniscient hand predetermining our every move.

If I have described our sense of conditional freedom with reasonable accuracy, then we have arrived at a basic difference between life and art. For in any work of fiction we know that just such a metaphysic is at work, that there is an omniscient hand—the author's—governing his imagined chessboard. Our feelings about the mimetic adequacy of any novel will, therefore, depend in large part upon the tact with which the pieces are moved. But this is emphatically *not* to reiterate the doctrine that the artist should as far as possible eliminate himself from his work; in any case, as we have seen earlier, the author's "second self" must be present in some way in the novel. Many authors have openly intruded into their novels without interfering with the illusion that their characters are free in the sequence of choices and actions they play out within their fictional world. The great novelist does not by his use of omniscience diminish his fictional world; rather he enlarges it to the magnitude of life itself. Our sense of the freedom of the characters does not depend simply on the overt or disguised omniscience of their authors; the problem is more complicated than that. For a fictional character lives in two dimensions of freedom where we live in only one; the character's freedom exists in relation to the author and in relation to the quality of the imagined fictional world. And the sense of this latter freedom may in fact be diminished by the author's efforts to eliminate or disguise himself. Fielding rushes with gusto into the world of *Tom Jones*; Conrad makes his crafty exit behind the figure of Marlow in *Lord Jim*. Yet most of us would agree, I think, that as a character Jim appears to us less free than Tom. How, then, can we explore further the mimetic relationship of fictional characters to our own sense of relative or conditional freedom?

I said earlier that this sense of conditional freedom depends upon our prior sense of some balance between Self and the World. In real life this sense is pretty much a donnée; depending upon individual temperament there will be some difference in emphasis upon one or other of these basic categories. But apart from pathological cases the difference is relatively slight; we tend, perhaps wrongly, to assume the relationship between Self and the World as a constant; we take it much as it comes. But in fiction the novelist is free—as in real life we are not free—to make much more radical adjustments in the balance between the Self and the World of his characters.

Novels which portray roughly the same equipoise between Self and World, which achieve the effect of conditional freedom that I have described, we may call *realistic*. They form, I believe, the central tradition of fiction as we know it; that is to say, of the post-Renaissance European novel. Granted the greater freedom of the novelist, he may then adjust the balance in one of two directions. He may stress the greater importance of the World, may give greater weight to all the various factors which limit our sense of freedom. That way lies determinism, which in its various forms is reflected in the kind of fiction we may call *naturalistic*. Or he may stress the greater importance of the Self, may allow his characters a greater freedom than we in fact discover in our commerce with the world; this kind of novel I wish for convenience to describe as the *subjective* novel.

Since the realistic novel is the main concern of this book, I wish here to glance briefly only at the naturalistic and subjective ends of the spectrum of fiction. In the naturalistic novel the determining forces are generally of three kinds—metaphysical, social and genetic. The categories are not clear-cut; social forces, for example, may often be thought of as quasi-metaphysical principles. Most naturalists stress more than one kind of determining force; in Zola and Dreiser, for example, we find a blended emphasis on the social and genetic.

There are three main points I wish to make about this kind of fiction. If we are primarily concerned with the mimetic adequacy of fiction and if this depends on our sense of an equipoise between freedom and necessity such as I have tried to describe, then it follows that the more a novel weighs down the see-saw of conditional freedom, the greater strain it places upon our assent to its credibility. We are more likely to reject it, to say that it is inadequate to our sense of what life is actually like. The purer the variety of naturalism, the more a novelist stresses *one* kind of determining force, the greater this strain will become. The danger is that we shall attend less to an imagined fictional world and more to some dogmatic philosophy of life which engages us in an area of controversy entirely outside the world of art.

We must, however, take care not to confuse the artistic inevitability of a novel with determinism as a philosophy. In so far as a novel is successfully created it will seem to have an inevitable tightness and finality; given these characters and this situation the outcome will have a logic and justness we cannot but accept. But this is a by-product of artistic success; it has nothing to do with naturalism as a literary kind nor with determinism as a world view. Of course in any particular case—*Madame Bovary* is an excellent example—it may be difficult or impossible to disentangle the two kinds of inevitability.

My last point is mere speculation. Many novels depict societies dominated by conventional patterns of behaviour; this again has nothing to do with naturalism or determinism since we know that such conventions are part of real life and that paradoxically they are often a condition of our very freedom. When we move from one kind of social *mores* to a different kind we merely exchange one set of possible freedoms for another. In *The Magic Mountain*, for example, life at the Berghof Sanatorium goes on in a society that in many ways is more artificial and limiting than life in the "flatland". Yet it encourages certain other things; one cannot imagine the Hans Castorp of Hamburg declaring his love for Madame Chauchat. If now we shift our attention from convention as part of the artist's subject matter to convention as a literary force governing any particular *genre* of literature, then the question becomes more complicated. Can we say that the more rigid the literary conventions of an age, the more deterministic the world view of that age is likely to be, or that the most stylized forms of art tend to occur in autocratically governed societies? Probably not—except in a negative form. It is perhaps significant that of all major art forms the novel is the most free from any rigid set of literary conventions and that the decay of the whole doctrine of kinds or *genes* coincided with the growth of an increasingly pluralistic world-view and an increasingly liberal social order. Conversely, it may be possible that the decline of a liberal sense of freedom is connected with certain technical changes in the modern novel, particularly with the relative inability of the modern novelist to create characters as vivid, abundant and self-sufficient as those of the classical novelists.

Let us now consider the subjective novel in which the author allows his character a greater degree of freedom than normal. The sort of thing I have in mind is illustrated by these passages from Yvor Winters's essay on Henry James:

> James displays in all his more serious works an unmistakeable desire to allow his characters unrestricted freedom of choice and to develop his plots out of such choice and out of consequent acts of choice to which the initial acts may lead. Now absolutely considered, no human complex is ever free from a great many elements which are without the control and even the understanding of the human participants. . . .
>
> Elements of this sort are what we call the given facts of the plot: they are the ineliminable facts of character

and of initial situation. We have a certain group of particularized individuals in juxtaposition, the particularity is destiny, the juxtaposition chance. But the understanding and the will may rise in some measure superior to destiny and to chance, and when they do so, we have human victory; or they make the effort and fail, in which case we have tragedy; or the failure having occurred, there may be a comprehension of the failure and a willed adjustment to it, in which case we have the combination of tragedy and victory. It is this combination, the representation of which Henry James especially tries to achieve.

Some novelists—Defoe, for example, or Hardy—make a conscious effort to give the human participant the smallest possible freedom of play; James endeavours to give him the greatest possible freedom, and he is so successful in the effort that in reading one of his better novels one is conscious almost exclusively of the problem of ethical choice.

Now the norm of human experience, in the matter of unhampered choice, is probably somewhere between the extremes of Moll Flanders and of Isabel Archer, and the novelist who goes to one extreme or the other simply refuses to consider intelligently certain aspects of human life. There is possibly greater educative value—there are wider ethical implications—in suffering the consequences of an ill-judged but unhampered choice than in any other department of experience; on the other hand, the person whose choice is normally unhampered may often appear to have an abominably facile existence in the eyes of him whose life is an unbroken and unavailing endurance of necessity, whose primary virtue must of necessity be fortitude.[1]

It is perfectly possible to agree with the general drift of Winters's remarks, as I do, and yet believe that he has completely misread Henry James. The particular case is not in point; one can easily substitute other novelists—Virginia Woolf, for example—whose work seems more relevant. The important thing to notice is that, paradoxically, the extreme

---

[1] Y. Winters, *In Defense of Reason*, pp. 306–8. London: Routledge, 1960.

ends of the fictional spectrum come full circle; the subjective novel has much more in common with the naturalistic novel than either has with the realistic novel. Sartre's philosophy is totally anti-deterministic, yet the effect of *Mort dans l'Ame* is very close to that of Zola's novels. If the see-saw of conditional freedom is tilted too far either way, the result is the same; too much or too little freedom given to the characters and our sense of mimetic accuracy—based upon the medial "norm of human experience" is strained.

The reason for this lies in a further paradox. Our sense of conditional freedom depends upon a combination of factors which, considered singly, may seem to determine us, but which in association tend to liberate us. When one considers the multiplicity of everyday experience one is, so to speak, a Montesquieux rather than a Rousseau. That is to say, one views the conditioning factors of self and non-self as an incredibly complex system of checks and balances; freedom lies in the interstices of this system, one force qualifying or negating another. (Hence my mention of social conventions as a positively liberating factor.) Our conditional freedom is then in part accidental (depending on chance permutations, on one thing just happening to cancel out another) and in part the result of our ability to manipulate these determining factors, to play them off against each other. The extreme naturalist is, metaphorically, a Rousseau rather than a Montesquieux in that he tends to narrow down the multiplicity of these determining factors to a few, or even to one factor. This we tend to reject; we know that not *everything* is explicable in terms of our genetic make-up or our Oedipus complex or the nature of the class struggle. In other words, the naturalist strains our sense of mimetic adequacy because he offers too *simple* an explanation. We perceive many effects and conceive of many causes; unlike the naturalist we are reluctant to trace all phenomena back to a single cause.

Precisely the same sort of objection may be levelled against the writer of extremely subjective novels. In the interests of granting his characters greater freedom, such a novelist ignores the trivial and mundane factors which apparently hamper ordinary mortals. But if he excludes too much, then his characters are liable to topple back into a state where they are governed by a few compelling factors, generally imagined in fiction as basic psychological drives. Isabel Archer is given money and thereby the liberty to taste experience; ironically her freedom proves her greatest trap. Again, is this not true of the characters in Virginia Woolf's novels? They are freed by her from the squalid world of objective reality which she found so obtrusive in Arnold Bennett's work; yet, much more than Bennett's characters, they are hag-ridden by a few obsessive fears and desires. Mrs. Dalloway joins hands with Septimus Smith. Thus both Bennett and Virginia Woolf, we may say, working from opposite extremes of the fictional spectrum, are alike in that they both exclude too much. The result strains our sense of mimetic accuracy, a strain that is only eased by the mediating vision of the realistic novelist who reconciles these opposites and restores the equipoise of conditional freedom.

II

In an interview, Pasternak defended *Dr. Zhivago* in these terms:

> In the nineteenth-century masters of the novel, Balzac, Tolstoy, Stendhal, if you take away the characters and characterization, the imagery, description and so on, you still have left *causality*, the concept that an action has a consequence. Flaubert's style is the ultimate, merciless verdict on this nineteenth-century causality. For me, reality lies not there, but in the multiplicity of the universe, in the large number of possibilities, a kind of spirit of freedom, a coincidence of impulses and inspirations. ... Even modern science and mathematics, about which I know little, or better, nothing, is moving in that direction, away from simple causality. Whatever happens, for example, loss or destruction in nature or life, is just one of many things that happen. There is always an enormous quantity of happenings. Nature is much richer in coincidences than is our imagination. If all these possibilities exist, reality must be the result of choice, of a choice deliberately made. Even in the novel, the totality of the work, the total conception, is important, not the details or the irrationality of the details. I have frequently been asked about the coincidences in the book, particularly

by young people of fifteen or sixteen, from whom I get many letters. Of course I made the coincidences on purpose, that *is* life, just as I purposely did not fully characterize the people in the book. For I wanted to get away from the idea of causality. The innovation of the book lies precisely in this conception of reality.[1]

Philosophically, it is not difficult to demolish the idea of causality. But like Hume, most of us in our everyday lives leave philosophy behind in the study and in this we agree with the novelist; there is little great closet-fiction. Our sense of conditional freedom is closely linked to our sense that "an action has a consequence". We know, of course, that an action may have multiple consequences; hence we rebel at the oversimple and stark concept of causality that underlies most varieties of determinism. On the other hand, we do not simply accept multiplicity as the final reality; we believe that we can perceive and make sense of causal patterns in both life and fiction. The interesting point is that here again we have an example of that convergence of the naturalistic and the subjective ends of the fictional spectrum. On the one hand, coincidence may be seen, so to speak, as the footprints of some otherwise invisible necessity, controlling the affairs of men. This, I believe—though the point is often overstressed and oversimplified—is true of some of Hardy's novels. On the other hand, coincidence may be seen as the index of a totally random and contingent world; this is true, for example, of the ironic twist in Sartre's short story, *Le Mur*. But most of us strike a balance between these two extremes. Clearly, however, a considerable problem is posed for the novelist who has to reconcile his vision of life with the formal demands of his art. How is he to render this common sense of balance and equipoise; how, in Ishmael's image, is he to render the casual blows of chance against the woof and warp of reality? For an example of successful reconciliation, I turn again to *Bleak House*.

I cannot think of another novel in which coincidence plays so essential a part as it does in *Bleak House*; Hardy's tragedies of circumstance are simple and crude by comparison. As an

---

[1] Pasternak as reported by Ralph E. Matlaw, "A Visit With Pasternak", *The Nation*, September 12, 1959.

example we may briefly recall Chapter 24. Richard has decided to join the army and is taking sword-lessons; his teacher turns out to be George Rouncewell, who is thus brought into contact with Esther and Jarndyce. Thus the various narrative strands converging on George (the reader particularly remembers Smallweed and his interest in Captain Hawdon) begin to tangle with the already tangled strands of Esther's past and future. (This is gently hinted by George's bewilderment at the familiarity of Esther's face; the reader has already encountered something like this when Guppy connected Esther with Lady Dedlock's portrait.) One coincidental connection, acknowledged as such by Esther, is almost immediately made—George's knowledge of Gridley. Esther then goes to the Court of Chancery; coincidentally Guppy is there with Mrs. Chadband, who turns out to be the Mrs. Rachael of Esther's childhood. George appears with a message from Gridley to Miss Flite; providentially Esther is there to introduce them. They go to George's shooting gallery and by chance Bucket turns up at this moment to arrest Gridley on a warrant from Tulkinghorn (one of the few times he is ever mentioned in Esther's narrative); thus Bucket meets Esther for the first time—an important detail since when much later Bucket finds Esther's handkerchief in Lady Dedlock's room he has to ask George where Esther lives in London in order that she may help him search for her mother. In the space of ten pages, then, several chance encounters—most of some consequence for the future of the novel—casually occur.

So casually, indeed, are these quite typical coincidences insinuated into the novel that I doubt whether any relaxed, non-analytical reader would recognize more than one of them (probably Mrs. Rachael—Mrs. Chadband) as coincidental. Certainly one does not feel that the characters are thereby made puppets or that the elaborate plot creaks with obvious contrivance; one accepts coincidence as a natural part of the *Bleak House* world. There are exceptions; Sir Leicester's visit to Jarndyce in Chapter 43 perhaps reveals Dickens in the act of contriving and faking. But by and large, coincidence is to the microcosm of the novel what the law of gravity is to the macrocosm of the real world. We accept both as natural laws and are largely unconscious of their operation.

Only very detailed analysis could properly show how Dickens attains this end. But we may note four main factors combining to merge the various coincidences into the very fabric of the story. The first of these is the interlocking twin narratives we have already examined. Many of the coincidences Esther takes for granted because she is ignorant of something of which the omniscient narrative informs us. But because she takes them for granted and because we trust her, therefore we tend to take them for granted too.

Second, Dickens *does* combine coincidence with a good deal of naturalistic, rational explanation. Clearly in a complex novel dealing so centrally with the consequences, anticipated or unforeseen, of human actions some such explanation will be needed. Dickens had failed badly when faced with this problem early in his career. In *Oliver Twist*, after the mystery of a powerfully imagined Fagin, we are offered in an undigested lump the tangled motivations of a feebly imagined Monks. In *Bleak House*, by contrast, such explanations are carefully broken-up, placed, and distributed. Frequently they occur long after the event to be explained has taken place; thus we rarely bother to check their validity. We are never offered too much explanation at one time; thus the Esther–Lady Dedlock relationship is cleared up relatively early. (By this stroke Dickens achieves many ends. He avoids cluttering up the end of the novel with too many climaxes and he misdirects the reader who thinks that the essential mystery is now cleared up and is thus unprepared for the subsequent mystery of Tulkinghorn's death. A similar tactic is central to *Our Mutual Friend* where the reader, having solved the problem of the hero's identity, is liable to take Boffin's pretence at its face value.)

Moreover, what seems coincidental is often the result of plotting and *Bleak House* is full of conspirators. The interesting thing to notice is how often their plots go astray, how often what man proposes is thwarted by the bias of chance, of unforeseen circumstances, of the merely random. No one, not even Bucket, is infallible. Partly because of this, because plotters, plots, and coincidences often cancel each other out, we accept Dickens's scheme of things. Coincidence is not the malign symptom of some metaphysical destiny inexorably hunting down a selected victim; we do not rebel because we feel Fate is unfair; chance reigns with fine impartiality over all.

Finally and paradoxically, it is because coincidence is so extensive in the novel that it becomes so natural. It seems true because it is congruent with the rest of the book. But more important, in the last analysis it expresses a truth about the real world. It expresses our sense that real life blends the casual and the causal, that things are connected and contingent, patterned and random, that we are both free and determined. This sense of life's contradictions is a common sense and we take commonsensically that which, if examined closely, would turn into wonder and mystery, into a world of speculation, dense with *ifs* and *perhaps* and *might-have-beens*. We walk in the real world as Esther walks, through a labyrinth of the conditional; we are surrounded, as she is, by other lives and other narratives; what seems to us a straight path is nothing but a series of crossroads.

So much is true and trite. Yet Dickens refreshed this cliché, expressed it with such imaginative force that it seems an original and profound intuition about the nature of things. At the heart of his work—beneath his immediate topical or satiric concerns—lie a number of such intuitions, darkly entangled with a number of private obsessions. Together they express something like Dickens's vision of the universal human predicament or, to be more modest and less portentous, the predicament of man in modern industrial society. Such, for instance, is his sense of the fragmented individual. One remembers here the sharp division between public and private, the official and the person; one recalls Bucket the person and Bucket the detective, Vholes the lawyer and Vholes as parent and child. The logical conclusion of this is the happy dichotomy of Wemmick in *Great Expectations*. In a different vein, one remembers Sir Leicester, decent enough but hopelessly locked within the prison of his class and caste; one remembers Lady Dedlock masking her guilt and suffering by a frozen disdain. As with the individual so with the fragmented society; what can the Boodles know of Jo or Jenny when Snagsby, who lives not far away, can be appalled by the unfamiliar hell of Tom All Alone's? Against isolation and alienation Dickens poses connection—whether of love, charity and responsibility or the sinister negations of these, embodied in the infections of Chancery and the slums.

Yet even such basic intuitions as these depend upon that sense of the world I have tried to describe. The most explicit expression of this sense occurs in Forster's frequently quoted report of Dickens:

> On the coincidences, resemblances, and surprises of life Dickens liked especially to dwell, and few things moved his fancy so pleasantly. The world, he would say, was so much smaller than we thought it; we were all so connected by fate without knowing it and people supposed to be far apart were so constantly elbowing each other; and tomorrow bore so close a resemblance to nothing half so much as yesterday.

This theme is heavily stressed in the opening chapters of *Little Dorrit*; in *Bleak House* it is given only brief and oblique expression by several of the characters. But it is implicit in the whole structure of the novel.

"Trust in nothing but Providence and your own efforts. Never separate the two," Jarndyce tells Richard Carstone and unconsciously sums up this deepest sense of the intricate meshing of chance and choice in the affairs of men. Dickens recognized, of course, that chance is often cruel and that there is a world where Jo and Jenny have no choice but to suffer and die. For them he could see no easy remedy; no trust was to be placed in the Boodles of his world. For the rest of us, all we can do—as Esther would say—is to perform our duty; freedom lies in the recognition of *that* necessity. This, then, is what I take to be the essential substance of *Bleak House* and the form of the novel is expressive of its substance. Here, at the deepest level, the twin narratives and the widespread use of coincidence unite; out of a world of mingled chance and choice Dickens had created the design necessary to a great work of art.

III

I wish now to consider in greater detail the nature of choice, perhaps the most crucial aspect of this particular problem of mimetic adequacy. We may usefully take as our

starting point some remarks on the problem by Professor
John Lawlor:

> If, firstly, we are to speak of free-will in the drama, we
> must mean the activity of choice, for drama is a doing.
> We are therefore to distinguish between the power of
> choice and the field of choice—between ability to choose
> and the things there are to choose from. Even where the
> centre of attention is in the refusal of choice, "the pale
> cast of thought" under which the name of action is all
> but lost, man must, as we have seen, still search earth and
> heaven for reasons why. For choice is proper to man; not
> to choose is not to be. Dramatic characterization can
> therefore be thought of as operating in two phases; firstly,
> the character must be introduced as a particular sort of
> chooser, one more disposed to certain choices than to
> others: and secondly, he must be established as such,
> given a past field of choice in the evidence of confidants,
> acquaintances and the like, from whatever standpoint
> (whether of approval or not) they speak. This second
> "phase" makes great demands upon skill; as it is the only
> kind of heredity and environment the character needs, so
> it is vital that it be lodged both effectively and, for the
> most part, indirectly, with the audience.[1]

Professor Lawlor is here commenting on *Macbeth*. His
remarks are, therefore, all the more useful since if we follow
them up we shall discover some important differences between our approach to character in drama and in fiction,
differences I believe to have been obscured by the interplay
of various forces in modern criticism.

The two most important factors determining the freedom
of any character are, we may agree with Professor Lawlor,
the range of choices open to the character and the kind of
chooser he is, as shown by the history of choices displayed
by him or imputed to him in the past. Let us consider,
abstractly, the simplest variety of these two factors. The
simplest field of choice is the clear-cut Either/Or situation,
wherein the character is free only to choose one of two alternatives. Correspondingly, the simplest kind of chooser is the

---

[1] John Lawlor, *The Tragic Sense in Shakespeare*, p. 112. London: Chatto and
Windus, 1960.

Either/Or kind of character, the man who *sees* all situations, no matter how complex they may in fact be, in terms of one of two clear-cut alternatives. From this we may derive the simplest form of dramatic action, that in which an Either/Or character is confronted with an Either/Or situation. This kind of combination will frequently be found in melodrama or in the products of a poor or crude imagination. But it will also be found in certain types of highly stylized and conventionalized drama and that it may be the basis of great literature is proved by the existence of French classical tragedy.

Few great dramatists, however, have been content with this simplest of dramatic actions and most have tended to complicate it in one of two ways. An Either/Or character may be faced with a situation which he mistakenly assumes is to be thought of in terms of two clear-cut alternatives. The audience, however, know better and will pity the deluded protagonist for persisting in error or will share with him his painful awakening to the true state of affairs. In their different ways, *King Lear*, *Othello*, *Coriolanus* seem to me examples of this type of drama. Conversely an Either/Or situation may be thrust upon a character who by nature refuses to see life in the simple categories of clear-cut alternatives; *Hamlet* immediately comes to mind. "To be or not to be"; Hamlet is forcing himself into the mould of an Either/Or character, but the same soliloquy dramatically renders the doubts, hesitations, qualifications of his mind; the simple issue is soon clouded; that is not, or not precisely, the question after all. And what the poetry enacts locally is conveyed by the total action and structure of the play. This particular dramatic configuration, it is worth noting, has been particularly popular on the modern stage and one may relate it to the crisis of liberalism I mentioned in the previous section. It is a particularly apt dramatic form in which to deal with the dilemma of a liberal (by definition a pluralist and therefore the antithesis of an Either/Or character) when confronted with the Either/Or dilemma of clashing monistic imperatives. Stephen Spender's *Trial of A Judge* is perhaps the clearest example.

Few plays, I think, will attempt a greater degree of complication than this. The reasons lie within the very nature of drama itself. A play must aim at concentration, compression;

K

there is simply no time to build up to and resolve more than one or two crises; in the interests of tension and conflict a paring away of inessentials is imperative. (Though, of course, with Shakespeare multiplicity miraculously asserts itself in the density of poetic texture.) Moreover, tempo and concentration must be reconciled with lucidity; if the audience is to grasp the experience embodied in the quick-flowing and irreversible sequence of the stage action, then the naked skeleton of the Either/Or structure must never be too obscured.

The novel, because of its length, because of its relative diffuseness of texture and because of the different mode of attention it demands of its reader, is not subject to these limitations. Certain important consequences follow, all of which allow the novelist to portray our sense of conditional freedom in all its intricate detail with a much greater degree of mimetic accuracy. In the first place the novelist does not have to be so skilful in establishing the nature of his chooser; he can, in a much more leisurely and detailed way, establish this necessary "heredity and environment". On the one hand, unlike the dramatist, he can, if he wants to, indulge in a great deal of direct description and analysis. Moreover, whereas the play has time only to create one or two crucial moments of choice, the novel, with its greater length and scope, can establish an entire sequence of choices and thus establish within itself the history, and therefore the identity of the chooser. For much the same reasons the novel can create a much wider and more complex field of choice at any given time; it is no longer tied to some variant of a basic Either/Or situation.

For these reasons the novel can, much more than the play, reflect one important aspect of our real life sense of conditional freedom. When we examine our own personal history and experience we can trace the actual line we have taken, can isolate what I may call the real trajectory of our lives. But because we live in a world where multiplicity is ever at our elbow we are aware that had we made different decisions at any given point different consequences would have followed. We sense that our actual life, the line that we do in fact follow, is surrounded by a network of possible lives that we might have led. This is surely not an uncommon

intuition; our lives follow a narrow line of light (our knowledge of the actual) through a shadowy penumbra of possibilities, of might-have-beens.[1] This is surely part of the
meaning of the opening lines of *Burnt Norton*:

> *Footfalls echo in the memory*
> *Down the passage which we did not take*
> *Towards the door we never opened. . . .*

A play, in all its brevity, can hardly express more than a
generalized sense of this what-might-have-been; we rarely
get more than a lament for some one unrealized alternative.
"Cut is the branch that might have grown full straight";
drama has room for little more than this. A novel, on the
other hand, can allow for a much fuller expression of this
sensed penumbra of unrealized possibilities, of all the what-
might-have-beens of our lives.

It is because of this that the novel permits a much greater
liberty of such speculation on the part of the reader than
does the play. Such speculation frequently becomes, as it
does in real life, part of the substantial reality of the identity
of any character. The character moves in the full depth of
his conditional freedom; he is what he is but he might have
been otherwise. Indeed the novel does not merely *allow* for
this liberty of speculation; sometimes it *encourages* it to the
extent that our sense of conditional freedom in this aspect
becomes one of the ordering structural principles of the
entire work.

What happens is this. In both play and novel, the protagonist follows a particular trajectory of action, a particular
history of choice, and thereby creates in us a sense of his
identity. In both play and novel he is surrounded by other
characters, less fully realized, who stand in a particular en-
lightening relation to him. Of such characters in a play we
generally express this relationship by saying that they act
as foils to the protagonist or that they set him in relief;
we rarely have the sense that they embody alternative possibilities in the hero. We hardly feel, I think, that Hamlet

---

[1] "I had thought, much and often, of my Dora's shadowing out to me what
might have happened, in those years that were destined not to try us; I had considered how the things that never happen are often as much realities to us, in their
effects, as things that are accomplished" (*David Copperfield*, Chapter 58).

could have been Horatio or that Macbeth *could* have been
Banquo; we should probably think it illegitimate to speculate about the hero in these terms. In the novel this is not
necessarily so. The novelist, because of his greater scope and
freedom, can create a much larger range of subordinate
characters, can establish their autonomy in much greater
detail and can analyse their relationship to the protagonist
in a much more complex way. Consequently we sometimes
feel that one of their functions is to embody unrealized
potentialities in the protagonist, to create the penumbra
of alternative histories around the actual history he creates
for himself.[1]

Lord Jim is a particularly rich example of this process;
here the clearest and most crucial instance is Jim's encounter
with Gentleman Brown, in whom he recognizes so much of
what he is and what he might become:

> And there ran through the rough talk a vein of subtle
> reference to their common blood, an assumption of
> common experience; a sickening suggestion of common
> guilt, of secret knowledge that was like a bond of their
> minds and of their hearts. (Chapter 42)

But Gentleman Brown is only one of a wide variety of
characters in the novel who create his penumbra of possibilities around the protagonist. Some, like the French lieutenant
stand in a simple and obvious relation to Jim; others, like
Captain Brierly function in a more oblique and obscure
manner. Nor is *Lord Jim* an exceptional novel in this
respect; many other novelists have contrived to render the
same effect. Thus, for example, Lydgate in *Middlemarch*
follows a particular trajectory, dependent on the choices he
actually makes, yet we feel it legitimate to speculate about
what might have happened to him if he had chosen slightly
different alternatives. *One* thing that might have happened
to him is that he *could* have turned into somebody rather
like the Reverend Mr. Farebrother. We sense this and feel
it to be a legitimate source of speculation because George
Eliot has had the time to create the Lydgate–Farebrother
relationship in some detail. It is part of the reality of her

[1] For a detailed exploration of this, cf. Barbara Hardy, *The Novels of George
Eliot*, Chapter 7.

fictional world, and hence part of the reality of Lydgate himself. As such it corresponds to an intuition we frequently have about our own status in a world of conditional freedom and hence makes for a much greater degree of mimetic accuracy. If we may adapt Mr. Eliot's formulation:

> *What might have been and what has been*
> *Point to one end, which is always present. . . .*

Present, that is, in the reader's imaginative response, both to the real world and to the world of fiction.

CHAPTER VII

Character, Essence and Existence

So far, the idea of character has been discussed in terms of what I earlier called a "liberal" viewpoint; an approach that is, I hope, empirical, pragmatic, pluralist and tentative. This viewpoint is by its very nature too unsystematic to be called an ideology; it is rather, as Arnold said, a tone and temper of mind. It is, perhaps unjustifiably, suspicious of philosophical rigour; it does not rest well on a Procrustean bed; it espouses common sense even at the risk of breeding confusion. I have also suggested that the cultural epoch characterized by this liberal temper may well be crumbling under various kinds of pressure and attack and I have pointed to certain mutations within the *genre* of the novel as possible evidence of this process. But clearly the "liberal imagination" is also directly challenged by hostile philosophies which contain or imply their own theories of art. For our purposes the most interesting of these is existentialism, since here we witness a quite unusual convergence of the philosopher and the creative artist. What I wish to attempt in this chapter, then, is an examination of the existentialist view of character.

Such a task imposes immense problems, quite apart from the exigencies of presenting a compressed but tolerably fair account of an intrinsically complex philosophy.[1] To start

[1] Though my mistakes and misunderstandings, at least, are my own, I owe much to several commentators on Sartre's philosophy. Apart from those cited later in notes to this chapter, they include two brief but useful introductions, by Iris Murdoch (Bowes and Bowes, 1961) and Maurice Cranston (Oliver and Boyd, 1962). But my main guide has been Wilfrid Desan's *The Tragic Finale* (Harper Torchbooks, 1900). I have used the following translations, to which all subsequent page references are made: *Being and Nothingness* (*L'Être et le Néant*), trans. Hazel Barnes (Philosophical Library, 1956). *What is Literature?*, trans. B. Frechtman (Methuen, 1950). *Literary and Philosophical Essays*, trans. A. Michelson (Rider, 1955). *Sketch for a theory of the Emotions*, trans. P. Mairet (Methuen, 1962). *Nausea* (*La Nausée*), trans. L. Alexander (Hamish Hamilton, 1962. Previously published by Lehmann as *The Diary of Antoine Roquentin*). *The Age of Reason* (*L'Âge de Raison*) trans. E. Sutton (Penguin Books, 1961). *The Reprieve* (*Le Sursis*) trans. E. Sutton (Hamish Hamilton, 1960). *Iron in the Soul* (*La Mort dans l'Ame*) trans. G. Hopkins (Hamish Hamilton, 1960).

with, as so often happens, the *ism* soon turns out to be a prism; there are many brands of existentialism with very different aesthetic consequences. Thus in this chapter I shall concentrate on the theory and practice of Sartre, and while within these limits it might be justifiable to make cross-references to Simone de Beauvoir, it would be quite inappropriate to extend the discussion to Camus. Something is lost by this exclusion since Camus seems to me indisputably the finer artist; but Sartre's philosophy is the obvious starting point and his creative achievement is sufficiently impressive to stand comparison with the novelists discussed earlier in this book. In such a context his novels dwindle but do not entirely disappear.

Many problems still remain, even within this narrowed scope. Sartre's thought cannot be considered as a static thing, neatly laid out for our inspection. It is primarily—as one might expect with any major thinker, but especially with an existentialist—a development in time. Some dates are necessary here. The philosophic work with which we shall be mainly concerned is *L'Être et le Néant* (1943); around this are clustered the novels, *La Nausée* (1938), *L'Âge de Raison* (1945), *Le Sursis* (1945) and *La Mort dans l'Âme* (1949). The last three novels in this list form part of a projected tetralogy, *Les Chemins de la Liberté*; a section of the unfinished fourth volume, *La Dernière Chance*, was published in *Les Temps Modernes* in 1949. By that date Sartre had also written most of the other relevant aesthetic and critical essays. It forms, then, a kind of watershed; the fact that the tetralogy remained unfinished is, I think, symptomatic of a major turning-point in Sartre's intellectual development; another symptom is the non-appearance of the ethical study which was to have developed from *L'Être et le Néant*. The development, briefly, is from existentialism to a peculiar brand of Marxism, of which the first major philosophic product is the *Critique de la raison dialectique* (1960). We shall concentrate on the work produced before 1949, though we shall have to consider some of the tensions which caused the intellectual leap and which, I believe, inhibited Sartre as a novelist.

Even within the work as we have further narrowed it down, there is still great complexity and variety. We may distinguish four levels; philosophy, general aesthetic theory, detailed literary criticism and finally the fiction itself. I shall, for convenience, consider these in turn, but it must be stressed that the work is all of a piece. Sartre's coat of thought is indeed a seamless garment. With this proviso, we may turn to *L'Être et le Néant*.

II

Sartre is a phenomenologist; that is, he is concerned with things as they appear to the consciousness. He short-circuits completely the traditional problem of epistemology, the relation of appearance to some reality behind or beyond appearance. The structure of his phenomenology is based on a dialectic between consciousness (the *pour-soi*) and whatever appears to the consciousness, the world of things-in-themselves (the *en-soi*). The characteristic of the *en-soi* is that it simply exists as brute being; it is *there*, it coincides with itself. It is massive and rich; it never exhausts its appearances but always reveals itself afresh as we experience it. Consciousness for Sartre is produced by a kind of fissionary process; the *pour-soi* has broken away and alienated itself from the *en-soi*. This it has done by negation. The modes of negation are complex and subtle, but essentially consciousness defines itself by knowing what it is not—I am not this table, I am not you, I am not what I was yesterday, and so on. The *pour-soi* cannot bear this alienation; it is, so to speak, fission longing to become fusion. It longs to become *en-soi* and at the same time remain conscious of itself; this it cannot do, since the *en-soi* is, by definition, non-conscious. Hence consciousness remains eternally alienated from the world; it is essentially alone. Moreover the fissionary process which sunders *pour-soi* from *en-soi* continues within the *pour-soi* itself. There are for Sartre two kinds of consciousness. There is first a pre-reflexive consciousness which composes most of our simple knowledge; for example, I am conscious of this table. But the *pour-soi*, by a reflexive act, can become aware of itself; thus, I am conscious of my consciousness of this table. It is partly because of this internal fission that the *pour-soi* can never achieve the massive self-coincidence of the *en-soi*. My self-consciousness can never quite coincide with that of which I am conscious; I can only be aware of what *was* my consciousness. If we introspect, we are forever chasing our own tails.

This double process of fission creates a tragic view of existence, complete with its own version of the Fall and Original Sin. The sense of alienation, and the vertigo or nausea which accompany it, is, according to Sartre, a reality which it is difficult for mankind to bear. Moreover, the recognition of his estate allows man to see that alienation has set him totally free and that therefore he is totally responsible. Again, for most men, this is an unendurable burden. Hence man flies from this sense of alienation, freedom and responsibility; he seeks in innumerable ways to ignore or evade it. He takes refuge in one form or another of what Sartre calls *mauvaise foi*; belief in God, in the conventional social order or in any kind of determinism are all examples of *mauvaise foi*. Sartre's emphasis on this point shifts from time to time. Sometimes he stresses that *mauvaise foi* is an inherent and ineradicable part of the human condition, that it is involved even in man's sincerest attempts to be sincere. At other times it becomes a more limited object of moral and satiric attitudes, particularly as it manifests itself in the comfortable, conventional, "solid" world of the bourgeois.

One other feature disturbs the basic dialectic of *en-soi* and *pour-soi*. This is the existence of what Sartre calls the Other; our awareness of another consciousness. Let us suppose that I am looking at a tree; I then become aware of another person looking at the scene which includes both the tree and myself. The whole situation is now altered. I am not simply myself, *pour-soi*, but I am also aware that I exist as a Self for the Other. My Self-for-the-Other is in fact a kind of *en-soi*. I am reduced to an object; conversely the Other so exists for me. Consequently there is a kind of battle between my Self and His, each resisting the metamorphosis from consciousness into Object. I may seek in various ways to dominate him, to "stare him down" and thus reduce him to an object, or I may allow myself in various ways to be dominated by him. This struggle is, for Sartre, the basis of all human relationships, even that of love. In love we wish to possess and to be possessed; to become one with the Other and yet to retain the autonomy of both as free selves. Such an attempt is, or course, doomed to failure. Love is a continually tilting see-saw which can never achieve the desired equilibrium.

If Sartre's existentialism had to be reduced to a slogan, one could not better his declaration that existence precedes essence. Sartre, like Lawrence, wishes to demolish the notion of the "old, stable Ego", the Cartesian "ghost in the machine". We exist from moment to moment, looking forward into the future; there is no such thing as a continuing ego which unifies the flux of our concrete experience; there is no underlying essence which determines our nature. For this is to confuse *pour-soi* with *en-soi* and to think of consciousness as a thing. If we try to think of ourselves as things, then we are guilty of *mauvaise foi*. It is true that our past *becomes* a thing, but we are not our past. We cannot, so to speak, add ourselves up and declare that the result is what we are; the equation is always open and is never completed until we die. Our consciousness is, as it were, the crest of a wave as it travels through time, continually toppling towards the future. It is for this reason that the *pour-soi* is totally free; it is free to make a rational and responsible choice of any one of its possible futures. If we are anything, then we are the sum of our possibilities. Any attempt to evade these facts of our existence and our freedom—by maintaining, for example, that the past determines us—is another example of *mauvaise foi*. Human reality is entirely conscious—Sartre rejects any notion of the unconscious—it continually faces its future and has the total responsibility of choosing what it will become. This "becoming" is a concrete and continuous process; as we move through time the future, by becoming the past, also becomes *en-soi*. While we cannot alter the past we are always free to alter its significance by a further act of choice.

We must be careful when we speak of total freedom. Sartre, though anti-deterministic, recognizes what he calls the "facticity" of any human situation. Some things are *a priori* in any given case; for example, we did not choose our birth, our sex or our historical epoch; our futures are always limited by the absurdity of death. Such factors create the concrete situation within which we exist; nevertheless, *within* this situation we are totally free to choose. This choice is always conscious—hence our total responsibility. At this point, in some way not entirely clear to me, Sartre makes the leap to Freedom as an absolute value. The assertion of our own freedom always delimits the freedom of the Other, in that for him we are part of the "facticity" of the world; our free choice creates the concrete situation in which the Other must make his free choice, and vice versa. Thus, concludes Sartre, we are not only responsible for our own freedom but for the freedom of all.

III

Antoine Roquentin, hero of *La Nausée*, is overwhelmed by the brute existence of things. The categories by which we make sense of our lives turn out to be fictions; the comfortable, solid world dissolves into a viscous flux:

> If anyone had asked me what existence was, I would have answered, in good faith, that it was nothing, simply an empty form which was added to external things without changing anything in their nature. And then all of a sudden, there it was, clear as day: existence had suddenly unveiled itself. It had lost the harmless look of an abstract category: it was the very paste of things, this root was kneaded into existence. Or rather the root, the park gates, the bench, the sparse grass, all that had vanished: the diversity of things, their individuality, were only an appearance, a veneer. This veneer had melted, leaving soft, monstrous masses, all in disorder—naked, in a frightful, obscene nakedness.[1]

Roquentin does not abandon himself to this vision without a struggle. As the novel progresses we watch, one by one, the crumbling of his defences. He has tried to make sense of parts of his life by conceiving it as a work of art. This underlies his notion of the "adventure", the sequence of experience which has a shape, "a beautiful melodious form" which is rescued from the daily routine. But he abandons this notion, realizing that "he tries to live his own life as if he were telling a story. But you have to choose: live or tell. . . . I wanted the moments of my life to follow and order themselves like those of a life remembered. You might as well try and catch time by the tail."[2] Similarly his ex-mistress Anny abandons

---

[1] *Nausea*, pp. 171–2.   [2] *Ibid.*, pp. 56–8.

her attempt to create "perfect moments" by acting out her life as though it were a theatrical performance.

Another useless prophylactic against la Nausée is the biography that Roquentin has been trying to write; this he abandons since "history talks about what has existed—an existant can never justify the existence of another existant."[1] One cannot make sense of one's own life by giving it a vicarious shape in the recreated life of another. Yet one thing seems to resist the viscous flux of existence; the work of art, as symbolized in the novel by the record of a jazz song. It is a precarious but triumphant achievement, Roquentin reflects, as he listens to it:

> A few seconds more and the negress will sing. It seems inevitable, so strong is the necessity of this music; nothing can interrupt it, nothing which comes from this time in which the world has fallen; it will stop of itself, as if by order. If I love this beautiful voice it is especially because of that: it is neither for its fulness nor its sadness, rather because it is the event for which so many notes have been preparing, from so far away, dying that it might be born. And yet I am troubled; it would take so little to make the record stop: a broken spring, the whim of Cousin Adolphe. How strange it is, how moving, that this hardness should be so fragile. Nothing can interrupt it yet all can break it.[2]

It is this record which at the very end consoles Roquentin with the hope that he, too, may achieve a work of art, a novel which when written will enable him to "remember my life without repugnance".

Why does the record console? We should note that it is not because of its human content or its mimetic relationship to the world. Indeed, Roquentin explicitly excludes this:

> Now there is this song on the saxophone. And I am ashamed. A glorious little suffering has just been born, an exemplary suffering. Four notes on the saxophone. They come and go, they seem to say: You must be like us, suffer in rhythm. All right! Naturally, I'd like to suffer that way, in rhythm, without complacence, without self-pity, with an arid purity. But is it my fault if the beer at the

[1] *Nausea*, p. 237.   [2] *Ibid.*, p. 34.

bottom of my glass is warm, if there are brown stains on
the mirror, if I am not wanted, if the sincerest of my
sufferings drags and weighs, with too much flesh and the
skin too wide at the same time, like a sea-elephant, with
bulging eyes, damp and touching and yet so ugly? No,
they certainly can't tell me it's compassionate—this little
jewelled pain which spins around above the record and
dazzles me. Not even ironic: it spins gaily, completely
self-absorbed; like a scythe it has cut through the drab
intimacy of the world and now it spins and all of us,
Madeleine, the thick-set man, the patronne, myself, the
tables, benches, the stained mirror, the glasses, all of us
abandon ourselves to existence, because we were among
ourselves, only among ourselves, it has taken us unawares,
in the disorder, the day to day drift: I am ashamed for
myself and for what exists *in front* of it.

It does not exist . . . it does not exist because it has
nothing superfluous: it is all the rest which in relation to
it is superfluous. It *is*.

And I, too, wanted to *be*. That is all I wanted; this is
the last word. At the bottom of all these attempts which
seemed without bonds, I find the same desire again: to
drive existence out of me, to rid the passing moments of
their fat, to twist them, dry them, purify myself, harden
myself, to give back at last the sharp, precise sound of a
saxophone note.[1]

Restated abstractly, this is basically an autonomy theory
of art. The song with its arid purity, its complete self-absorp-
tion, *is* for Roquentin because it has shed the contingency
and superfluity of the viscous world of existence. It *is*, autonomous and whole, because it creates its own strict necessity,
its own world of internal coherence and order.

I stress this point because many critics, regarding
Roquentin as a mouthpiece for his creator, have found it
difficult to reconcile this theory of art with Sartre's aesthetic
views as expounded elsewhere, particularly with his notions
of *la littérature engagée*. But surely there is in fact no evidence
for any simple equation between character and author?
Surely it is truer to the achievement of *La Nausée* to see this

[1] *Nausea*, pp. 233–4.

aesthetic as the dramatic expression of yet one more stage in Roquentin's development? The remarkable resonance and openness of the novel then reside in this final ambiguity— that we are left equivocally poised between Roquentin's views seen either as a truth finally arrived at or as a still imperfect, partial notion from which he must still go on. This ambiguity then enacts both the substance and the form of the novel; Roquentin's insight becomes both a terminus to which the rest of the book has been drawn, and a fresh point of departure. His final meditation thus has much the same dramatic status as Stephen's exposition of *his* aesthetic theory at the end of *A Portrait of the Artist as a Young Man*. For evidence of this we must look elsewhere, at Sartre's essays in aesthetic theory.

IV

At first glance, Sartre's *What Is Literature?* might seem to support the identification of his own views with those of Roquentin. For he begins by allowing that painting and music are not "committed" arts; this he does by a distinction drawn in terms very close to the idiom of *La Nausée*:

> A cry of grief is a sign of the grief which provokes it, but a song of grief is both grief itself and something other than grief. Or, if one wishes to adopt the existentialist vocabulary, it is a grief which does not *exist* any more, which *is*.[1]

He continues by placing poetry in the same category. Poets do not *use* words; the poetic attitude

> considers words as things and not as signs. For the ambiguity of the sign implies that one can penetrate it at will like a pane of glass and pursue the thing signified, or turn one's gaze towards its reality and consider it as an object. The man who talks is beyond words and near the object, whereas the poet is on this side of them . . . the speaker is *in a situation* in language; he is invested with words. They are prolongations of his meanings, his pincers, his antennae, his spectacles . . . he is surrounded by a verbal body which he is hardly aware of, and which ex-

[1] *What is Literature?*, p. 3.

tends his action upon the world. The poet is outside language. . . . If the poet injects his feelings into his poem,
he ceases to recognize them; the words take hold of them,
penetrate them, and metamorphose them; they do not
signify them, even in his eyes. Emotion has become thing,
it now has the opacity of things; it is compounded by the
ambiguous properties of the words in which it has been
enclosed. . . . The word, the phrase-thing, inexhaustible
as things, everywhere overflows the feeling which has
produced them.[1]

So far we are in much the same world as that of *La Nausée*.
But there is one important difference. Whereas Roquentin
thinks of his projected novel in the same way as the recorded
song, Sartre draws a sharp distinction:

> Prose is in essence utilitarian . . . the words are first of
> all not objects but designations for objects.[2]

By making this distinction, Sartre directs his argument
towards the notion of *la littérature engagée*; the writing of
prose is an *act*, an act of revelation and disclosure:

> The writer has chosen to reveal the world and particu-
> larly to reveal man to other men so that the latter may
> assume full responsibility before the object which has been
> thus laid bare . . . the function of the writer is to act in
> such a way that nobody can be ignorant of the world and
> that nobody may say that he is innocent of what it is all
> about.[3]

This distinction is extremely odd since it simply draws a
line between poetry and prose. The argument might hold if
the distinction were between imaginative and non-imagina-
tive modes of discourse, and if novels were held to be of the
same order of things as poems; but Sartre nowhere indicates
that this is what he means. What he proposes, in fact, is a
truncated variant of an autonomy theory. One way of distinguishing between autonomy and mimetic theories is to consider works of art either as *making* or as *saying* something;
Sartre here merely restates a traditional view. But put thus

---

[1] *What is Literature?*, pp. 5–6, 10.
[2] *Ibid.*, pp. 10–11.   [3] *Ibid.*, p. 14.

bluntly, few of us would be willing to make such an absolute division as Sartre; most of us, I imagine, would prefer to see artistic works as doing both or as oscillating between these two functions. If one looks at concrete examples, then one soon discovers the inadequacy of Sartre's distinction. Few of us, for example, would deny that the element of *saying* is very strong in *Religio Laici* or *The Dunciad*. Yet Sartre's distinction would involve us in denying these works the status of poems, which they obviously are. The truth is that Sartre's theory is historically conditioned; it only begins to work reasonably well with symbolist and post-symbolist poems from which, in fact, he draws most of his examples. Sartre himself at one point seems to recognize this:

> The crisis of language which broke out at the beginning of this century is a poetic crisis. Whatever the social and historical factors, it showed itself in an attack of depersonalization when the writer was confronted by words. He no longer knew how to use them . . . finally, they became things themselves, or rather the black heart of things. And when the poet joins several of these microcosms together the case is like that of painters when they assemble their colours on the canvas. One might think that he is composing a sentence, but this is only what it appears to be. He is creating an object.[1]

It is indeed true that many modern novels aspire to the status of this kind of poem. But it is not true of Sartre's own novels. How Sartre reconciles theory and practice and how he works from an autonomy theory to the notion of *la littérature engagée* are topics too large for adequate treatment here; we can concentrate only on one crucial point—the notion of freedom as it is relevant to the novel.

While the novelist in creation "meets everywhere only *his* knowledge, *his* will, *his* plans, in short himself", nevertheless "the object he creates is out of reach; he does not create it *for himself*".[2] The created artefact transcends the subjectivity of the writer by becoming an object for the reader: "it is the joint effort of author and reader which brings upon the scene that concrete and imaginary object which is the work of the

---

[1] *What is Literature?*, p. 8.   [2] *Ibid.*, p. 29.

mind. There is no art except for and by others."[1] It is in this way that Sartre escapes from a simple autonomy theory which would emphasize the isolation of the artefact. The novel *is* an artefact, "the object is essential because it is strictly transcendant, because it imposes its own structures",[2] but equally essential is the subjectivity of the reader since this alone makes it possible for there to *be* an object. The work of art is like an object, a massive *en-soi*, in that it contains a multitude of relations and appearances which the reader will never exhaust at one reading. Nevertheless:

> The literary object has no other substance than the reader's subjectivity; Raskolnikov's waiting is *my* waiting which I lend him. Without this impatience of the reader he would remain only a collection of signs. . . . On the other hand the words are there like traps to arouse our feelings and to reflect them towards us. Each word is a path of transcendence; it shapes our feelings, names them, and attributes them to an imaginary personage who takes it upon himself to live them for us and who has no other substance than these borrowed passions; he confers objects, perspectives and a horizon upon them.[3]

In this process the freedom of the reader's subjectivity must be respected:

> All feelings which are exacted on the basis of this imaginary belief are like particular modulations of my freedom. Far from absorbing or masking it, they are so many different ways it has chosen to reveal itself to itself. Raskolnikov, as I have said, would only be a shadow, without the mixture of repulsion and friendship which I feel for him and which makes him live. . . . Thus, the reader's feelings are never dominated by the object, and as no external reality can condition them, they have their permanent source in freedom. . . . Thus reading is an exercise in generosity, and what the writer requires of the reader is not the application of an abstract freedom but the gift of his whole person, with his passions, his preposses-

[1] *What is Literature?*, pp. 29–30.
[2] *Ibid.*, p. 30.   [3] *Ibid.*, pp. 31–2.

sions, his sympathies, his sexual temperament, and his scale of values.[1]

But if the reader is to be generous, if he is to give his subjectivity freely to the novel and thus endow its characters with reality, he must not feel that his freedom is circumscribed or dominated by the novelist. Hence Sartre develops an attack on the omniscient author as found in the traditional novels of his predecessors:

> They had chosen literary idealism and had presented us with events through a privileged subjectivity. For us, historical relativism, by positing the *a priori* equivalent of all subjectivities, restored to the living event all its value and led us back, in literature, to dogmatic realism by way of absolute subjectivism. They thought that they were justifying, at least apparently, the foolish business of storytelling, by ceaselessly bringing to the reader's attention, explicitly or by allusion, the existence of an author. We hope that our books remain in the air all by themselves and that their words, instead of pointing backwards towards the one who has designed them, will be toboggans, forgotten, unnoticed, and solitary, which will hurl the reader into the midst of a universe where there are no witnesses; in short, that our books may exist in the manner of things, of plants, of events, and not at first like products of man. We want to drive providence from our works as we have driven it from our world.[2]

The most striking development of this viewpoint is to be found, of course, in the brilliant and perverse attack on Mauriac. "Do you want your characters to live?" asks Sartre, "see to it that they are free." But Mauriac by his omniscient intrusions limits the freedom of his characters and thus inhibits the generous gift of the reader's subjectivity. Mauriac exhibits the subjectivity of his heroine, yet at the same time forces us to view her as an object:

> Seated in the centre of her consciousness, I help her lie to herself and, at the same time, I judge and condemn her, I put myself inside her, *as another person.*[3]

---

[1] *What is Literature?*, pp. 35–6.   [2] *Ibid.*, p. 169.
[3] *Literary and Philosophical Essays*, p. 12.

Mauriac, says Sartre:

> Wrote that the novelist is to his own creatures what
> God is to His. And that explains all the oddities of his
> technique. He takes God's standpoint on his characters.
> God sees the inside and outside, the depths of body and
> soul, the whole universe at once. In like manner, M.
> Mauriac is omniscient about everything relating to his
> little world. What he says about his characters is Gospel.
> ... The time has come to say that the novelist is not God.[1]

V

We encounter here a head-on collision between Sartre's
viewpoint and the thesis developed earlier in this book. For I
have maintained that the novelist's relation to his work cannot be anything but god-like. What Sartre condemns as a
fault—our double view of character as both subject and
object—I have, through the notion of varied perspectives
and contexts, considered to be a virtue. Where he maintains
that it destroys the illusion of freedom, and therefore the
character's reality, I have argued that it does not *necessarily*
impair our sense of freedom and that, on the contrary, it
constitutes in large part the reality of fiction. In view of this
contradiction it is clearly necessary to consider Sartre's
theories critically, both in themselves and in relation to his
creative practice.

At the heart of Sartre's theory there exists, so it seems to
me, an insoluble contradiction. For him, the work of art is a
transcendent object which at the same time demands the
free play of the reader's subjectivity if it is to exist at all. The
work is transcendent "because it imposes its own structure".
But who imposes the structure? Natural objects impose
their own structure and Sartre wishes us to think of the work
as a kind of natural object, free, detached, gratuitous. The
reality of such artefacts lies in an illusion such that we do not
think of them "at first like products of man". At first? But
what happens thereafter? We may agree with Sartre that the
work exists as the recreation of the reader that for example,

> the degree of realism and truth of Kafka's mythology,
> these are never given. The reader must invent them all in

---

[1] *Literary and Philosophical Essays*, p. 14.

a continual exceeding of the written thing. To be sure the author guides him, but all he does is guide him. The landmarks he sets up are separated by the void. The reader must unite them; he must go beyond them. In short, reading is directed creation.[1]

It is precisely this emphasis on the reader's activity that is the valuable element in Sartre's theory. But once he has allowed the notion of guidance and direction, then it seems to me that he has excluded the existence of the work as a free, gratuitous, transcendent object. For this is a special kind of object, an artefact; therefore the argument from design *does* hold good; the artist *is* a kind of god. A tree and a spade are both objects, but we do not regard them in the same way. A spade only makes sense if we regard it as designed for a particular use. And, as we have seen, prose is for Sartre a kind of tool to be used, though not in any crude, didactic fashion.

We may focus Sartre's difficulties more precisely. What happens, he asks, if the god-like author is banished from his creation?

Our technical problem is to find an orchestration of consciousnesses which may permit us to render the multidimensionality of the event. Moreover, in giving up the fiction of the omniscient narrator, we have assumed the obligation of suppressing the intermediaries between the reader and the subjectivities—the viewpoints of our characters. It is a matter of having him enter into their minds as into a windmill. He must even coincide successively with each one of them. We have learned from Joyce to look for a second kind of realism, the raw realism of subjectivity without mediation or distance. Which leads us to profess a third realism, that of temporality. Indeed, if without mediation we plunge the reader into a consciousness, if we refuse him all means of surveying the whole, then the time of this consciousness must be imposed upon him without abridgement. If I pack six months into a single page, the reader jumps out of the book.

This last aspect raises difficulties that none of us has re-

---

[1] *What is Literature?*, p. 31.

solved and which are perhaps partially insoluble, for it is
neither possible nor desirable to limit all novels to the
story of a single day. Even if one should resign oneself to
that, the fact would remain that devoting a book to
twenty-four hours rather than to one, or to an hour rather
than to a minute, implies the intervention of the author
and a transcendent choice. It will then be necessary to
mask this choice by purely aesthetic procedures, to prac-
tise sleight of hand, and, as always in art, to lie in order to
be true.[1]

Sartre provides his own comment on the problems of
temporal realism and we need discuss them no further. But
his comment applies equally well to *all* aspects of narrative
art. All art, he says, lies in order to tell the truth; all readers
know this and all novelists accept the fact as the necessary
framework within which they must labour to create a sense of
reality. If the novelist chooses to abolish his god-like powers,
this is still *his* choice and in choosing he is still god-like. We
abolish omniscience, for example, by entering directly into
the consciousness of a character. But why *this* character
rather than that? In *L'Âge de Raison*, for instance, some
characters like Mathieu or Daniel, are revealed in their subjectivity; others, notably Ivich, are seen consistently as objects, opaque and mysterious. If we can accept this without
loss of reality, then I do not see why we cannot accept
Mauriac's double view of his characters. The truth is surely
expressed by Jean-Louis Curtis:

> Lire un roman, en effet, c'est avoir conclu un accord
> tacite avec le romancier. Un accord suppose l'agrément
> de deux parties, un consentement mutuel. Or, qu'est-ce
> que le lecteur peut concéder au romancier? D'être un
> romancier, justement. C'est-à-dire un démiurge. D'être
> celui par qui les fables romanesques existent. Celui grâce
> à qui les créatures, légitimement qualifiées de "fictives"
> sont suscitées du néant au moyen d'un sortilège de mots
> et de phrases. Le lecteur sait fort bien que le démiurge est
> tout puissant et qu'il avait d'avance tout prévu. . . . Le
> point de vue divin n'est plus ici principe de séparation,

---

[1] *What is Literature?*, p. 229.

mais d'intégration et d'unité. On peut donc affirmer que
l'existence romanesque—c'est-à-dire l'apparence de vie
et d'autonomie qu'assument pour les lecteurs les person-
nages de romans réussis—n'est pas nécessairement liée
par un relation causale aux techniques tendant à voiler
l'omniscience et l'omnipotence du romancier.[1]

The truth of this is evident if we turn to Sartre's novels
and notice the discrepancies between his theory and practice. By close analysis of passages from *L'Âge de Raison*,
M. Curtis has no difficulty in showing how Sartre, although
he has masked his omniscience, controls the consciousness
of his characters in a way not essentially different from that
of Mauriac. When we read phrases like "He had dreamt that
he was a murderer, and something of his dream *still lurked in
his eyes*", or "Boris *from habit* did not protest", or "They
drew together, *feeling like a pair of orphans*", we cannot locate
such phrases within the consciousness of any one of the
characters; we have moved outside them and are viewing
them, like the author, as objects. Similarly Sartre's fecundity
of metaphor—one of his strong points—overflows the
consciousness of his characters. Thus, while Mathieu is a
very literary and self-conscious character, it is difficult to
locate within his consciousness, as part of the natural flow of
his thought, an image like, "And then—it happened in an
instant, just as a sleeper suddenly finds himself on his feet
in the morning without knowing how he got there." A great
many of the images in *L'Âge de Raison* have this ambiguous
status; they hover equivocally between the characters and
their creator.

Indeed, I should wish to extend the argument and maintain that the author's effort to eliminate himself may sometimes reveal his presence in the novel even more acutely than
direct intervention. If the author manages his presence on-
stage with sufficient tact, then we soon get used to him and
accommodate him to the rest of the novel. But if he is disguised then we are liable to be shocked when we stumble
across him. For example, early in the first chapter of *L'Âge
de Raison*, Mathieu sees his mistress Marcelle, "sitting on
the edge of the bed, blankly naked and defenceless, like a

[1] J. L. Curtis, *Haute Ecole*, pp. 171–3. Paris: Julliard, 1950.

great porcelain vase". Aesthetically, the comparison is only there because it anticipates his memory, a little later, of having as a child gratuitously broken a precious Chinese vase. We may accept this as natural since both image and memory belong to Mathieu's consciousness, but a little later still Marcelle thinks of Mathieu, "he really feels angry as if he had broken a vase". Sartre is scoring a point here but scoring it too obviously; attention is distracted from the characters to their creator.

This is even more evident in *Le Sursis*, Sartre's most strenuous attempt "to find an orchestration of consciousness which may permit us to render the multi-dimensionality of the event". Here Sartre shows one central event—the Munich crisis—refracted in the consciousness of scores of individuals scattered across Europe, including both fictional and historical characters. Syntax overflows personality; the jump from one character to another is often made within the same sentence. Sartre's conjuring trick is here a very old one; he conceals his art by revealing it. No technique could be more blatantly omniscient than this, but one does not object to it on these grounds. A more pertinent criticism is that such fragmentation and juxtaposition is really a very crude technique, capable of only a very limited range of ironic and satiric effects which are soon exhausted and incapable of sustaining a long novel. Sartre can extract from it a good deal of simple knockabout fun like this, in which the English Prime Minister is mixed up with a record request programme:

> Ellen Birnenschatz laid down her fork, tilted her head back and said: Well, I don't believe there'll be a war. *I will wait till you come back*: the aeroplane was flying above a flat expanse of dusty glass: at the extremity of that expanse, very far away, could be seen a patch of resin, Henry leaned towards Chamberlain and shouted in his ear: That's England, England and the crowd at the aerodrome gates, waiting till you come back, darling, waiting till you come back, he felt slightly faint, it was so hot, he wanted to forget the fly-headed conqueror, and the Hotel Dreesen, and the memorandum, he wanted to believe—he really did—that something could surely be

arranged, he closed his eyes, *My darling doll*, at the request of Mme Duranty and her little niece. . . .[1]

But too much of this rapidly becomes boring and though
the tempo of juxtaposition gradually slows and the narrative
evens out, we are rarely allowed to stay within one consciousness long enough for our interest to quicken. But the important thing to notice is that our awareness of the fiction as
schematic, and of the novelist as puppeteer, *increases* when
Sartre tries to mask his omniscience. Take, for example, this
conversation between Mathieu and Gomez:

> "Take a shepherd in the Cevennes. Do you think he
> would know why he was fighting?"
> "In my country the shepherds are the keenest hands,"
> said Gomez.
> "Why are they fighting?"
> "That depends. I've known some who are fighting for
> the opportunity to learn to read."
> "In France everyone can read," said Mathieu.[2]

The irony of this depends on our knowledge, and the
characters' ignorance, of Gros-Louis, the illiterate French
shepherd. But the point is too obviously scored, the target is
hit with such a palpable thud, that one winces at its crudity.
The same thing happens on a larger scale; thus at the end of
the book the sexual violation of Ivich is made to coincide
neatly with the political violation of Europe. The result is
again far too schematic; we cease to attend to the fiction in
our quarrel with the author about the over-simplicity of his
technique.

Such criticisms cannot be levelled at *La Nausée*, firmly
located as it is within the consciousness of a single character.
Yet even here there are elements in the novel which go beyond the character and imply the brooding presence of the
author within his work. For example, the coincidence of
Anny abandoning her "perfect moments" just as Roquentin
has abandoned his "adventures" is a little too schematic and
contrived; the parts click together rather too neatly. But I
am thinking mainly of the element of literary parody in the
novel; this is not an accurate term but I can think of no

[1] *The Reprieve*, p. 108.   [2] *Ibid.*, p. 252.

other for the intellectual sophistication which plays over the surface of the whole novel, creating a series of dazzling jokes which explode and shoot off at a tangent from its manifest content. They are permissible because they are at least anchored in the extremely literary consciousness of Roquentin. Thus, when he sits in the cafe reading Balzac, and a passage of conversation from *Eugenie Grandet* is stranded like an artificial island in the chaotic sea of random chatter all around him, we may agree with Philip Thody that

> the target of the satire is the attempt of so-called "realist" literature to express life as it is. Before the novelist has remodelled it, Sartre maintains, all real experience is formless and incomprehensible and the pretensions of realist literature are a lie.[1]

We may agree with Mr. Thody that Sartre is present here but we do not find his control objectionable since he has successfully masked himself behind Roquentin. But there is another area of literary reference of which Roquentin is quite unaware and which we can only refer to the author himself; I mean the pervasive Proustian parallels. As Mr. Thody says:

> The idea has been tentatively put forward by some critics that *The Diary of Antoine Roquentin* is itself the book which Roquentin intended to write, and that the whole work is a kind of poor man's Proust. In this interpretation, "Some of These Days", represents the phrase from the Vinteuil Sonata which gave Marcel his first realization of the value of art, and Roquentin's final decision to write his *Diary* corresponds to Marcel's own discovery of the artistic vocation which leads him to write *À La Recherche du Temps Perdu*. However tempting this may be for the connoisseur of literary curiosities, it does not explain the fact that *The Diary of Antoine Roquentin* is not at all the kind of book that Roquentin wanted to write.[2]

One may agree with Mr. Thody's last sentence—though can one be so sure, after all, that *À La Recherche du Temps*

---

[1] P. Thody. *Jean Paul Sartre*, p. 10. London: Hamish Hamilton, 1960.
[2] Thody, *op. cit.*, p. 14.

Perdu is the kind of book that Marcel wanted to write? But even if one accepts the essential difference between these two works, the Proustian parallels still remain valid. They are, of course, not meant to be taken seriously; they are savage, comic or satiric. Roquentin is a parody of Marcel; the gigantic perversions of Sodom and Gomorrah dwindle to the dwarfishly timid and futile passions of the Self-Taught Man. Many other examples could without strain or over ingenuity be found; cumulatively they fill *La Nausée* with what Mary McCarthy has called the "arcane laughter" of the novelist.[1] When we detect this laughter we are in the presence not of Roquentin but of his creator. *La Nausée* is an entirely serious novel, but it is also a huge joke.

Nowhere is this "arcane laughter" more brilliant or dazzling, and nowhere is it more successfully wedded to a serious purpose, than in a trick played by Sartre in so simple a fashion that, so far as I know, it has been ignored by his critics. The mastery of the trick lies in its timing; it is over almost before the show has begun and the audience has composed itself. I refer, of course, to all the hocus-pocus at the beginning of the book, in which the anonymous editors solemnly present Roquentin's diary, tentatively assembling the evidence with a full parade of introduction and footnotes. The device is ambiguous and has complex functions. We may take it at its face-value as a straightforward attempt to assert that what follows is reality, the thing itself, untouched by the novelist's omniscient hand. But equally well, we may take it as a parody of similar devices used by other novelists in presenting what is transparently fiction. Beyond this initial equivocation, the device contributes immensely to the reality of Roquentin by helping to create the wonderful sense of openness to the future that so characterizes the novel. On this sense Roquentin's liberty depends; the novel is not like one of his "adventures", it has no real beginning or end; as we close the book Roquentin is about to plunge into a dark and undetermined future. Yet the device of the diary unifies what would otherwise be a mere continuum, a slice of

---

"There is an element of the private game, even of the private joke, in this kind of writing—a secret and comic relation between the author and his character. An arcane laughter, too infernal for the reader to hear, quietly shakes such books."

[1] Mary McCarthy, *On the Contrary*, p. 287.

time out of Roquentin's life. And the editorial apparatus leaves us with a final ambiguity; why, we may ask—matching the author's straight face with our own—was the diary edited and published at all? Was it because Roquentin achieved his project of writing a novel—are these the pious literary remains of a great novelist? Or are they, ironically, all that is left of him, the shreds and detritus of his hopeless desires? Such speculation would be idle and irrelevant if we actually sought an answer; it must remain the play of the reader's mind answering the play of the novelist. But the mere fact that we are prompted to speculate at all indicates Sartre's success in realizing *his* project.

In *La Nausée*, then, Sartre's sleight of hand comes off; he has successfully manipulated his relation to the life of his protagonist. Roquentin is left free to go through his experience, yet around him flickers and flashes that "arcane laughter" which indicates the presence of his creator. The one achievement does not inhibit the other, as we feel it sometimes does in *L'Âge de Raison*.

But whether successful or not, the main point still holds; the author cannot be banished from his creation. If he withholds his direct intervention, then he is still present in all the choices which determine his creative act and in all the tricks which characterize his art. It is only when the effects of either intervention or elimination are too obvious that we object. The contradiction at the heart of Sartre's literary theory becomes a paradox of creation; the more absolute the illusion of freedom, the more absolute the real, though disguised, artistic control. We can apply to Sartre's own work his comment on Camus:

> Absurdity means divorce, discrepancy. *The Outsider* is to be a novel of discrepancy, divorce and disorientation; hence its skilful construction.[1]

And of *La Nausée*, at least, we can ask Sartre's own question:

> How are we to classify this clear, dry work, so carefully composed beneath its seeming disorder, so "human", so open, too, once you have the key?[2]

---

[1] *Literary and Philosophical Essays*, p. 33.
[2] *Ibid.*, p. 41.

VI

Finally, we must consider the novels in relation to Sartre's general philosophical view, briefly expounded earlier in this chapter. While, of course, it is possible to read and enjoy the novels while remaining totally ignorant of the philosophy, such a reading would miss a great deal. The novels are what they are, for better and for worse, because of the philosophy behind them. Fiction and philosophy are twin facets of the same view of the world.

There are three closely-related questions to be asked. The first, oddly enough, is not often asked of a philosopher's work—how *true* is his philosophy? By this I do not mean the tightness of his logic, the intellectual coherence of his system. Nor do I mean to imply that we ever accept or reject a philosophy lock, stock and barrel; clearly many philosophies —Berkeley's, for example—which we would never accept in our mundane, unreflective lives may nevertheless have considerable interest and value. All I mean by the truth of a philosophy is its adequacy to our own rough and ready sense of what life is like. This is surely not an unreasonable demand to make of a philosopher who, as a phenomenologist, is primarily concerned with the accurate descriptions of things as they appear to be. Nor could we expect a mimetically adequate fiction if the antecedent philosophy seemed to us to be false. Again, this is not to deny other kinds of value and interest to mimetically inadequate fiction—a novel written directly, say, from a Berkeleyan viewpoint might be very interesting indeed. But since Sartre claims to be giving a true picture of the real world, then we must take his claims seriously.

Secondly, we may ask how *useful* is the philosophy to the novelist? Whether it is true or false, does it help or hinder the creation of "real" characters? It is tempting here to say that the truth or falsity of the philosophy is irrelevant to the value of the imagined creation; that what matters with Lucretius is the poetry of *De Rerum Natura* and not the world-views of Epicurus, or that the value of Yeats's *Byzantium* does not depend upon the truth of *A Vision*. But although critics commonly and fruitfully work on this assumption, it does not, in the last analysis, seem to me to be valid.

We may grant that poems are not propositions, that good or bad views do not *necessarily* make good or bad art, that in any particular case it is extremely difficult to relate the value of a poem to the philosophy behind it. Yet it is also true that ultimately the *kind* of philosophy a man holds determines the *kind* of art he produces; it allows him to do certain things, ask certain questions and give certain answers, while it inhibits him from other kinds of achievement. If this is true, as I believe, of any kind of art, even the most apparently self-contained lyric poem, then it is more true of the novel than of any other art form, and certainly true of a writer like Sartre who believes, as we have seen, that the novelist is committed to *using* language for a moral purpose. It is only after we have considered the problem that we may ask the properly aesthetic question; how successful has Sartre been in transmuting his philosophy into art? Is he a genuinely creative artist or are his novels merely rather sophisticated variants of the *roman à these*?

As I have said, I am not concerned with strictly philosophical objections to Sartre's views; these have been made, forcefully, elsewhere. But there are three points which are especially relevant to any consideration of character; the attack on essence, the notion of the *pour-soi* and the relationship between our Self and the Other.

Sartre's attack on essence is valuable in so far as it corrects our tendency to think of the ego as a stable, solid *thing*. But most of us, I imagine, would stubbornly cling to the notion of personal identity and would probably deny the Sartrean cleavage between what I am (my *pour-soi*, my present consciousness) and what I was (my past considered as *en-soi*). My past is uniquely mine and I feel its continuity with my present. "Could Sartre speak of a past without something which was yesterday and is still to-day?"[1] Sartre's own characters, despite their existential anguish, continually think in these common sense terms. Thus Daniel:

> War would be just the same. Horrors always come next day. Myself married, and a soldier, I come upon nothing but my own self. Scarcely that: a succession of small impulses, darting centrifugally here and there, but no focus.

[1] Desan, *The Tragic Finale*, p. 153.

And yet *there is* a focus: that focus is myself, and there the horror lies.[1]

And thus Mathieu:

> And yet, up to that minute, there was still something that could call itself Mathieu, something to which he clung with all his strength. Something, indeed, beyond analysis. Perhaps some ancient habit, perhaps a way of choosing his thoughts in his own likeness, of choosing *himself* from day to day in the likeness of his thoughts, of choosing his food and clothes, the trees and the houses that he looked at. He relaxed his grip and let it go: all this happened deep in his inmost self, in a region where words possess no meaning.[2]

But it is always dangerous, and especially here, to take the views of dramatically realized characters as evidence; we can never be certain that what they seem to assert as truth is not in fact another misconception on their part. Thus these reflections of Daniel and Mathieu precede what we may call their crucial epiphanies—in Daniel's case, his belief that he exists eternally as an object before the gaze of God; in Mathieu's case, his realization of his authentic freedom. Both their views of their own identity might seem to accord with our own common-sense views. Yet there are clear differences; thus Daniel *wants* to become an object while Mathieu merely *feels* that war has reduced him to an object. Daniel's view is clearly to be taken as a perversion, a peculiarly complicated case of *mauvaise foi*. Even with Mathieu we are left in doubt; he continually slides into what seems to be an existentialist truth only to slide out again. This process is necessary to Sartre's view that freedom is not a permanent state which we achieve once and for all, but that we have continually to re-create our freedom in a sequence of choices. Yet it certainly makes Mathieu a slippery and evasive character; we find it difficult to gauge our own responses to him. We are, in fact, in constant danger of mis-reading Sartre's novels because of a tension between his philosophic purpose and his creative talent. Thus what is "unreal", philosophically considered, is often realized in fictional terms

[1] *The Reprieve*, p. 120.   [2] *Ibid.*, p. 314.

more vividly than "reality" itself; Daniel is a much more powerfully rendered character than Mathieu. Sartre's very success as a novelist may obscure his philosophical burden.

But even if we turn to Sartre's own exposition, we find that he has difficulty in banishing the notion of a continuing personal identity. As Desan points out:

> There is in Sartre's Existentialistic psychoanalysis a concept which he uses quite often. It is expressed by the term "fundamental project" and can be described as the essential and basic attitude of a person towards the world.[1]

Our particular projects—the multitude of day-to-day choices that we make—are, so to speak, the spray which falls from the steady jet of our "fundamental project", the constant pressure of what we are. If we accept this, then Sartre's concept of absolute freedom must be modified. As we have seen, Sartre allows that we are limited by the "facticity" of the world and the *en-soi* of our individual past is for each of us part of this "facticity". Already we have begun to swing towards the notion of conditional freedom outlined in an earlier chapter. The truth, as Desan says, is "that all choice supposes a certain number of data; I can choose among these data but the data themselves I have not chosen."[2] Sartre would not dispute this, but he would dispute the notion that our past not only determines the date from which we can choose but is also a constituent in our power of choosing. Yet surely this is a fact of life that most of us accept?

We can see Sartre's difficulties if we examine a question which he dismisses as metaphysical and beyond discussion— the question of origin. Authentic freedom presupposes a free consciousness. But where does this come from? It is not merely a question of the origin of human consciousness in the evolutionary process; it is also a question of individual growth, something which affects each personal identity. At what stage in our lives do we enter the condition of free, reflexive consciousness? Sartre's short story *L'Enfance d'un Chef* and his studies of Baudelaire and Genet suggest that he would place it early in childhood, but he is nowhere quite clear on this point. Yet surely the process of growth involves

---

[1] W. Desan, *op. cit.*, p. 164.   [2] *Ibid.*, p. 170.

an imperceptible change from object to subject; whether or no we endorse Freud's theories, we should surely agree that there is some human state prior to that described by Sartre which nevertheless acts as a conditioning factor on our mature existence? In this sense, alone, we can maintain that we are in part determined without being guilty of *mauvaise foi*. Sartre's concept of absolute freedom is useful in that it spotlights *certain* aspects of the human condition. Its moral consequences seem to me entirely beneficial in so far as it demands that we *try* at least to be fully responsible as we face the future. But we can only try; the future is never *quite* of our choosing; in this sense Sartre's view does not entirely match the everyday texture of our lives, the *feel* of conditional freedom.

Many of the difficulties so far encountered derive from a basic tension in Sartre's thought. The clash between the novelist and the philosopher is not simply to be found in the novels; it is also present within *L'Être et le Néant* itself. On the one hand the impulse of the novelist—and of the strict phenomenologist—is to render experience in all its rich concreteness. Thus *L'Être et le Néant* is enlivened with subtle analyses of complex human states. These often tend to disguise weaknesses in the argument. Their persuasive force is such that we often leap from a convincing particular case to an unconvincing general principle without noticing it. On the other hand, there is a strong rationalistic, almost Cartesian strain in Sartre which tends to reduce the contradictions of experience to the simplicity of a few basic abstractions. No sooner is essence ejected through the front door than it creeps back, suitably disguised, through the back window.

This tension is nowhere more apparent than in Sartre's description of the *pour-soi*. Consciousness is evacuated of all human content; it is refined to a chemical purity. Thus what we normally think of as the psyche, with its complex burden of passions and memories, is in fact relegated to the status of *en-soi*. Elsewhere, in his *Sketch for A Theory of the Emotions*, Sartre explains emotion away as a magical rather than a rational apprehension of the world, a refuge in which the consciousness shelters when it cannot endure its situation. Again, we protest, human reality is simply not as Sartre depicts it. The translucent consciousness is always clouded

and coloured with the full spectrum of the human psyche.
As Professor Ayer observed:

> Against him, I should argue that to say that a feeling is
> conscious may be pleonastic; it does not necessarily add
> anything to the statement that it is a feeling. If the feeling
> is mine, it forms part of my "conscious history"; but it
> enters into this history as a *constituent* and not necessarily
> as an *object* of consciousness.[1]

For most of us consciousness of a Sartrean purity is a point
to which we may aspire but which we hardly ever attain. A
great part of our lives is spent in unreflexive consciousness, a
great part in what Sartre would dismiss as *mauvaise foi*;
authentic and pure self-reflection is quite exceptional. In his
novels Sartre tacitly recognizes this; his characters are depicted as struggling and failing to achieve this uncluttered
and unclouded consciousness which bears about as much
relation to common human experience as do moments of
mystical ecstasy. And like the mystical poet, Sartre has the
well-nigh insoluble problem of expressing this state in
language which is clogged and contaminated by ordinary
human experience. The remarkable thing is not that he fails
but that, by vivid and powerful metaphors, he comes so
close to succeeding.

The same rarefied and abstract quality characterizes
Sartre's account of human relationships. No doubt we try
sometimes to reduce the Other to an object or suffer ourselves to be so reduced. But can we derive *all* personal relationships to this single principle? While his philosophical
framework allows Sartre to display considerable psychological insight, Professor Ayer's comment nevertheless
seems just:

> These analyses of human behaviour seem to be of con-
> siderable psychological interest, but, to my mind, they
> are open to the serious objection that they do not corre-
> spond empirically to the way that most people actually be-
> have.[2]

[1] A. J. Ayer, "Novelist-Philosophers: Jean-Paul Sartre", *Horizon*, Vol. 12,
1945, p. 19.
[2] Ayer, *op. cit.*, p. 110.

How far can we convert these criticisms of Sartre's philosophy into aesthetic terms? Oddly enough, the novel which remains most immune is *La Nausée*, the most thoroughly philosophic of them all. This is because the novel is no fictional illustration of existentialism; philosophy is re-created as lived experience, felt on the pulses and along the nerves. The real subject and value of *La Nausée* is dramatization of a human process—what it is like to become an existentialist. The human journey we can share, irrespective of the philosophic goal. Sartre's fidelity to this human process releases within the relatively narrow scope of this novel a greater range of feeling than is usual in the more ambitious canvas of his later novels. Concurrent with the vein of existential anguish, for example, there is a vein of something like broad comedy which modulates not merely into mockery of society but also of the protagonist. The integrity of Roquentin's vision is somehow preserved by the fact that he can be ironic at his own expense; in this passage for example, the laugh is not merely at the Self-Taught Man:

> The Self-Taught Man laughs candidly, but his eyes stay wicked:
> "You are too modest, Monsieur. In order to tolerate your condition, the human condition, you, as everybody else, need much courage. Monsieur, the next instant may be the moment of your death, you know it and you can smile: isn't that admirable? In your most insignificant actions," he adds sharply, "there is an enormous amount of heroism."
> "What will you gentlemen have for dessert?" the waitress says.
> The Self-Taught Man is quite white, his eyelids are half-shut over his stony eyes. He makes a feeble motion with his hand, as if inviting me to choose.
> "Cheese," I say heroically.[1]

This contrasts sharply with Sartre's characterization of Mathieu, at least in *L'Âge de Raison*. Mathieu's extreme self-consciousness dissolves the rich content of human experience into a thin, analytic abstraction; as a result he comes across to the reader as drab, priggish and boring. There is,

[1] *Nausea*, p. 163.

moreover, a corresponding impoverishment in human relationships; as Iris Murdoch has observed, other people are
for Mathieu either completely opaque, mysterious, *en-soi*, or
they are rendered transparent, made case-studies within his
subjective consciousness. There is no middle-ground between these two extremes; yet it is between them that the
dense tangle of human relationships flourishes in reality.

If *L'Âge de Raison* tilts the balance too far in the direction
of subjectivity, then *Le Sursis* is equally drastic in reducing
human beings to objects. No doubt this accords with Sartre's
philosophic purpose; thus he wishes to emphasize the
"facticity" of the human situation and to demonstrate how
individual choice merges into collective responsibility. This
is a note struck again and again in *Le Sursis*:

> A vast entity, a planet, in a space of a hundred million
> dimensions: three-dimensional beings could not so much
> as imagine it. And yet each dimension was an autonomous
> consciousness. Try to look directly at that planet, it would
> disintegrate into tiny fragments, and nothing but con-
> sciousnesses would be left. A hundred million free con-
> sciousnesses, each aware of walls, the glowing stump of a
> cigar, familiar faces, and each constructing its destiny on
> its own responsibility. And yet, each of those conscious-
> nesses, by imperceptible contacts and insensible changes,
> realises its existence as a cell in a gigantic and invisible
> coral. War: everyone is free and yet the stakes are set.
> It is there, it is everywhere, it is the totality of all my
> thoughts, of all Hitler's words, of all Gomez's acts: but
> no one is there to sum that total. It exists solely for God.
> But God does not exist. And yet the war exists.[1]

But again the philosophic emphasis demands too radical an
adjustment to accord with our sense of human reality. In *La
Mort dans l'Ame* the see-saw comes closer to the desired
equilibrium. Again the "facticity" of the human situation is
stressed; again human beings, the crowd of prisoners, are
reduced to helpless objects; yet within this situation freedom
quickens and life starts to grow again. As Mathieu makes his
exit with a final, gratuitous act of defiance, he is replaced by
Brunet. Brunet's development within the total work, *Les*

[1] *The Reprieve*, p. 292.

Chemins de la Liberté, is sketchy and tentative, but it points in a promising direction. In *L'Âge de Raison* Brunet has done what Daniel wishes to do; he has made himself an object by committing himself totally to the Communist Party. In *Le Sursis* his rock-like stability begins to be shaken; he is troubled by the bourgeois background which separates him from the proletariat. In *Mort dans l'Ame* this process continues; in the prison camp his faith in the rightness of his actions is further shaken. At the same time Sartre begins to develop a human relationship—the friendship of Brunet and Schneider—which has a complexity and a human depth previously absent from his work. This continues in *La Dernière Chance*, the fragment of the unfinished fourth volume. Whatever the reasons for Sartre's abandoning of the work, *Les Chemins de la Liberté* stops abruptly just at the point when it seems likely that the fiction must break free of the philosophic framework.

Although, as I have argued, this framework limits the range of Sartre's achievement and is sometimes inadequate to human reality, it is still to facile a judgment to dismiss *Les Chemins de la Liberté* as a *roman á thèse*. Only intermittently is the fiction badly warped by the need to provide a neat illustration of some theoretic position. This generally happens under some moral or satiric pressure, notably Sartre's impulse to regard the bourgeoisie as a collective example of *mauvaise foi*. When this is generalized and impersonal, as it often is in *La Nausée*, we accept it; but when it is localized in an individual character, like Mathieu's brother, Jacques, we tend to feel that Sartre has loaded the dice or has over-simplified things; we protest at his arbitrary abrogation of the character's autonomy. For Sartre does sometimes subvert his desire to preserve the illusion of his character's freedom; sometimes he does use his god-like powers and reduce them unmercifully to exemplary objects, mere case-studies. If we can trace the artefact back to the subjectivity of its author, then we have to say that co-existent with Sartre's intellectual penetration there is a certain coldness and lack of generosity towards his creation.

Most of this chapter has been critical of Sartre: I prefer to end by stressing the considerable degree of his achievement. One notes first his talent for creating a sense of time, place and physical presence; striking, too, is his gift for vivid and abundant metaphor; together these enable him to create many wonderful scenes—tableaux almost—beginning with the bourgeois Sunday and Roquentin's visit to the Art Gallery in *La Nausée*. These are carried off with such élan and energy, almost with such high spirits, that by contrast much of his later work seems heavy and flagging. *L'Âge de Raison*, in particular, has a kind of monochrome monotony, but even there one remembers the nervous vitality of Daniel and his sackful of cats or Mathieu at the night-club. One remembers, too, Sartre's capacity for intricate moral analysis; sometimes the concept of *mauvaise foi* seems to impose itself as a rigid blueprint, distorting the fluid contours of human reality, but at his best—with Daniel or Philippe— Sartre's dissection of the perverted mind is deft and delicate. It is enriched, too, by a curious kind of sympathy which is almost entirely lacking in his treatment of Mathieu, a hero perhaps too like his creator for Sartre to risk compassion. Similarly one notices how often a quality of tenderness suffuses those characters who are reduced to helpless objects; one remembers Charles and Catherine, the evacuated stretcher-cases of *Le Sursis*, or the defeated army of *Mort dans l'Âme*. These also illustrate Sartre's command of crowds and masses; perhaps it is in his depiction of the prison camp that he reaches his peak as a novelist.

Nevertheless one feels that he is not naturally a novelist; there is something constrained and withdrawn about his fiction; his achievements are triumphs of intelligence and will. He is happiest when working at a certain remove from the full body of human reality, when his story allows him to deal with characters or situations that are in some way abnormal and exceptional. Abnormal and exceptional, that is, from the viewpoint of the liberal imagination; Sartre might justly argue that Hitler was hardly the spokesman of a normal world. Nevertheless, all critics have agreed that Sartre is a novelist of extreme situations; it is perhaps this that led him to the compression of the short story and the play. Most of us live most of the time at a relatively low pressure; Sartre constantly forces the pressure up. Generally speaking, as the opportunities for choice increase so the pressure to choose diminishes. Sartre's extreme situations, because they narrow the field of choice, force a man to be free. What the liberal regards as the normal condition of freedom, namely the incredibly complex compromises that we constantly and unreflectively make, Sartre would dismiss as trivial or as *mauvaise foi*. Where we impose a tentative armistice upon a multitude of minute conditioning factors, the moral life of Sartre's characters has all the clarity of a cold war. Where we preside over a shifting and unstable coalition of private interests, Sartre's characters inhabit the stage of tragedy or debate. For him the norm of a situation is so pure that the liberal regards it as the abnormal or exceptional case. The moral life for the liberal is like a crowded and cluttered chessboard, where the permutations of movement are infinite, where pieces advance and retreat, threaten but rarely take each other. By contrast, Sartre's world is a perpetual end game, where isolate kings and queens starkly confront each other on an otherwise naked board. They live in the condition of total victory and defeat or else, as in *Huis Clos*, go through the mechanical routines of a perpetual stalemate.

As such, the world of Sartre's fiction is distinct and unmistakable; it is uniquely his. As such, and quite apart from its intrinsic worth, it remains permanently valuable as a challenge to the liberal imagination. Sartre is perhaps as good as any novelist can be without achieving real greatness; when we read his novels we say, "Yes, this is the Sartrean world"; but when we read one of the great masters we say, simply, "Yes, this is the world". The difference in our response may perhaps seem slight; in fact, it is crucial.

CHAPTER VIII

Conclusion: an End to Theory

WHEN we say of a novel, "Yes, this is the world," our act of recognition and surrender transcends all our critical theories. Most aesthetic systems, after all, are either rationalizations of taste or weapons in a continuing critical debate. Unlike scientific theories, they cannot offer the hope of fresh knowledge or become the basis for prediction; at best they can help to prevent error by clarifying what in a sense we already know. For this reason the prime necessary condition of a good aesthetic theory is that it be not *a priori*, that it come after our experience of works of art. If, like some neoclassical theories, it comes first, then it can only narrow taste and blinker comprehension.

As a rationalization of my own taste the mimetic theories implicit in this book can be of little interest to others. But these theories, to use Sartre's term, transcend my subjectivity by becoming part of a current and general critical debate which, to avoid clutter, I have relegated to an appendix. But briefly, my position is summed up in the title of an extremely relevant essay by Iris Murdoch, "Against Dryness"[1] —the dry novel being that which is neat, precise, formally watertight, which sees life as something to be beautifully bottled rather than as something to be swum in. It is the kind of novel envisioned by Roquentin; the hard, jewel-like object, immune from the viscous flux of existence. It is in this flux that the "loose, baggy monsters" of the great tradition wallow and flounder; my book is a plea for them, antediluvian though the species may be. It is a plea for any novel which dares to remain open to life, which dares to say, "This is the world".

In pleading thus I do not wish, of course, to make a crude distinction between content and form, cast my vote for content and neglect the formal properties of the work of art. Indeed, I have tried in this book to concentrate on those formal qualities of fiction by which life is revealed rather

[1] I. Murdoch, "Against Dryness", *Encounter*, Vol. 16, 1961.

than incapsulated. I wish only to suggest that criticism deriving from autonomy theories of one kind or another has been overstressed and that the time has come to redress the balance. Of course, such criticism is often valuable and as I suggested in my first chapter, that critic is a fool who, leaving behind the rigorous climes of theory, would deny himself *any* useful critical method.

Thus the same critical point may be equally well made in terms of autonomy or mimetic theories; a book may be equally well judged as internally incoherent or as simply untrue to life. An instance of this occurred in Chapter 4, with the discussion of *The Princess Casamassima*, but to focus the point we may look briefly at a more radical failure of the same kind, *Oliver Twist*.

Is Dickens's belief in radical innocence a tenable belief? Is it credible that a boy with the childhood environment of Oliver should remain so consistently pure of speech and mind? In asking these questions we appeal from art to nature; we are working within a mimetic theory. But we can restate these objections by saying that the book is internally fragmented, that the element of realism does not cohere with the element of fairy-tale, or that there is an aesthetic discrepancy between a vivid intensity in some parts of the novel and a sentimental blur in other parts. This is to work within an autonomy theory; the results are pretty much the same. All we need notice here is that though the emphasis may be on formal blemishes, the appeal is ultimately once again to truth and nature. For what we note in formal terms is the incongruity of two mimetic angles—realism and fantasy—within the same book.

In the first appendix to this book I have stated some of the historical reasons why autonomy theories have recently flourished. But apart from these I would say that there is built into *any* critical theory—simply *because* it is a theory—a dislike of muddle and loose ends. If I incline to mimetic theories this is in part because they are rather more tolerant of the loose-ends and muddle which seem to me a part of all experience, whether of art or nature. Of course, our own tolerance of muddle is again a matter of personal taste and temperament.

Correspondingly, I am a little suspicious of the novels

which display too much formal precision, in which the parts are too neatly articulated, and which too triumphantly make a coherent whole. The danger is that unity may be bought at the cost of excluding too much. In the present study my suspicions have catalysed in the word *schematic*, but again I would not wish to use the term in a totally or consistently pejorative sense. My unease is acute only when attention is distracted from the life portrayed to the obtrusive formal properties of the work. Even here there are exceptions; thus in certain works, as I tried to show with *Death in Venice*, an intense and even oppressive sense of the novel's artifice may be essential to the total effect. This is also true wherever the novel inclines to fable or to the kind of fantasy which, as E. M. Forster says, consists of "muddling up the actual and the impossible until the reader isn't sure which is which".[1] And apart from fantasy, there are other kinds of fiction designed by their very intricacy and complication to give the effect of an endless regression of opposing mirrors, so that the reader's sense of distinction between art and reality is deliberately blurred or distorted.

Clearly each case of the schematic must be considered on its merits; let us look again at the work of Sartre which I criticized in the previous chapter largely on these grounds. When the formal qualities of his work harden into the schematic, one objects not merely because the artifice is obtrusive but because Sartre betrays his own pretensions, limiting the freedom of his characters and revealing a god-like presence in a creation from which the omniscient author has allegedly been excluded. Yet even here one accepts the schematic as justified if some effect of intensity or vividness is thereby achieved. In *Mort dans l'Ame*, for example, the situations of Mathieu and Brunet are very carefully paralleled as the narrative passes from one character to the other. Mathieu makes his exit in a blazing and occupied village; Brunet is captured in a situation so similar that the reader may think the two villages are one and the same. The reader is relieved when he comes to realize that he is not, after all, being asked to accept such an extreme coincidence; it is perhaps because of this relief that he is willing to accept the formal parallels. Once accepted, the schematic structure is

[1] E. M. Forster, *Two Cheers for Democracy*, p. 222.

seen to reinforce the meaning of the novel; the story passes from one character to another almost like the baton in a relay race and we realize that deep below the surface is the cliché, potent because disguised, of "handing on the torch". As war changes into defeat, so Mathieu's final and futile blaze of defiance modulates into Brunet's unspectacular but enduring form of resistance—a theme, no doubt, which would have broadened and deepened had the tetralogy been completed.

Here, then, is a case where the schematic comes off, but generally it fails unless it satisfies two conditions. Firstly, the *characters* must not be conscious of the formal patterns to be inferred from their experience; thus, if Simone de Beauvoir's *Les Mandarins* at all transcends the case-study nature of her other fiction, it is because her psychoanalyst heroine, Anne, remains largely unconscious of the parallels between her and the neurotic Paula. Secondly, the *reader* must not be too conscious of the formal patterns; they must remain submerged beneath the complicated texture of the rendered experience. Very often this is a by-product of simple mass; thus, Sartre's three novels cumulatively build up many powerful parallels and contrasts which do not seem schematic because they are dispersed throughout the total work. A similar but simpler example occurs in *Wuthering Heights*. Early in the novel Lockwood has a dream of the dead Cathy knocking at the window to be let in:

> Terror made me cruel; and finding it useless to attempt shaking the creature off, I pulled its wrist on to the broken pane and rubbed it to and fro till the blood ran down and soaked the bedclothes.

At the very end of the novel Nelly describes her discovery of the dead Heathcliff:

> I could not think him dead: but his face and throat were washed with rain; the bedclothes dripped, and he was perfectly still. The lattice, flapping to and fro, had grazed one hand that rested on the sill; no blood trickled from the broken skin, and when I put my fingers to it, I could doubt no more: he was dead and stark!

Surely the tremendous poetic force of this is effective only because the echo is muted in our minds by the intervening mass of the novel? Had it been more closely juxtaposed, then its reverberations would have become intolerable and we would have rejected it as schematic, a sensational Gothic cliché.

Even within this discussion of the schematic we have begun to move towards a view of the formal nature of fiction which transcends any autonomy theory. But clearly, any mimetic theory based on the naïve proposition that art directly imitates the formlessness of nature would be absurd; most of us, I imagine, are content to rest at the half-way house inhabited, for example, by E. M. Forster. I quote, for convenience, the summary of his views made by F. C. Crews:

> Forster's position on every question of theory is a middle one, involving a vital balance between extremes that threaten to "tyrannize" the novel. A novel should exist simultaneously in a world of time and a world of value, without giving itself wholly to either measure. It must be "sogged with humanity" (*Aspects of The Novel*, p. 43), but must possess formal unity. It must be beautiful without aiming at beauty; impressive, but never at the expense of truthfulness. Pattern is desirable, but not beyond the point where it begins to restrict "the immense richness of material which life provides" (p. 233). And a great part of this richness, for Forster, is unavailable to logical categories; it falls under the heading of "muddle", and is hence perceivable only by a sense of the incongruous. For this reason the "charmed stagnation" of *Tristram Shandy* is more congenial to Forster's taste than the relentless purposefulness of *The Ambassadors*. "The army of unalterable muddle" (p. 164) lies behind Sterne's masterpiece and provides its appeal.[1]

Yet even as we retreat from the chaotic flux of existence into this comfortable and liberal compromise, we should notice that a mimetic theory may reconcile a sense of the formless plenitude of reality to the discipline of art. Energy, variety, abundance—these are the characteristics of the very greatest novels; their authors display an appetite and pas-

[1] F. C. Crews, *E. M. Forster: The Perils of Humanism*, p. 93. London: O.U.P., 1962.

sion for life which threatens to overwhelm the formal nature of their art.

The result is that characterization often overflows the strict necessities of form:

> We mean by character just the element in excess of plot requirements, the element we call *individual* because it eludes and defies classification. The paradoxical defiance of classification does not so much describe the individual element by creating a new, more refined category as it alludes symbolically to its ultimately enigmatic nature— to that unlit area behind the Aristotelian agent in sensing which we sense what we mean by the character's *life*. This area provides the mysterious, life-giving dimension of those "three-dimensional" characters the reviews of fiction are always talking about.[1]

While Professor Langbaum is here describing how the novel evades or transcends specifically Aristotelian categories, his remarks may be generalized to include almost any kind of formal requirement.

A surplus margin of gratuitous life, a sheer excess of material, a fecundity of detail and invention, a delighted submergence in experience for its own sake—all these are observable in the work of the great novelists. It is this exuberance of creative play that gives their fiction its ultimate power of lying open to the world, of suggesting that the boundaries of art are marked by no sharp frontiers, but that the contours of fiction merge into those of life itself. Form thus recognizes and pays tribute to its opposite; even while it subdues the turbulent chaos of experience it acknowledges the always transcendent, ever elusive nature of the reality it renders. Once we recognize this then we can understand the final paradox of such fiction, that the apparently formless has in fact a multitude of formal functions. By it the novelist may afford the reader relief and relaxation, or he may render the contingency of the world, or he may express the sense of life simply going on, here and elsewhere; the sense described by Auden.

[1] R. Langbaum, *The Poetry of Experience*, pp. 223-4. London: Chatto and Windus, 1957.

About suffering they were never wrong,
The Old Masters: how well they understood
Its human position; how it takes place
While someone else is eating or opening a window, or
just walking dully along. . . .[1]

Such works achieve that sense of reality attributed by Dr.
Johnson to Shakespeare's plays; they, too, exhibit:

the real state of sublunary nature, which partakes of good
and evil, joy and sorrow, mingled with endless variety of
proportion and innumerable modes of combination; and
expressing the course of the world, in which the loss of
one is the gain of another; in which, at the same time, the
reveller is hasting to his wine, and the mourner burying
his friend; in which the malignity of one is sometimes defeated by the frolick of another; and many mischiefs and
many benefits are done and hindered without design.[2]

Nowhere is this more apparent than in the greatest of all
novels, *War and Peace*, and no critic has come closer to
stating this sense of reality than Isaiah Berlin in his study of
Tolstoy. I conclude by quoting him at some length, since
what he lays bare are the basic strata of our experience. Great
fiction is rooted deep in this soil and unless, as critics, we dig
our foundations there, all our theories will be so many castles
in the air. As it is, the passage which follows applies as much
to criticism as to any form of rational enquiry; hence we may
learn from it the humility which is the first step towards
understanding:

We—sentient creatures—are in part living in a world
the constituents of which we can discover, classify and
act upon by rational, scientific, deliberately planned
methods; but in part (Tolstoy and Maistre, and many
thinkers with them, say much the larger part) we are immersed and submerged in a medium that, precisely to the
degree to which we inevitably take it for granted as part
of ourselves, we do not and cannot observe as if from the

---

[1] W. H. Auden, "Musée des Beaux Arts", *Collected Shorter Poems*, p. 19. London:
Faber and Faber, 1950.
[2] "Preface to Shakespeare"; *Johnson on Shakespeare*, ed. W. Raleigh, pp. 15–16.
O.U.P., 1940.

outside; cannot identify, measure and seek to manipulate; cannot even be wholly aware of, inasmuch as it enters too intimately into all our experience, is itself too closely interwoven with all that we are and do to be lifted out of the flow (it *is* the flow) and observed with scientific detachment, as an object. It—the medium in which we are— determines our most permanent categories, our standards of truth and falsehood, of reality and appearance, of the good and the bad, of the central and the peripheral, the subjective and the objective, of the beautiful and the ugly, of movement and rest, of past, present and future, of one and many; hence neither these, nor any other explicitly conceived categories or concepts can be applied to it—for it is itself but a vague name for the totality that includes these categories, these concepts, the ultimate framework, the basic presuppositions wherewith we function. . . . It is "there"—the framework, the foundation of everything, and the wise man alone has a sense of it.[1]

[1] I. Berlin, *The Hedgehog and the Fox*, pp. 67–71.

The Retreat from Character

"When we think of the works of Tolstoy or George Eliot, we are not remembering Tolstoy and George Eliot, we are remembering Dolly, Kitty, Stiva, Dorothea and Casaubon."

IRIS MURDOCH[1]

THOUGH I am quoting Miss Murdoch out of context, the general assumption behind her remark, namely that great novels are chiefly memorable for the characters they portray, is not likely to be disputed by any common reader. Yet if we survey the criticism of fiction of the last thirty years we find more often than not that Miss Murdoch's proposition, unless it is hedged around with qualifying clauses and other syntactical escape routes, is treated with uneasiness, suspicion, embarrassment or downright contempt. This is an odd situation and worth exploring. What I have called simply "the retreat from character" is, of course, a state of affairs so complex that analysis can only hint at the interaction of many different forces. But however complicated the process, the results have been quite simple and I do not think that the title of this appendix does them any injustice.

I start from the assumption that most modern criticism of fiction has been largely determined by five shaping forces.

(*a*) The example of modern (i.e. post-Jamesian) creative practice.

(*b*) The rationalizations of modern novelists based either on their own work (e.g. James's *Prefaces*) or on their own special view of past and contemporary achievement—special because the creative artist is an interested party, his view of others being largely determined by what is viable, usable in his own terms or by what he feels as a threat to his own artistic individuality. As an example of attraction one may quote James on Turgenev—"an artistic influence extraordinarily valuable and ineradicably established"; as an example of fear James may serve again, this time on Tolstoy—"his own case is prodigious, but his example for others dire: disciples not elephantine he can only mislead and betray."

---

[1] Iris Murdoch, "The Sublime and the Beautiful Revisited", *Yale Review*, Vol. 49, 1959, p. 226.

(c) The way in which the evidence provided by these first two factors has been converted by critics—generally academic critics—from mainly descriptive statements into mainly prescriptive assertions.

(d) The overflow into the field of fiction of that whole impulse towards close scrutiny and analysis of particular texts that we conveniently if crudely term the "new criticism".

(e) The overflow into the field of fiction of this new criticism as it has particularly concerned itself with drama and, more narrowly still, with the Shakespearian mode of poetic drama.

Each of these factors or each combination of them has proved useful and illuminating at times, yet if I were forced to sum up for good or ill, I should say that the final result has been to distort our view of the novel as an art form, to produce a lopsided version of the great tradition in fiction and to render much criticism pedantic, sterile, mechanical and utterly remote from the concerns of any intelligent common reader.

One symptom of this has been the subject of this book. If the common reader supposes that the creation of interesting, lively and lifelike characters is one of the chief concerns of the novelist, he is likely soon to be disabused of such notions by the modern critic. Modern criticism, by and large, has relegated the treatment of character to the periphery of its attention, has at best given it a polite and perfunctory nod and has regarded it more often as a misguided and misleading abstraction. Plenty of "character sketches" still appear which serve only as easy targets for such hostility. But if I wish to refer my students to a wise and substantial general treatment of character in fiction there is relatively little to which I can direct them since E. M. Forster's deceptively light treatment of the subject more than thirty years ago. What has been said about character since then has been mainly a stock of critical commonplaces used largely to dismiss the subject in order that the critic may turn his attention to other, allegedly more important and central subjects—symbolism, narrative techniques, moral vision and the like.

These are sweeping assertions; what I hope to do in this appendix is to justify them by citing evidence which will at the same time explain why this retreat from character has taken place. Most modern critics are neither knaves nor fools and the reasons why the concept of character has fallen into disrepute may help to illuminate the problems which must be tackled if the term is to be rehabilitated. Let us look again at the five shaping forces I isolated at the beginning of this appendix.

THE EXAMPLE OF CREATIVE PRACTICE

No one, I suppose, would deny that the period since about 1880 has been one of unprecedented technical experiment in the novel. Literary historians may well discover odd and ancient analogues for these experiments, but cumulatively they amount to nothing less than a revolution. James, Conrad, Proust, Gide, Joyce, Virginia Woolf, Faulkner—such novelists have explored the frontiers of their form, have pushed ahead into regions of craft and imagination still waiting to be settled and made habitable by the less daring. If, in this rush of exploration, the common reader has sometimes been left behind, the critic has trekked laboriously in the trail of the pioneers, constructing maps that don't quite tell the truth about the imaginative landscape, erecting signposts that point in not quite the right direction—but on the whole doing a useful job of consolidation.

Two points may be briefly made about the effects of this revolution. First, it should be clear that the critical techniques evolved in response to an age of extreme experiment may, precisely *because* they work admirably with Joyce or Gide, work less well with Fielding or Balzac. Moreover, the critic does not merely use a critical technique; frequently he spends a great deal of time creating or refining it in response to the creative challenge. What the critic himself creates he will tend to cherish and be loath to discard.

It is almost as difficult to describe the heart of the critical process as it is the creative, and the submerged metaphor beneath my prose at the moment—a metaphor of the critic and the tools of his trade—is liable to distortion. A critic's intelligence and sensibility are not in any way mechanical. True; but if I may risk pushing my metaphor a little further, I would say that any particular critical technique is rather like a lens. It enables the critic to see certain things with greater precision and intensity—but only *certain* things. The same lens may distort or blur other objects; if it does so and if the critic, because he has polished the lens, is reluctant to discard it, then he may be tempted to do one of two things. He may either declare that the blurred object is not worth observing or he may deny that it is blurred at all. If one's critical lens, for example, focuses perfectly on the novels of Virginia Woolf, then one is quite likely not to think very highly of Arnold Bennett. Or, again, if one thinks highly of Kafka, then one may try to applaud the novels of Dickens by stressing those elements in his work most

N

assimilable to Kafka. The circumlocution office, for example, may seem less a direct satire on Victorian bureaucracy and more a symbol of man's helplessness in an alien and incomprehensible universe. To sum up, then; a critical system or method which deals finely and justly with the modern novel may well deal clumsily and unjustly with older types of fiction, simply because of the radical differences wrought by modern experiment.

The second point to be noted about the experimental novel is that its technical features which so intrigue critics—the complication of narrative methods, the elimination of the omniscient author, the expressive manipulation of style, the greater stress on image and symbol, stream of consciousness techniques and so on—that all of these reflect a changed conception of the relation of art to reality, a change largely determined by the modern novelist's sense of increasing alienation. Behind this changed conception often lie radical doubts about the very nature of reality. We are no longer certain of the world we live in; physics, psychology, politics and philosophy all conspire to dissolve the comfortably solid boundaries of our everyday world. Reality becomes flickering, evanescent.

> What is meant by "reality"? It would seem to be something very erratic, very undependable—now to be found in a dusty road, now in a scrap of newspaper in the street, now a daffodil in the sun. It lights up a group in a room and stamps some casual saying. It overwhelms one walking home beneath the stars and makes the silent world more real than the world of speech—and then there it is again in an omnibus in the uproar of Piccadilly.[1]

Such a conception of reality would hardly have been understood by Fielding or Jane Austen or George Eliot. Many of the finest aesthetic effects in the modern novel come from the deliberate exploitation of ambiguity—what are we, for example, *finally* to make of Lord Jim or the Ververs or Joe Christmas? This kind of effect is comparatively rare in the traditional English novel—though it is sometimes there in the French and frequently in the Russian—and equally rare is this distinctively modern kind of ending which suggests a precarious equipoise, a momentary peace before renewed conflict:

> "Why aren't I enough?" she said. "You are enough for me. I don't want anybody else but you. Why isn't it the same with you?"

[1] Virginia Woolf, *A Room of One's Own*, p. 165. London: The Hogarth Press, 1946.

"Having you, I can live all my life without anybody else, any other sheer intimacy. But to make it complete, really happy, I wanted eternal union with a man too; another kind of love," he said. "It's an obstinacy, a theory, a perversity."

"Well—" he said.

"You can't have two kinds of love. Why should you!"

"It seems as if I can't," he said. "Yet I wanted it."

"You can't have it, because it's false, impossible," she said.

"I don't believe that," he answered.[1]

Given this new conception of reality and given, therefore, a changed conception of mimesis—I used the word to denote not simple imitation but the general relation of art to life—it is not difficult to see why critics will tend to shy away from a discussion of character in the modern novel. For character itself so often dissolves or becomes symbolic and the mimetic nature of the modern novel is so often tenuous, distorted or abstract, that the critical lens may quite naturally be focused elsewhere—on thematic patterns or image clusters, for example.

THE NOVELIST AS CRITIC

One thing shown by Miriam Allott's useful collection, *Novelists On The Novel*, is the difference in quantity and quality in the remarks made on their own craft by novelists before and after James. Without agreeing with Mrs. Allott that "only the practitioner can speak with final authority about the problems of his art", it is obviously true that the critical remarks of James, Conrad, E. M. Forster, D. H. Lawrence, Edith Wharton, Virginia Woolf and many others must have had an immense influence on modern critical attitudes to the novel.

Although many of these novelists have been greatly interested in the problems of characterization—for example, James on Isabel Archer in his preface to *Portrait of A Lady*—it is nevertheless true to say that the general effect of their remarks has been to distract attention to other aspects of the novel.

This, I think, is because novelists have inevitably been interested primarily in the creative process. Without entering into an elaborate discussion of the ontological status of a work of art, let us agree for the moment that any work may be viewed from three points of view. These are the creative process (the situation of the novelist), the created artefact and the recreative process (the situation of the reader). It

[1] D. H. Lawrence, *Women in Love*, Chapter 31.

should be clear that for a critic interested in the mimetic nature and function of character, the emphasis will be on a balance between the artefact and the recreative process. Moreover, it seems that to many novelists—acutely aware of the difference between imaginative processes and any subsequent critical rationalization—the creation of character remains a more or less impenetrable mystery, a *donnée* they are content to accept. They are perhaps *afraid* to investigate too closely, lest critical scrutiny should dry up the mainsprings of their creative talent. They are thus less reluctant to throw the emphasis on other more technical, perhaps more public, aspects of their art—questions of structural composition, formal arrangement, style and so on. When they do discuss the mimetic nature of their characters, it is noticeable how often they are content merely to deny any simple imitative intent, any crude one-to-one relationship between a character and an actual person. This aspect of mimesis—the relation of fictional characters to historical originals—is not one I shall discuss further since my emphasis in this book has been on the relation between the artefact and the recreative processes of reading and critical study.

Many novelists have subsequently commented on their characters *as if* they were real people. Sometimes this is mere whimsy, sometimes a serious index of their involvement in the experience they are articulating. This *as if* may even be a necessary component in any act of artistic creation. But in any case, testimony of this kind is irrelevant to the judgment a reader makes about the mimetic sufficiency or insufficiency of the characters he confronts when reading a novel. It is the reader's exclamation, "How real!" or "How true to life!" that I have tried to explore. What do we mean when we talk of a character being real, true, authentic, flat out three-dimensional? In discussing questions of this kind, evidence derived from a concern with the creative process is inadmissible.

THE NOVELIST AND THE CRITIC

To describe the process by which critics have converted particular observations into general assertions and descriptive statements into touchstones of value would, in the case of the novel, be a more intricately difficult task than to analyse the parallel fate of Aristotle's *Poetics*. It would require a long and detailed piece of literary history quite outside the scope of this book. In my study of George Eliot I tried to outline briefly the way in which this happened in the case of the omniscient author convention as opposed to the fashionable stress on point of view. In general, three points may be made.

(*a*) For the conversion to take place at all a considerable body of critical statement by novelists must *a priori* exist. If, as I have said, most of this criticism has been by novelists interested in technical experiment and therefore liable to over-emphasize the formal aspects of their craft, then it is likely that non-creative critics will maintain a similar emphasis.

(*b*) That this is so is proved by the immense stress laid on technical factors of all kinds. Modern criticism has developed a rhetoric comparable only to Puttenham or Quintillian and this is because analytical methods have been evolved precisely to cope with technical complications.

(*c*) The transition in criticism from an *is* to an *ought* is a very easy one to make. The history of many critical terms (e.g. *irony*, *ambiguity*, *paradox*) frequently follows this slide from description to judgment. As with terms, so with method; if one has elaborated a technique of analysis to deal with the complex, oblique or subtle then it may be difficult to remember that the simple, direct or obvious is sometimes the better.

A clear and indeed self-conscious example of this tendency in modern criticism can be seen in Guerard's stimulating study of Conrad. After a few pages of entirely sensible comment on some problems of characterization, he continues:

> *Lord Jim*, then, rests on the bedrock of a great story and an important human situation; *it has some appeal even for the casual reader who moves through a novel as clumsily as he moves through life.* And yet it is, of course, an art novel, a novelist's novel, a critic's novel—perhaps the first important one in England after *Tristram Shandy*. This means that it becomes a different novel if read very attentively; or becomes a different novel when read a second or third time. The usual Victorian novel surrenders most of its drama and meaning at a first rapid reading *and thereafter becomes inert.* If we return to *David Copperfield* after a year or twenty years and find it a different book from the one remembered, this is not because the book has changed. It is we who have changed. But certain novels —*Benito Cereno* as a mild example, *Absalom, Absalom!* as an extreme one, *Lord Jim* as somewhere between the two—do change. They do become different novels at a second attentive reading.[1]

This, if one ponders it, is an amazing statement. How can anyone demonstrate in one instance that *we* have changed and in the other that

[1] A. Guerard, *Conrad the Novelist*, pp. 129–34. Cambridge, Mass., 1958.

the *book* has changed? If we regard a novel *simply* as an artefact, it never changes. Of course, we hardly ever do think of it simply as an artefact since it only takes on meaning as an experience in the reader's mind. This being so, then of course it is *always* the reader who has changed; the mere fact of having read the book—any book—must change him since he has experienced something new.

However, I do not want to chop logic since the interest of Mr. Guerard's position deserves more than mere quibbling. The two points I take to emerge from his paragraph are:

> (*a*) That different kinds of novels elicit or demand different kinds of attention from the reader. This is obviously true and I would go beyond Mr. Guerard and maintain that this is so *even* at a first reading. I would say that it is quite easy for an intelligent reader to give a relaxed or casual first reading to *David Copperfield*, quite difficult to do so with *Lord Jim* and quite impossible to do so with *Absalom, Absalom!*
>
> (*b*) Mr. Guerard's second point is that a casual or relaxed reading will yield a lot with some novels and little with other novels. This again is clearly true but proves nothing about the changed quality of response at a second or third reading.

In both these instances Mr. Guerard is, I believe, attempting a neutral and descriptive statement of what he calls the "generic" difference between types of novels. But his special interest in the complex and the intricate—in the art novel, the novelist's novel, the critic's novel—leads him to smuggle value judgments into his description. These come out particularly in the phrases I have italicized. I could, of course, argue that he has given wrong examples and that *David Copperfield* is just as complex in its way as *Lord Jim*. Indeed, I believe this to be so. But even supposing that the best Victorian novels were technically as simple as Mr. Guerard maintains, it would still be wrong to say that they rapidly exhaust their meaning and interest and after "a first rapid reading" become "inert". Complexity and technical skill cannot be equated with wisdom or mature insight into the true nature of things. If wisdom and mature insight are our concern, then *David Copperfield* or *Middlemarch* (another novel mentioned by Mr. Guerard) are no less easily exhausted than *Lord Jim* and are probably less so than *Absalom, Absalom!*

I have countered Mr. Guerard's assertions with assertions of my own and clearly to go further we would have to argue particular cases. But I hope I have at least clarified my basic assertion—that particular critical techniques, because they work well with certain kinds of novels may tend to distort our judgment of other kinds with which they don't work so well. The kind of novel that tends to get blurred by the modern critical lens includes those which are, in Mr. Guerard's words, "a clear, orderly imitation of life". In other words, it includes the novel where greater stress and value will be placed on characterization. To depreciate this kind is therefore to depreciate characterization which is thus relegated to the periphery of the critic's attention. Yet most fictional masterpieces are of this kind. *War and Peace* is the greatest novel ever written, yet it is certainly not "a critic's novel"; indeed, it stubbornly resists the kind of approach so usefully made by Mr. Guerard to Conrad. This being so, I would prefer to stress the limitations of the critical approach rather than the limitations of the recalcitrant masterpiece.

THE NOVEL AND THE NEW CRITICISM

It follows from what I have said that distortion is even more likely to occur when critical techniques developed to deal with an entirely different kind of literature are applied to the novel. The New Criticism was centrally concerned to apply close and rigorous analytical methods to lyric poetry; it is noticeable how ill at ease its practitioners have been when they have approached the bulky, diffuse and variegated world of the novel. There is no point in piling up examples; one, by a particularly eminent critic, will suffice. John Crow Ransom, in an essay called *The Understanding of Fiction*,[1] asks the very question, "to what extent can the understanding of poetry be applied to the understanding of fiction?" His aim is to apply intensive methods of analysis to selected passages of prose which will be "like fictional analogues of lyrical moments". For his examples he chooses roughly twenty-five lines from *Mansfield Park*, thirty lines from *Daisy Miller* and sixteen lines from *War and Peace*. Of this last passage—quoted in translation—he says, "It's author does not possess fully the technical advantages of a style. For concentration he substitutes repetition." Leaving aside the propriety of stylistically comparing a translation with passages from English novels, there is still the odd assumption that style equals concentration. But why should this necessarily be so? It can only be the result of a concern with other kinds of literature where such a stylistic feature is more commonly encountered.

Ransom's view of fiction (and really of the long poem as well; he

---

[1] J. C. Ransom, "The Understanding of Fiction", *Kenyon Review*, Vol. 12, 1950, pp. 189–218.

seems here to be reviving Poe's theory of pure poetry) is one of passages of "plain prose" serving as a context for "concentration effects . . . requiring an exceptional prose and taxing the stylistic resources of the artist; they will be the prose equivalents of true or short poems."

After this—mercifully perhaps—he does *nothing* with his selected passages. The real interest of the essay lies in the implicit confession that such critical methods can really do very little to help towards the understanding of extended works of fiction. They may work better with the short story; at any rate the proliferation of new-critical textbooks using the short story as raw material would suggest this to be the case.

In so far as the critic is encouraged to verify his assertions by close and careful reference to the text, he will always be indebted to the variety of techniques lumped together under the name of the New Criticism. But these techniques can do little with the problems of characterization since they must concern themselves with comparatively short passages. Characterization, on the other hand, is often a quality of the whole book and nearly always a quality of long passages of the prose continuum. What we might expect is in fact the case; the new critic, when dealing with fiction, is thrown back upon an interest in imagery, symbolism or structural features which have little to do with characterization.

DRAMA AND THE NOVEL

At first glance the drama obviously seems a better source of analogies for the novel than the lyric poem. Both are extended literary forms; both deal with characters developing and conflicting, both deal with man alone and man in society, with motive and with consequence. Yet ultimately the comparison if profitably suggestive is also dangerous.

The analogy is relevant to our present study in two ways. First, many great novelists have been fascinated and deeply influenced by the stage. This fascination has entered criticism largely through the theoretical aspirations and frustrations of Henry James. It needed only a slight re-emphasis by his commentators to make the injunction, "Dramatize!" the central fiat for modern novelists. By contrast, the injunction "Narrate!", which might equally seem the business of the novelist, has been heard but feebly during the last thirty years.

The second point of relevance derives from the tremendous revolution in the criticism of Shakespearian drama during the last thirty years. Interests, emphasis, techniques that have so rightly and so fruitfully been applied here have been transferred, largely without examination, to the criticism of fiction. What has happened, for good or ill, because of that transference, we must examine in some detail. But roughly I would say that the reaction against the Bradleyan approach to Shakespearian drama has been taken too far. Modern critics have rightly and emphatically denied that a dramatic poem is a psychological novel. They have not so frequently remarked that a psychological novel is not a dramatic poem.

This conclusion is not, however, entirely fair since it drastically oversimplifies a very complex state of affairs from which we may learn much. In justice to this complexity, therefore, I wish to quote in detail a good deal of evidence, reserving comment until the evidence is assembled.

If there exists an orthodox modern approach to Shakespeare, it is typically expressed in this passage from an early essay by Professor L. C. Knights:

> It should not be necessary to insist that in *Troilus and Cressida* the real interest centres not in the "characters", such as they are, but in the themes of which the play is composed and the way in which Shakespeare handles the language to obtain an unusually complex emotional response. Unfortunately, for over a hundred years, critics have tended to follow the spirit of Hartley Coleridge's naïve advice on *Hamlet*: 'Let us, for the moment, put Shakespeare out of the question, and consider Hamlet as a real person, a recently deceased acquaintance'. Let us, in short, abstract him from the language which gives him his vitality and from the play in which he has his proper being. Let us consider anything but the poem which Shakespeare wrote and fitted for the stage, and pursue the chimera of our own imagination. This is not criticism.[1]

Behind this statement lies the reaction against the Bradleyan approach—or what is taken to be the Bradleyan approach—to Shakespeare's characters. This approach, in caricature, has been called a "D.N.B." approach to the plays; that is to say, the characters are assumed to be exactly like historical personages, autonomous beings with a life independent of the plays that contain them. They are seen as beings living before and beyond the time sequence of the dramatic action. This private life is seen as a proper object of speculation; such speculation may be relevant to the play in that the private life may provide motives for actions which are otherwise inexplicable in terms

[1] L. C. Knights, *The Criterion*, Vol. 11, 1931-2, p. 624.

of the play itself. In other words, such a critic brings overwhelmingly naturalistic assumptions to his reading of Shakespeare. *How Many Children Has Lady Macbeth?*, the title of L. C. Knight's famous essay, sums up what is supposed to be the concern of the naïve Bradleyan. How far this squares with what Bradley actually maintained, I do not intend to discuss. But it should be obvious that there could equally well exist a similarly naïve anti-Bradleyan school of criticism. Shakespeare, on these terms, would be seen as completely non-naturalistic. Such a viewpoint does indeed exist and provides at times an equally proper subject for caricature. Since, however, we are concerned with criticism and not caricature, I would prefer to cite *in extenso* a much more cautious and discriminating approach, that of F. R. Leavis. *Othello*, Leavis maintains, is something of a special case in the Shakespearian canon:

> Even *Othello* . . . is poetic drama, a dramatic poem, and not a psychological novel written in dramatic form and draped in poetry, but relevant discussion of its tragic significance will nevertheless be mainly a matter of character-analysis. It would, that is, have lent itself uniquely to Bradley's approach if Bradley had made his approach consistently.[1]

Shakespeare's art in general, he continues: "derives from his imaginative grasp of concrete human situations in their complexity and particularity; his power of realizing the vivid here-and-now of experience as part of an intricate and coherent context."[2] This art expresses itself in many ways; it creates a spectrum of technique ranging from the naturalistic through the conventional to the strikingly symbolic and non-mimetic. Leavis establishes Shakespeare's mixture of modes by contrasting Othello with Leontes in *The Winter's Tale*. With Othello, "no development will be acceptable until the behaviour it imposes on him is reconcileable with our notions of ordinary psychological consistency".[3] Or again:

> As Shakespeare presents him, it is not so very elusive a datum about Othello, or one that ordinary experience of life and men makes it difficult to accept, that his past history hasn't been such as to test his proneness to sexual jealousy—has, in fact, thereby been such as to increase his potentialities in that respect.[4]

[1] F. R. Leavis, *The Common Pursuit*, p. 136. London: Chatto and Windus, 1952.
[2] *Ibid.*, p. 156.   [3] *Ibid.*, p. 157.
[4] *Ibid.*, p. 159.

Leontes, by comparison, is a relatively conventional and non-naturalistic figure; *The Winter's Tale* does not "anywhere ask us to endorse dramatic illusion with the feeling of everyday reality. But to impose jealousy by mere convention on Othello is another thing. What end would be served? What profit would accrue?"[1] For Leavis, *The Winter's Tale* is, in general:

> a supreme instance of Shakespeare's poetic complexity—of the impossibility, if one is to speak with any relevance to the play, of considering character, episode, theme and plot in abstraction from the local effects, so inexhaustibly subtle in their interplay, of the poetry, and from the larger symbolic effects to which these give life . . . we quickly see that what we have in front of us is nothing in the nature of a novel dramatically transcribed. The relations between character, speech, and the main themes of the drama are not such as to invite a psychologizing approach; the treatment of life is too generalizing (we may say, if we hasten to add "and intensifying"); so large a part of the function of the words spoken by the characters is plainly something other than to "create" the speakers, or to advance an action that can be properly considered in terms of the interacting of individuals.[2]

There are two points to be noticed about Leavis's position as I have briefly, but I hope not unfairly, summarized it. First, it is clear that most considerable writers will range up and down a spectrum somewhat like Shakespeare's, mixing the realistic, the conventional and the abstract. Certainly within an art form as diverse as the novel there is plenty of room for these different modes of imagination. For example, George Eliot is solidly at the naturalistic end of the spectrum and Kafka at the non-naturalistic. But between the two fine shades and interminglings are to be expected. Where, for example, would we place a work like Camus's *La Peste*? (And, of course—I hasten to forestall objections—isn't it too simple to dismiss Kafka as simply non-naturalistic? Many of his parables are clearly rooted in social observation and their total effect is often paradoxical—a naturalism of the fantastic.) Clearly, then, in any discussion of character we must take into account the various kinds existing within the novel as a general art form. Moreover, just as Shakespeare's is a mixed mode, so is the art of any considerable novelist. Even in so centrally naturalistic a novelist as George Eliot there are many passages in which realism is married to a non-realistic effect (e.g. Maggie drifting down the stream

---

[1] Leavis, *op. cit.*, p. 158.   [2] *Ibid.*, p. 175.

with Stephen) or even passages which are overtly abstract and symbolic (e.g. Romola drifting down the river to the plague-stricken village). Given this complexity, it is clearly important to discriminate. Leavis's position thus prompts a further question. What criteria have we for discriminating between the mode of *Othello* and the mode of *The Winter's Tale*? The *motive* for discriminating is a desire to do justice, to rescue the play. (This emerges in Leavis's "What end would be served? What profit would accrue?") But motives are not criteria; we might agree in our discrimination of kind and yet still disagree in our judgment of value. Presumably, in the case of Shakespeare, our criteria will derive from our response to the language itself, to those "local effects, so inexhaustibly subtle in their interplay, of the poetry". Shakespeare's poetry is sufficiently rich and concentrated to support our criteria. But is this the case with the novel, so much greater in bulk, so much more diffuse and relaxed in texture? The answer must be—sometimes, yes. Leavis, I suspect, would maintain that ultimately it always is. I shall maintain that there are cases in which criteria based on the use of language are insufficient, and that the kind of approach which works well with Shakespearian drama breaks down when applied to the novel.

It is surprising how much, in his essay on *Othello*, Leavis concedes to the Bradleyan approach; he emerges, in his own terms, as an intelligent Bradleyan though he reaches very different conclusions about the play. The point I wish to stress is the place he allows speculation and inference. I am not thinking here so much of his remark about Othello's past history making him prone to sexual jealousy—there is no doubt warrant for this in the text. But when, for example, he discusses Othello's nobility as manifested in relation to external circumstance—the storm, for example—he says: "With that kind of external stress Othello is well qualified to deal (if he went down—and we know he won't—he would go down magnificently)."[1]

This is certainly not speculation of the what-did-Hamlet-study-at-the-university variety. But it *is* a regard for and interest in a character, a human being, as something more than a creation of language or a function in the total context of the play. "He is the sort of man who in such-and-such a situation would do so-and-so"—this is the kind of remark we constantly use in real life, when discussing somebody's character. If this is permissible with a Shakespearian character it is even more legitimate when applied to the larger scope of the novel. The novelist, because he has more time and space, can frame the

[1] Leavis, *op. cit.*, p. 144.

situation to justify the *would do such-and-such* in our reaction. Indeed he may do more than this; as we have seen he may also leave room enough for us to speculate and to frame other situations than those actually existing in the novel. In other words we may sometimes legitimately assume a character's autonomy and there may be a proper place for a kind of speculation and inference not vulnerable to the anti-Bradleyan critic's attack. Such speculative activity may, in fact, compose a large part of the character's reality for us.

We should not neglect the real gains that may emerge from a comparison of drama and the novel. Leavis's insights into *Othello* can legitimately be used by the critic of fiction. But ultimately it is the differences rather than the analogies that need to be stressed. Leavis's emphasis is, after all, ultimately the same as that of Professor Knights—"the themes of which the play is composed and the way in which Shakespeare handles the language to attain an unusually complex emotional response". The novel is too unwieldy to sustain for any length of time the necessarily detailed analysis which can be given to the concentration of Shakespeare's poetic texture. Ultimately, therefore, the dramatic poem (the constant use of this term instead of simply "play" is deliberate and significant) differs (only in degree) from the lyric poem when seen in relation to the novel.

To sum up, we may say that while few great novels are *merely* a "clear, orderly imitation of life" and that while there have always existed novelists—for example, Dickens—whose work could never be described in these terms, nevertheless such a mimetic intention would have been thought the central concern of the novel until the end of the nineteenth century. But during the twentieth century the mimetic relation of the novel to life has been radically changed, both in the object of imitation (the kind of life thought "real" or important) and in the nature of the imitation itself. Obliquity, deliberate distortion, a retreat from the merely representational—these, in very general terms, are the characteristics of the modern novel. Following and combining with this change in creative practice, the critical forces I have tried briefly to describe have acted to direct attention away from problems of characterization. More than this: they have also been the source to certain positive objections to the discussion of character and it is with these objections that I wish to deal in the second appendix.

The Attack on Character

W E may agree at once that a naïve conception of mimesis often leads to imbecilites of rhapsodic gush, to simple and static character sketches (the "D.N.B." approach), or to criticism which is merely disguised confession and autobiography. These excesses helped to provoke the historical reaction which I analysed in the preceding appendix. If we discount this reaction, then we may say that attacks on the concept of character as the basis of a critical approach generally fall into one or more of the following categories:

(1) That such an approach may be morally unhealthy in that it encourages day-dreaming, fantasy and wish-fulfilment, and leads to the reader identifying himself in the wrong way with the hero or heroine.

(2) That it allows the critic to evade the proper task of criticism, the formation of value judgments, by offering instead descriptive sketches or character studies.

(3) That it operates on the basis of a concept which because of its generality and abstraction is false to the concrete experience of any particular book.

(4) That it ignores the real object of critical attention, which is the moral vision of the artist as manifested in a particular and concrete pattern of words.

(5) That it deflects attention from the unity of the total work by encouraging us to see the part as larger than the whole; to talk, for example, of Hamlet the prince rather than of *Hamlet* the play.

(6) That it denies the autonomy of the successfully created artefact and confuses real emotions with aesthetic emotions.

Clearly these categories are to some extent artificial; clearly there is a good deal of interaction between them. An answer to any one of them tends to turn into an answer to them all; thus for convenience I shall reserve the last point, which includes an alternative aesthetic theory, for the second half of this appendix; in the first half I will try to deal briefly and generally with the other objections.

II

Q. D. Leavis, commenting on one frequent response to popular fiction—"Your characters *live*. They become one's friends"—says:

> This readiness to respond to "characters" will bear some investigation. It almost entirely explains the undoubted popular appeal which Shakespeare makes, even to an uneducated public incapable of reading poetry. The fascination his plays have had for various bestsellers is notorious and genuine; for them, indeed for most people, Shakespeare is the "creator" of characters, and they translate his dramas into novels, so that nearly all Shakespearian criticism is a discussion of the suppostitious lives of the dramatis personae. This kind of interest leads critics to compare the merits of novelists by the size of the portrait gallery each has given to the world.[1]

In so far as Mrs. Leavis attacks an undisciplined and indulgent reaction to character, then this is well said. But her comment is obviously loaded. One may agree with her that plays should not be read as novels but not with her implication (one notices the logical elision in *so that*) that the criticism of fictional characters is simply a "discussion of the suppostitious lives of the dramatis personae". Indeed, the universal interest in Shakespeare as a creator of character should make us pause; should we not, like Dr. Johnson, "rejoice to concur with the common reader"? If we attend to the poetry, does not the poetry create character? If we attend to the "theme" or to the "moral vision" of the plays, what significance have these in abstraction, divorced from our primary sense of a human context? Isn't the term "portrait gallery" far too static to square with our sense of change, process, development in fictional characters?

One's unease about the polemic intent of Mrs. Leavis's comment is sharpened when she goes on to assume that "the highbrow novelist" does not create characters who:

> lend themselves to fantasying but cause disturbing repercussions in the reader's emotional make-up. Worse still, it is a fact that many highbrow novelists do not choose even to outline plausible characters, and this expectation of meeting recognisable people in fiction, amounting to a conviction that the novelist's first duty is to provide them, is generally at the bottom of failure to respond to the finer

[1] Q. D. Leavis, *Fiction and the Reading Public*, p. 59. London: Chatto and Windus, 1932.

novels. The confusion of fiction with life and the demand that fiction should compensate for life prevents enjoyment of Emily Bronte and Jane Austen, among others (*Jane Eyre* was admitted to literature long before *Wuthering Heights*), and nowadays of D. H. Lawrence and T. F. Powys; it causes the resentful bewilderment one notices in the objections to such novelists as Virginia Woolf and Henry James, who do not offer anything in the nature of "character".[1]

This is a tricky passage, full of concealed shifts of emphasis—for example, from "many highbrow novelists" to "the finer novels", and from "plausible characters" to "recognisable people". One simply can't accept Mrs. Leavis's degradation (for her own laudable tactical purposes) of the notion of character. Henry James, we protest, *does* offer a very rich range of characters, and if we feel Virginia Woolf does not, then we may surely criticize her for the resultant narrowing of sensibility and vision.

Of course, what Mrs. Leavis is attacking through her notion of character is a habit of bad reading. Of course, the validity of a critical method will not guarantee good criticism and, of course, bad reading will produce bad results whether we attend to character, plot, theme, language, moral vision or whatever. No one ever supposed otherwise. Why, then, single out character as the villain of the piece? Indeed, I would say that it is less easy for the bad critic to conceal himself in a consideration of character than in any other aspect of the novelist's art, since such a consideration raises most urgently and comprehensively the adequacy of the novel's relation to life. Our sense of that adequacy is surely the deepest foundation of our understanding and judgment of any work of art. Of course, this adequacy may manifest itself in forms other than that of a relatively simple mimetic relationship—but equally, not all novelists aspire to the condition of a Virginia Woolf or a T. F. Powys. The notion of mimesis, as I have tried to show, covers a very complex network of relationships and values, to which terms like *plausible, recognizable, portrait gallery, fantasy*, do less than justice. It is precisely by a serious examination of the idea of character that the critic may prevent that "confusion of fiction with life" so deplored by Mrs. Leavis.

But is not the notion of character so abstract that it is liable to falsify our experience of any particular book? Of course it is, unless we are careful—but then, this danger is inherent in all those terms whereby

[1] Q. D. Leavis, *Fiction and the Reading Public*, pp. 60-1.

we seek to interpret the raw data of our lives. As Sartre points out in his essay on Camus:

> What we call a feeling is merely the abstract unity and the meaning of discontinuous impressions.
>
> I am not constantly thinking about the people I love, but I claim to love them even when I am not thinking about them—and I am capable of compromising my well-being in the name of an abstract feeling, in the absence of any real and immediate emotion.[1]

Character, in itself, is no more dangerous an abstraction than any other critical term; we are just as liable to compromise our critical well-being in the name of *symbol* or *vision* or *theme*. To those who maintain that we can avoid this danger by concentrating on the work of art simply as an organized pattern of language, it seems to me that the final answer has been given by John Holloway:

> The question is: would this kind of approach, studying the language, exclude *anything* from our consideration of a play; or would it even tell us that some things were unimportant, others specially important? Certainly not: there is nothing whatever in a play—not plot, not characterization, not even the Girlhood of Shakespeare's Heroines, even, which we could conceivably study in any way save by a study of the language of the play. There is nothing else to study. Whatever aspect of the play we study—relevant or irrelevant to true criticism—where we have to study it is in the language. If we study the language loosely and vaguely, our results are loose and vague; an exact and sensitive study gives exact and sensitive results. So this general principle gives no guide at all as to what things will be important in a play. It leaves every question completely open. In fact, it is a truism.[2]

Precisely: the whole question is what we do with the raw data—the organized pattern of language—and how well we do it. It hardly needs to be added that of all art-forms the novel depends least upon its verbal medium; thus the novel loses least of all in translation. *War and Peace* is still the greatest novel, in English as in Russian. Moreover, there are some novelists—Dreiser, for example—who triumph over every kind of linguistic atrocity.

The value of the linguistic emphasis lies, of course, in its making us relate our necessarily abstract conceptions as closely as possible to the

[1] J. P. Sartre, *Literary and Philosophical Essays*, p. 31.
[2] J. Holloway, *The Charted Mirror*, pp. 220-1. London: Routledge, 1960.

o

given data and to the "discontinuous impressions" they create. Like any other approach, the study of character may lead to the wrong kind of abstraction; it is not hard to find examples of this in currently fashionable critical practice. Psychological interpretation, for example, often leads to disappointing results. When it is not concerned with the author or with the genetic processes of creation, it tends to fall into one of two errors. Either it leads to a naïve kind of naturalism, seeking to supply motives and explanations for characters who in fact are being used conventionally; or it tends to translate the character into its own terms. But this is reductive and wrongly abstract; Falstaff or Heathcliff, we protest, are *not* dramatizations of the id; Mr. Knightly is *not* a super-ego.

A similar reduction may be seen in the modern practice of considering the "mythic" significance of characters. This method, it is true, is a natural response to certain trends in modern fiction. It is quite possible that the simple and delighted creation of characters is viable only when the framework—social and ideological—which contains them is relatively stable and taken for granted. When the author is driven back to consider the framework himself, then the characters may indeed come to be loaded with mythic significance; the novel is concerned less to create individuals than to explore the general human condition. Nowhere is this more true than of the work of Thomas Mann, who himself speaks of

> my own growing inclination, which as I discovered was not mine alone, to look upon all life as a cultural product taking the form of mythic clichés, and to prefer quotation to independent invention.[1]

But even here the larger mythic meanings of *The Magic Mountain* or *Dr. Faustus* depend upon their successful incarnation in a number of concrete settings and individual characters. These are still the prime concern of the critic and he ignores them at his peril. An example of the dangers risked is to be found in Philip Rahv's extremely interesting essay, *The Cult of Experience in American Writing*. Rahv is concerned to analyse the American devotion to the "facts of the case" which involves a distrust of abstract formulation. Having used Goethe's *Faust* as a way of illustrating his thesis, he continues:

> James's heroines—his Isabel Archers and Milly Theales and Maggie Ververs—are they not somehow always being victimized by the "great world" even as they succeed in mastering it? Gretchen-

[1] T. Mann, *The Genesis of a Novel*, p. 125. London: Secker and Warburg, 1961.

like in their innocence, they none the less enact the Faustian role in their uninterrupted pursuit of experience and in the use of the truly Mephistophelean gold of their millionaire fathers to buy up the brains and beauty and nobility of the civilization that enchants them?[1]

Is it too naïve to object that James's heroines never exist in the plural, that there is in fact only *one* Isabel Archer? As Rahv's cultural generalization unfolds we lose contact with the individual characters; his description fits Maggie Verver perhaps, but not the other two; it simply imposes on them a pattern which just isn't there in the novels themselves.

Here, on the primacy of the individual character, I rest my case. There is obviously a danger that in stressing the part we may neglect the whole. But this results from a defective use of the method, not from a defect in the method itself, and I hope I have, with my stress on the importance of contextual relationships, sufficiently related part to whole. And I would maintain that such an approach brings us closer and more directly to the living heart of any novel. What do we care for theme or for moral vision, except in so far as these are incarnated in human realities? In our response to and our exploration of these we extend and explore ourselves; it is here that our deepest sense of value, belief, allegiance, sympathy and understanding are engaged; it is here that we are compelled to judgment. And since every critical judgment is also a judgment on the critic, then let us be generous.

III

We come finally to the notion that a concentration on character—and particularly on the character's mimetic relation to reality—ignores the essential autonomy of the artefact. Just as the concept of mimesis may easily degenerate into a crude "slice-of-life" view of fiction, so it is not difficult to discover and demolish equally crude and dogmatic versions of an autonomy theory of art. But I have chosen as representative the writings of Ortega y Gasset since they are not only high-spirited but also humane, wise as well as witty. They are also radical and comprehensive and their influence, I suspect, though diffused and oblique, has been considerable. Thus, though I would not suggest any simple causal relation, there are remarkable parallels, both of concept and metaphor, between Ortega's views and the aesthetic theories of Sartre, considered in an earlier chapter.

[1] P. Rahv, *Image and Idea*, p. 13. London: Weidenfeld and Nicolson, 1957.

Ortega's particular remarks on the novel must be related to certain more general ideas expounded in *The Dehumanization of Art*. Fundamentally, Ortega sees the distinguishing characteristics of modern art as resulting from an autonomy theory. The traditional view, he says, is that we find value in the rendered human content of a work of art, in its depiction of human actions and passions which so engage our imagination that we respond to it as to a "lived" reality. Art imitates life so that we respond to the imitation in terms of life itself. The modern view, on the contrary, is that:

> Not only is grieving and rejoicing at such human destinies as a work of art presents or narrates a very different thing from true artistic pleasure, but preoccupation with the human content of the work is in principle incompatible with aesthetic enjoyment proper.[1]

A human response is thus hostile to an aesthetic response since the "lived" reality of an old-fashioned work of art is too overpowering not to evoke a sympathy which prevents us from perceiving the work as a properly aesthetic object. "Instead of delighting in the artistic object people delight in their own emotions, the work being only the cause and the alcohol of their pleasure." Where the nineteenth century poet wished to be human, his twentieth-century counterpart wishes simply to be a poet: "life is one thing, art is another . . . the poet begins where the man ends." Although pure art is a theoretical absolute, impossible of complete attainment, modern art represents a process of relative purification which has resulted in the distortion or elimination of the "lived" human content.

To distinguish between the emotion one feels in a "lived" situation and aesthetic emotion, Ortega invokes the idea of aesthetic distance. Let us imagine, he says, a human situation—a death-bed scene, for example, when those present include the widow, a doctor, a reporter and an artist. All see the event in a different way; as many points of view, so many diverse realities. Which is the real, authentic "reality"? Any choice must obviously be arbitrary. But at least we can distinguish the degrees of emotional involvement in the event. The widow will be the most deeply engaged in the situation; hers will be the "lived" human reality. The doctor and the reporter will be less involved since theirs is primarily a professional concern. The painter will be involved least of all; he will be primarily concerned, *qua* artist, with mass, texture, colour, light and shade.

[1] Ortega y Gasset, *The Dehumanization of Art; and Notes on the Novel*, pp. 9–10. Princeton University Press, 1948.

In this scale, the degree of closeness is equivalent to the degree of feeling participation; the degree of remoteness, on the other hand, marks the degree to which we have freed ourselves from the real event, thus objectifying it and turning it into a theme of pure observation.[1]

As the widow and the artist have different perspectives on the same event which result in different degrees of emotional involvement, so different perspectives are possible as between the reader and the work of art. Ortega explains this in terms of a metaphor of looking through a window at a landscape, the glass here standing for the work of art and the landscape for the human content of its subject-matter, for that which is imitated. If we focus on the landscape, the objects we see will be distinct and "natural"; the pane of glass will be perfectly translucent and we shall not notice it. But if we focus on the glass itself, then the landscape beyond it will seem quite different; it will appear blurred and distorted in various ways—in other words, it will be dehumanized. We cannot focus on both glass and landscape:

> Perception of "lived" reality and perception of artistic form, as I have said before, are essentially incompatible because they call for a different adjustment of our perceptive apparatus. An art that requires such a double seeing is a squinting art. The nineteenth century was remarkably cross-eyed.[2]

If we now turn to *Notes on The Novel* it may at first seem that Ortega contradicts himself, for he concludes that "not in the invention of plots but in the invention of interesting characters lies the last hope of the novel". How can this possibly be reconciled with his thesis about the dehumanization of art; how can it be contained within an autonomy theory? No summary can be adequate to the series of dazzling paradoxes and logical elisions by which Ortega performs this feat; one can only hope to stress some of the main points.

We may start with a distinction that again recalls Sartre's aesthetic theories, a distinction between novels and poems. Ortega maintains that we look at lyric poems from the outside, as though they were objects. By contrast:

> the novel is destined to be perceived from within itself—the same as the real world in which, by inexorable metaphysical order, each man forms, in each moment of his life, the centre of his own universe.[3]

[1] Ortega y Gasset, *The Dehumanization of Art; and Notes on the Novel*, p. 171.
[2] *Ibid.*, p. 25.   [3] *Ibid.*, p. 96.

If each of us in real life is the centre of a universe, that universe has a horizon. No novelist can ever compete with the reader in the scope of his horizon; therefore he must "see to it that the reader is cut off from his real horizon and imprisoned in a small, hermetically sealed universe". Moreover:

> No horizon, I repeat, is interesting for its content. Any one of them is interesting through its *form*—its form as a horizon that is, as a cosmos or complete world. Microcosm and macrocosm are equally cosmos; they differ only in the size of their radii; but for a being that lives inside, each has a constant absolute size. . . . Were we allowed to compare the inner world of the book with outer reality and invited to "live", the conflicts, problems and emotions the book has to offer would seem so small and futile that all their significance would be lost . . . no writer can be called a novelist unless he possesses the gift of forgetting, and thereby making us forget, the reality beyond the walls of his novel. Let him be as realistic as can be; that is to say, let the microcosm of his novel consist of unquestionably true-to-life elements—he will have lost out if he cannot keep us from remembering that there exists an extra mural world.[1]

Here Ortega arrives at a final paradox concerning the novel:

> To enjoy a novel we must feel surrounded by it on all sides; it cannot exist as a more or less conspicuous thing among the rest of things. Precisely because it is a preeminently realistic genre it is incompatible with outer reality. In order to establish its own inner world it must dislodge and abolish the surrounding one.[2]

Before we are entirely cozened by Ortega's intellectual sleight-of-hand, let us pause to take stock of what has been so far outlined. It might first be objected that his views simply do not square with historical reality. Cross-eyed or not, the great novels of the nineteenth century are what they are—great novels, far greater than their modern successors. It may be argued, in Ortega's metaphor, that the windows of the great houses of fiction are indeed translucent, that form exists not for itself but only to reveal content, and that we should indeed focus on the landscape beyond the formal frame. To this it can be answered that Ortega is in fact describing distinctive developments in modern fiction and that his perception of dehumanization (parallel to

[1] Ortega y Gasset, *The Dehumanization of Art; and Notes on the Novel*, pp. 90–2.
[2] *Ibid.*, p. 96.

Sartre's emphasis on depersonalization) is remarkably accurate. This is undeniably true, so far as it goes. ("So much the worse for modern fiction," we may, parenthetically, mutter.) But one can easily slide from description to prescription, and I do not think that Ortega escapes this process; the significance and application of an autonomy theory is imperceptibly extended. Consequently the objection holds; we are left with a theory of art which simply does not cover most of the major triumphs of the genre—which seems, to say the least, an odd state of affairs.

Nor do I think that the psychology of aesthetic response implied by an autonomy theory is adequate. Some variants of this theory imply the operation of a special aesthetic sense, but I have never been able to discover of what this sense consists. If it lies in our perception of form alone, in our response to balance, mass, proportion, rhythm, then this, while it may be more or less adequate to some arts, like abstract painting or music, can only result in a trivial reading of fiction. Ortega is not so crude; nevertheless his psychology implies a complete imaginative surrender on the part of the reader; we are so captured within the hermetically sealed microcosm of the novel that we forget the reality of life outside. This is an important half-truth; we *do* make a kind of imaginative surrender. But it is only a half-truth; the other side of our response is surely that described by Dr. Johnson:

> Fiction loses its force when it departs from the resemblance of reality. . . . It is false, that any representation is mistaken for reality; that any dramatick fable in its materiality was ever credible, or for a single moment, was ever credited. . . . The truth is, that the spectators are always in their senses, and know, from the first act to the last, that the stage is only a stage, and that the players are only players. . . . Imitations produce pain or pleasure, not because they are mistaken for realities, but because they bring realities to mind.[1]

This, again, is in itself only a half-truth, but no account of aesthetic response is complete without it. We *do* lend imaginative belief to fiction but at the same time we know it to be fiction. Ortega may call this impure and cross-eyed, while I may call it the richness of a double vision—but no amount of name-calling will alter the facts.

Finally, I can find no adequate basis within an autonomy theory for a general standard of critical judgment. This theory can answer the question, "How well was the thing done?" but not the further

[1] Dr. Johnson, *Preface to Shakespeare*, pp. 25–8.

question, "Was it worth doing?" If each work is completely autonomous and if its truth derives simply from its internal coherence, then
no work can properly be compared with another. One can easily
imagine a work which is completely self-consistent and beautifully
formed into a coherent whole, yet which is still trivial or worthless.

By what criteria can we judge one critical theory to be better than
another? Granted that no one theory can provide final answers to all
questions and that a false theory may still issue in good practice, I think
that we may test a critical system in three ways—by asking how wide
is the range of works it covers without strain, how many aspects of a
single work it covers without distortion and how adequate an account
does it give of the reader's various satisfactions. On these three grounds
it seems to me that any autonomy theory is inadequate.

Are we left, then, caught between autonomy and mimesis, two
irreconcilable theoretical extremes? Of course not. As I said at the
outset a practising critic rarely works at this level of abstraction and
can find plenty of middle-ground in which to manoeuvre. Moreover,
even at a theoretical level we may possibly find ways and means of
bridging the gap. Clearly a great deal depends on agreement about
terms; in particular the idea of *form* seems crucial. This is where
Ortega's insight and dialectical skill prove so valuable.

At first Ortega seems merely to reiterate standard doctrine:

> The material never saves a work of art, the gold it is made of
> does not hallow a statue. A work of art lives on its form, not on its
> material; the essential grace it emanates springs from its structure,
> from its organism. The structure forms the properly artistic part of
> the work and on it aesthetic and literary criticism should concen-
> trate.[1]

This does not sound very promising. One is disposed to argue, to
point out that gold is not the material of a statue in the same sense
that the content of a novel—the truthful depiction of society, say—
is the material of the work. Ortega confuses material and medium in
order to score his point. But almost at once he begins to modify his
position; speaking of the cunning art of Dostoievski's novels, he points
out that Dostoievski seems to introduce each character with a definitive
biography, but no sooner do his people begin to act and talk than the
reader is disconcerted by their refusal to behave according to these
initial definitions. Hence the reader tries to find his own definition of
them; he tries to reconcile these disparities into a unified picture and

[1] Ortega y Gasset, *op. cit.*, p. 75.

this, says Ortega, is precisely what we do in our daily intercourse with real people.

Chance leads them into the ambit of our life, and nobody bothers officially to define them to us. What we have before us is their intricate reality not their plain concept. We are never quite let into their secret, they stubbornly refuse to adjust themselves to our ideas about them. And this is what makes them independent of us and brings it home that they are an effective reality transcending our imagination. But is not then Dostoievski's "realism"—let us call it that not to complicate things—not so much a matter of the persons and events he presents as of the way the reader sees himself compelled to deal with these persons and events? Dostoievski is a "realist" not because he uses the material of life but because he uses the form of life?[1]

Precisely. Ortega here is very close to the notion of the constitutive category by means of which I have in this book tried to give a firmer basis to the theory of mimesis. If we can reinterpret *form* in this manner to mean "the form of life", the syntax of our experience, then surely we have begun to compose our quarrel and to draw both sides towards a critical armistice, a treaty of mutual toleration and respect?

[1] Ortega y Gasset, *op. cit.*, p. 78.

Index